A Far, Far Better Thing

A Far, Far Better Thing

*Did a Fatal Attraction Lead
to a Wrongful Conviction?*

Jens Soering and Bill Sizemore

Lantern Books ● New York
A Division of Booklight Inc.

2017
Lantern Books
128 Second Place
Brooklyn, NY 11231
www.lanternbooks.com

Permission to use the photographs on pp. xv–xxii has been granted as follows: cover
photo of Jens Soering at Brunswick Correctional Center, by the *Virginian-Pilot*. The
following photos, by Filmperspektive GmbH: Jens Soering and Elizabeth Haysom
in the 1980s (two versions, on the cover and inside the book); Loose Chippings, the
Haysoms' retirement cottage; Elizabeth Haysom testifying at her sentencing hearing
in 1987; Judge William Sweeney at Jens Soering's trial in 1990; Richard Neaton, the
lead defense attorney during Jens Soering's trial; Gail Starling Marshall, a former
deputy state attorney general; Major Ricky Gardner at the Bedford County Sheriff's
Office; Gail Ball, Jens Soering's parole lawyer and David Watson, retired master
detective; Prosecutor James Updike; Steve Rosenfield, Jens Soering's current lawyer;
Chuck Reid, the original lead investigator in the Haysom murder case; Ed Sulzbach,
FBI criminal profiler; and Jens Soering at Buckingham Correctional Center.

Printed in the United States of America

Library of Congress Cataloging-in-Publication Data

Names: Soering, Jens, 1966– author. | Sizemore, Bill, author.
Title: A far, far better thing : did a fatal attraction lead to a wrongful conviction? /
    Jens Soering and Bill Sizemore.
Description: New York City : Lantern Books, [2017]
Identifiers: LCCN 2016047270 (print) | LCCN 2017002254 (ebook) | ISBN
    9781590565643 (pbk.) | ISBN 9781590565650 (ebook)
Subjects: LCSH: Murder—Virginia—Bedford County—Case studies. | Trials
    (Murder) —Virginia—Bedford County—Case studies. | Haysom, Derek, –1985
    | Haysom, Nancy, 1932–1985.
Classification: LCC HV6533.V8 S67 2017 (print) | LCC HV6533.V8 (ebook) |
    DDC 364.152/309755675—dc23
LC record available at https://lccn.loc.gov/2016047270

Contents

About the Authors
About the Publisher

Acknowledgments

To a variety of friends and supporters, we owe a debt of gratitude that can never be adequately repaid. Since one of us is in prison, much of the help we received pulling this book together took very basic forms. The ever-faithful Bernadette Faber has been a marvel at archiving records, research, and communication, and providing moral support. Attorneys Steve Rosenfield, Gail Starling Marshall, and Gail Ball have devoted vast quantities of time to the case, most of it uncompensated. Filmmakers Karin Steinberger and Marcus Vetter did groundbreaking research for their documentary *The Promise*, and generously made the fruits of their labors available to us.

Many key players in the case graciously gave interviews for the book, including Tony Buchanan, Major Ricky Gardner, Andrew Griffiths, Chuck Reid, Judge William Sweeney, and former sheriff Carl Wells. Deacon Tom Elliott has been a rock-solid source of support and comfort. M. K. Sizemore performed yeoman's service as a sounding board and fount of editorial advice and technical support. And Martin Rowe, our editor at Lantern Books, will have our everlasting gratitude for his perceptiveness, sensitivity, and care in guiding the book into print.

—*Jens Soering and Bill Sizemore*

Foreword

Martin Sheen

My first encounter with Jens Soering came by way of his extraordinary book *The Convict Christ* (2006), a twenty-first-century North American take on liberation theology. Although I had heard of Soering from several Catholic social-justice activists, including our mutual friend Bishop Walter Sullivan of Richmond, Virginia, I did not know any of the details of his case. But clearly, here was a unique writing talent that captivated my interest with his spiritual insight, deep compassion, and a disarming sense of humor. Of course, this work was achieved under extremely difficult circumstances, to say the least. Not many people in prison write books to begin with, let alone people serving life sentences. So with my interest piqued, I began a correspondence with Soering and a friendship developed.

Along the way I learned more about his life and the details of his case. He was not only a brilliant and prolific writer who had converted to Catholicism behind bars, he was a German citizen enduring the harshest and most unforgiving punishment our country can offer—a life sentence without a realistic hope of release, which some refer to as "the other death penalty."

Soering had been incarcerated since 1986 for a crime he clearly did not commit. Nevertheless, he found a way to unite the will of the spirit with the work of the flesh to become a powerful voice for prison reform and an advocate for the more than two million men and women lost in the maze of the American prison-industrial complex.

His next book was the uniquely revealing *One Day in the Life of 179212* (2012), a personal prison diary written at Brunswick Correctional Center in Lawrenceville, Virginia, where Soering escorts the reader through a "typical" day. But obviously there is nothing at all typical about a single minute of it, and despite struggling to survive in such a dark and degrading place, Soering again projects compassion, intelligence, and a deep spirituality—along with his indefatigable sense of humor. Dare I mention there is even a mysterious level of *enviable joy* escaping between the lines, despite the strict control of the prison's security system, and we are left to wonder?

From Brunswick, Soering was transferred to Buckingham Correctional Center in Dillwyn, Virginia, where he continues serving time, and it is from here that this most recent work, *A Far, Far Better Thing*, emerges to command our attention. Despite the power and grace of his earlier works, it is only this book that spells out in minute detail and scrupulous honesty every aspect of his case, including new evidence and DNA analysis so compelling that a new trial is warranted at the very least. *A Far, Far Better Thing* appears here in tandem with "The Evidence" by Bill Sizemore, who presents an equally compelling case for Soering's innocence and release.

With this foreword it is my purpose to join the ever-growing number of knowledgeable and conscientious advocates supporting Jens Soering's immediate release from prison and repatriation to Germany. Anything less would add to the horrible and continuing miscarriage of justice dealt to him so long ago.

Thirty years of suffering behind prison walls in a tiny cell have taken a significant toll on Soering's body, mind, and soul. Human suffering is universal and unavoidable, of course, and Soering discovered that personal suffering is necessary for spiritual growth. But to suffer for a just cause is one thing; to endure inflicted suffering is quite another. And the worst suffering of all is to suffer alone.

Malibu, California,
November 2016

Introduction

Bill Sizemore

THE GENTEEL SUBURB of Boonsboro, nestled just outside Lynchburg in the shadow of Virginia's Blue Ridge Mountains, had never seen anything like it.

In early April 1985, in their cozy retirement cottage set back from a winding rural road, a prominent local couple were found brutally murdered in a style reminiscent of the notorious Charles Manson cult slayings in California years before.

Derek Haysom, a seventy-two-year-old retired steel executive, lay sprawled in the doorway between the living room and dining room, the victim of thirty-six stab wounds. His wife Nancy, fifty-three, a scion of an old Virginia family and a distant relation of Lady Astor, was lying on the linoleum kitchen floor, stabbed six times. Both victims had been nearly decapitated. Blood was everywhere.

"It was like stepping inside of a slaughterhouse," one sheriff's detective said later. "You know: What gang of people did this?"

Such a crime scene was unthinkable in bucolic Bedford County, a haven of fundamentalist Christianity. Initially, there were fears that the killings were the work of a satanic cult. At one point, desperate for suspects, detectives even consulted a psychic.

Eventually, the investigation turned in the direction of the Haysoms' twenty-one-year-old daughter Elizabeth and her eighteen-year-old boyfriend Jens Soering, even though at first blush neither seemed a likely candidate for murder. Both were brilliant honors students at the University of Virginia. Elizabeth had attended prestigious boarding schools in England and Switzerland. Jens had attended an exclusive church-affiliated school in Atlanta, where his father was a mid-level diplomat in the German consulate.

But the detectives' suspicions were confirmed that fall when the young lovers fled the country and spent six months on the run through Europe and Asia. Their flight ended in April 1986 when they were arrested in London for check fraud. When British detectives searched their flat, they found diaries and letters that contained oblique references to the murders. Over four days of interrogation in London, without a lawyer present, Jens confessed to the killings. Elizabeth, too, confessed briefly but quickly reversed herself, saying Jens carried out the crime at her behest.

In 1987, Elizabeth waived extradition, pled guilty as an accessory to murder, and was sentenced to ninety years in prison. Jens, facing capital murder charges, fought extradition and was brought back to Virginia only after a precedent-setting decision from the European Court of Human Rights took capital punishment off the table.

At his 1990 trial—a media spectacle broadcast gavel to gavel on cable TV—Elizabeth was the star witness for the prosecution, testifying that she goaded her boyfriend into butchering her parents. But in a dramatic turnabout, Jens recanted his confession and said Elizabeth was the real killer. He had falsely confessed, he said, to save his girlfriend from the electric chair.

From that day to this, Jens has continued to proclaim his innocence. As a lovestruck and misguided teenager, he says, he was inspired by the sacrifice of Sydney Carton, the character in Charles Dickens' *A Tale of Two Cities* whose love for Lucie Manette is so deep that he takes the place of her husband, Charles Darnay, on the guillotine. As he waits on the platform, he celebrates his unselfish act: "It is a far, far better thing that I do, than I have ever done; it is a far, far better rest that I go to than I have ever known." Hence the title of this book.

The jury, however, accepted the prosecution's theory that Jens committed the murders at Elizabeth's instigation. He was convicted and sentenced to two life-terms.

Over the three decades since his trial, a series of new revelations and experts' conclusions have emerged to support Jens' story. The most compelling new evidence was only discovered in the summer of 2016 when a DNA analysis eliminated Jens as the source of blood found at the crime scene. That revelation undercuts the prosecution's theory of the case and bolsters Jens' long-time contention that Elizabeth carried out the murders with one or more unknown male accomplices. The DNA evidence is discussed in detail in Chapter 19.

The original lead investigator in the case now says he believes that Jens is innocent. He gives his reasons in Chapter 20.

Also in 2016, a world-renowned expert on police interrogations conducted a months-long investigation of the case and concluded that Jens' confession—a linchpin of the evidence against him—should have been regarded as unreliable. Those findings are covered in Chapter 21.

This is an unusual book. It is the product of two authors, each with a distinct voice and mission.

Part I is Jens' first-person account of his obsessive love affair with Elizabeth, the events leading up to and after the murders, the couple's international flight from the authorities, their arrest, and trial.

Part II is my account of the cascading revelations in the years since the trial that throw the verdict into question. It is based in part on my own investigation of the case, which I began in 2006 as a newspaper journalist. It also draws heavily on the work of others, most notably the filmmakers Marcus Vetter and

Karin Steinberger, whose compelling documentary *The Promise* premiered in 2016.

Over my four decades as a journalist, I came to believe that sometimes the criminal justice system seems more about winning and losing than about finding the truth. This book is an attempt to get at the truth about this case.

In the end you, the reader, will be the judge.

Williamsburg, Virginia
September 2016

Jens Soering and Elizabeth Haysom in the 1980s

Virginia Press Service News Clipping Bureau/Filmperspektive GmbH

Jens Soering and Elizabeth Haysom met as fellow honor students at the University of Virginia in 1984.

Virginia Press Service News Clipping Bureau/Filmperspektive GmbH

Derek Haysom, a South Africa–born industrialist, and his second wife Nancy, a distant relation of Lady Astor, were married in 1960.

Jens Soering

Loose Chippings, the Haysoms' retirement cottage, was set back from a rural road outside Lynchburg, Virginia, in sight of the Blue Ridge Mountains.

Filmperspektive GmbH

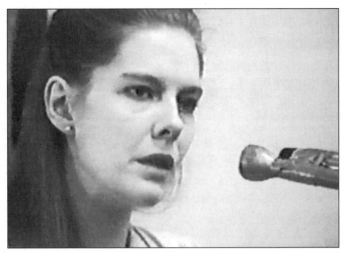

Elizabeth Haysom testifying at her sentencing hearing in 1987

WSET 13 News, Lynchburg, Virginia/Filmperspektive GmbH

Richard Neaton, the lead defense attorney during Jens Soering's trial and direct appeals, lost his law license in 2001.

Filmperspektive GmbH

Judge William Sweeney at Jens Soering's trial in 1990
Filmperspektive GmbH

RISQUE LINDGREN BENEDICT
Playful, lovable, but at business, brisk;
You'll find it profitable to bank on Risque.
Vice-President, Chemistry Club; Civics Club; Athletic
Association; Debating Club; Honor League; "Crest";
"High Times"; Chairman Community Chest 212, '44;
National Honor Society.

WILLIAM WHITNEY SWEENEY
Good in football, smart in books.
From everybody he gets the looks.
Chemistry Club; Civics Club; Football Squad; Varsity
Club; Quill and Scroll; Spanish Club; David Garrick
Players; Assistant Feature Editor, "Critic" '44, Co-
Editor '45; Athletic Association; Honor League; National
Honor Society.

Judge Sweeney was a high school classmate of Risque Benedict, Nancy Haysom's brother. In addition to their senior pictures above, the 1945 E. C. Glass High School yearbook included the uncaptioned photo (right).

The Crest, E. C. Glass High School, Lynchburg, Virginia, 1945

Gail Starling Marshall, a former deputy state attorney general who took over Jens Soering's defense in 1994, has said she believes "to a moral certainty" that he is innocent.

Filmperspektive GmbH

Gail Ball, Jens Soering's parole lawyer, hired David Watson, a retired police master detective, to investigate the Haysom murder case in 2011. He concluded that the sockprint evidence was "completely unscientific and prejudicial" and that Elizabeth Haysom was the more likely perpetrator.

Filmperspektive GmbH

Major Ricky Gardner displays a copy of the bloody sockprint at the Bedford County Sheriff's Office. He remains convinced that Jens Soering is guilty of murder.

Filmperspektive GmbH

In his closing argument, prosecutor James Updike emphasized the presence of type-O blood—Jens Soering's type—at the crime scene. Later DNA analysis eliminated Jens as the source of the blood.

Filmperspektive GmbH

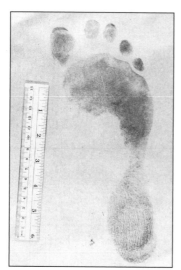 

The smeared bloody sockprint at top was decisive in Jens
Soering's conviction. A prosecution witness paired it with a
transparent overlay of Jens' footprint, above left. Elizabeth
Haysom's footprint is at right.

Jens Soering

Chuck Reid, the original lead investigator in the Haysom murder case, now says he believes Jens Soering is innocent of the killings.

Filmperspektive GmbH

Ed Sulzbach, a longtime FBI criminal profiler, says in the documentary film *The Promise* that he settled on Elizabeth Haysom as the most likely perpetrator of the murders. Sulzbach died in 2016.

Filmperspektive GmbH

Steve Rosenfield, Jens Soering's current lawyer, says the DNA evidence shows that Jens is innocent and "the real killer, a man with type-O blood, is still out there."

Filmperspektive GmbH

Andrew Griffiths, a retired British police officer and expert on police interrogations, investigated the Haysom case in 2016 and concluded that Jens Soering's confession should have been regarded as unreliable.

Andrew Griffiths

Jens Soering, now housed at Buckingham Correctional Center fifty miles from where the Haysoms were murdered, admits he is not totally innocent because he helped cover up the slayings.

Filmperspektive GmbH

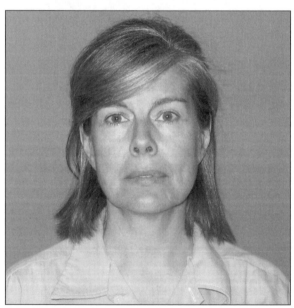

Elizabeth Haysom, housed at Fluvanna Correctional Center for Women, shuns most media interviews and has seldom pled her case in public.

Virginia Department of Corrections

—Part I—

A Far, Far Better Thing

Jens Soering

Falling in . . . Love?

"I would make a man humiliate himself to obtain me."

August 1984–December 1984

E VEN NOW, so long afterward, I keep returning to the night I met Elizabeth Roxanne Haysom, picking over the memories again and again. Memories are all I have now, after more than thirty years in prison. Every morning, when I open my eyes and see the thick bars across my window, I cannot help but think back to that evening at the end of August 1984: the evening my downfall began.

Darkness was falling on our first day at the University of Virginia. Across the campus, in old dorms and new, the air seemed to vibrate with that thrilling mixture of joy and trepidation that sweeps through all first-year students upon their arrival at college. Earlier, our mothers had cried while unpacking our suitcases, our fathers had given us long lists of emergency telephone numbers, and we had more or less gently hustled them back to their station wagons and waved good-bye. Now we were free at last, free at last! But, we all asked ourselves, could we really handle the responsibilities of our new lives as independent adults? Or would we overdose on cold pizza and endless midnight replays of our roommates' record collections?

An amazing thought, looking back more than thirty years later: in 1984, all we college kids had were LP records. No CDs, no MP3 players, no Internet, no cell phones. President Ronald Reagan was still in his first term of office and in my home country of Germany, Helmut Kohl was still chancellor. In fact, my country was still two countries then: West and East Germany.

Even in those long-ago days, however, incoming university students needed guidance and reassurance, so on that first evening at U.Va. all of us first-year students had to attend orientation lectures conducted by college administrators. The two hundred or so honors students, called Echols Scholars, who had been assigned to Watson dorm were scheduled to be oriented together in Webb lounge, in the basement of the new dorm adjacent to ours. Herded along by third- and fourth-year volunteer counselors, we poured into the long, low room a buzzing mass of frazzled nerves and forced smiles. All around us there were so many faces, dozens and dozens, and not one of them familiar!

Wait . . . there, in the corner, that Korean-American girl, I knew her, that was Christine Kim! Reminding her of our first encounter during the Jefferson Scholars competition five months ago, I reintroduced myself and congratulated her on winning one of those sixteen academic scholarships. Christine, however, was not pleased to see me again; unlike me, she had not been named a Jefferson Scholar but had decided to attend U.Va. anyway as a regular honors student. Preferring a conversational partner who did not recall past failure, Christine quickly handed me over to her roommate, Liz Haysom. She had won a scholarship, too, and Christine informed me with lip curled in a smirk that hers was a scholarship to Cambridge University, England. All three of us, having recognized each other immediately as snobs, knew that Cambridge's reputation exceeded the University of Virginia's.

Suitably chastened for unintentionally offending Christine, I turned to her distinguished roommate. Elizabeth certainly did not look prepossessing. She was pale and skinny beneath her purple denim jeans and wore a T-shirt that would have been white if she had washed it more frequently. But the dubious impression created by her appearance was soon dispelled by her manner. Standing at right angles to Christine and me, she threw a sharp sideways glance in my direction, so she would not have to look up at someone whose scholarship was inferior to her own. Then her blue-gray-green eyes turned back to the crowd, measuring everyone coolly from beneath the fringe of short, unkempt, dirty-blond hair. One leg was cocked to the side; one hand rested on its hip; and the other hand slowly brought a cigarette to her lips for a long addict's drag.

"Yah," Liz drawled in her pure BBC–British accent. She had won a scholarship to Cambridge. But she had turned it down. Things had come up. . . .

Few could have made a success of such a performance, but Elizabeth did. Her secret was, I think, her innocent knowingness. That bored look as she blew smoke through her nostrils was designed to remind us that she was experienced, while we were merely fresh-faced ignorant teenagers, interchangeable in our eager naiveté. Yet Liz's face, with its high cheekbones and impish upturned nose, had retained some childlike softness of its own. Though the hard-boiled act clearly was not pretense, she had to work at it, and occasionally she would steal quick glances at our reactions when she thought we were diverted. Elizabeth need not have worried; she had the natural actor's gift of enlisting her audience to cheer her on, to want her performance to succeed.

But before she could continue to impress and entertain, the first of a gaggle of professors stepped up to the microphone on the lectern at the other end of the room. Having coughed and gurgled the meeting to order, the professor and his learned colleagues proceeded to induce that familiar hypnotic trance that overcomes all teenagers when they are forced to hear lectures on "the responsibilities of being student leaders, and the challenges and risks of independence." All I could remember from my orientation session was U.Va.'s most sacred campus rule: freshmen are never called freshmen, but always first-year students. It is possible, I suppose, that the professors did mention that there might be one future double-murderer and one future accomplice to double-murder with us in Webb lounge, and that we should consequently be circumspect in our choice of friends. But if such a warning was given, I missed it.

After the professors had completed their duties as soporific Cassandras, we students drifted back to Watson dorm and tried to shake off our drowsiness. It was Elizabeth, I believe, who suggested that a small group of us should climb Observatory Hill behind our dormitory. Although that night changed my life so completely, I can now only remember one other participant in our excursion: Christine Kim. Even then, Liz was the absolute center of my and the others' attention.

The black pines along the narrow road soon wrapped us in darkness as we embarked on our journey. But we climbed on steadily, leaving the mundane world of dormitories and classes far behind and below us. Our only guides were the moon and the starlight and the sound of Elizabeth's soft British accent, charming us like a pied piper's tune. The higher we rose on our way to the summit, the deeper we penetrated those dark woods, the more we felt strangely privileged to be there with Elizabeth—apart from the others at the foot of the hill.

In the black night she told us of her past: her birth in Salisbury, Rhodesia, now called Harare, Zimbabwe; her family's ties to English aristocracy and the Astors; her education at exclusive Swiss and English boarding schools; her vacations at her parents' estate in Nova Scotia, Canada, where her father had been chairman of a steel company; the prize-winning plays and novels she had written; the plaudits she had earned as an actress at the Royal Academy of Dramatic Arts in London, England; the skiing medals and field hockey championships she had won before her knee injury; the piano and saxophone and cello recitals she had mastered; and, naturally, her academic scholarship to Trinity, the most exclusive of Cambridge University's colleges.

We who climbed Observatory Hill with Elizabeth that night were awed by her accomplishments. As first-year honors students, all of us had been high achievers before coming to U.Va., but none of us could compare with her. My father, for instance, was no steel baron but merely a mid–level German diplomat. Like Elizabeth, I had grown up around the world—in Thailand, Cyprus, Germany, and Atlanta. But unlike her, I apparently allowed the many moves to hinder me. I could boast of no more than being editor of my school newspaper, as well as being named Best English and Best Art Student of my graduating class at my church-affiliated private high school. My musical talent did not extend beyond playing the electric guitar with my friends in a couple of rock bands, and my acting career had been limited to the role of the dim-witted killer in the tenth-grade production of *Arsenic and Old Lace*. No prizes, awards, or championships for me. And Elizabeth's scholarship to Cambridge was not only superior to mine here, but she had also refused to accept hers—a coup of snobbery so enormous that I could only quiver with envy.

But, at least for a while, we were distracted from Liz's wondrous past by a strange orange light glowing through the trees ahead. Soon the light was joined by a mysterious humming sound, which also grew louder as we approached, and I for one was beginning to feel just a little nervous. Who knew what could happen in dark woods at night? But it was only an electric power substation, protected by security lights and high fences with signs reading, DANGER! HIGH VOLTAGE! We walked past quickly to return to the blackness of our narrow road and the shadowy embrace of the pines. The night was what was familiar and comfortable now, while the artifacts of everyday life, like electric substations, seemed an intrusion.

So Elizabeth began playing her piper's magic tune again, but this time in a darker, melancholy key. Now she told us of her beautiful lover, Melissa, who had not won a scholarship to Cambridge and thus could not join Liz there; her decision to run away to Europe with Melissa, so they could be together and free; her thieving and dealing and using heroin in Italy; her dossing in an anarchist commune near the Berlin Wall; her capture, after an accident, by a friend of her parents in U.S. Army Intelligence; her involuntary return to Lynchburg, where her mother's family came from and to where her parents had now retired; and her delayed enrollment at U.Va., which made her two years older than the rest of us first-year students.

How many times in the coming months would I listen to Elizabeth use her voice magic, bewitching me and others again and again! I know that we who followed Liz into the black woods on Observatory Hill that evening believed her every word. She was a messenger from a world of excitement and adventure, a world whose existence we had so far only suspected. Our parents and teachers had sheltered us too perfectly from lesbians and anarchists, so we thirsted desperately for Elizabeth's knowledge of such delicious dangers. We believed her because we needed to.

As Liz finished her tale, we rounded a turn on our road and finally reached the clearing at the top of Observatory Hill. There was nothing to see in the darkness, and the small observatory itself was closed and blind to the stars overhead. But the long journey to the summit had been worth the effort. In Liz's presence we all felt our lives more sharply: the pines by the clearing smelled sweeter, the lights of the cars far below twinkled more brightly, the wind around us tasted fresher, the grass on which we sat to rest felt softer and richer, even the silence seemed to echo with messages meant only for us. It was our first day at college, our first night as independent adults—a time of portents and omens for the future that stretched ahead. And it was Elizabeth who made that night special.

Sometimes when I lie in my cell and feel depressed, I wonder about those portents and omens for the future. I wonder whether some mysterious deity with a sick sense of humor was indeed trying to send me a message. Elizabeth and I lived in a dorm called Watson; twenty months later, when we were arrested in London, we lived in a flat just off Baker Street, the home of Sherlock Holmes and Dr. Watson. The place where she spun the first snare, the fantastic story of her scholarship to Cambridge, was a lounge called Webb, and this one was not as innocuous as Charlotte's. Liz led us to an observatory where nothing could be observed and persuaded us to feel grateful for the experience. On the way to the summit we passed those signs warning of Danger! High Voltage!, prefiguring the large role Virginia's electric chair would play in my future. Oh, I was warned, I was warned.

But looking back, I realize that no warning could have saved me because I would not have listened to it. Like all self-respecting eighteen-year-olds, I was convinced that bad things only happened to other kids, that I was somehow blessedly immune. Like all self-respecting Jefferson Scholars, I believed that I really, truly was smarter and better than everyone else, and that my superiority would protect me. And like all self-respecting virgins (in every sense), I thought my innocence was a kind of shield against the wicked ways of the world, not a gap in my armor. In other words, I was ignorant, arrogant, and naive—that is, I was young! If a wise adult or a more experienced teenaged friend had sat me down and slowly explained the dangers ahead, I would have paid absolutely no attention. So I only have myself to blame for all that followed.

In my ignorance, arrogance, and gullibility, I believed in the autumn of 1984 that Elizabeth was of a completely different, superior caliber to the rest of us first-year students. It was only natural for her to disappear from dormitory life during September and much of October, spending all her free time with third- and fourth-year students her own age.

Occasionally, I caught a glimpse of Liz running to some party in her old, baggy clothes, a style I thought of as Salvation Army chic. Her hair changed colors frequently, though her personal hygiene remained as dubious as on that first night. When Elizabeth began writing a book about her travels in Europe, some of her dorm-mates were allowed to type a few chapters, since such mundane tasks were beneath her. Otherwise, the only traces of her existence were the love-struck, stoned, pseudo-artistic young men and women who left desperate messages with her roommate, Christine Kim.

It never occurred to me during those first few weeks at college that Elizabeth and I might soon fall in love. But I was having too much fun to feel her absence from my life. Although I took too many courses at far-too-advanced levels, I achieved good grades with relatively little work. On weekends I stumbled from one beer-sodden fraternity party to the next, like everyone else. My second band's drummer from high school was now living in a nearby dorm, so we made grand plans for a new rock band.

To my complete astonishment I also discovered that I had a small following among the girls in Watson dorm. Throughout high school I had been forced to restrict my dating to summer vacations in Germany. Only there had I found girlfriends who could hold a conversation about the *nouvelle vague* of the French cinema or the pros and cons of Pershing Missile deployment. The girls at my very preppy private school in Atlanta, on the other hand, had been as dull and uninspired as our school uniforms.

But at the honors-student dorm at U.Va., I was suddenly surrounded by scores of intelligent and attractive girls. And a few of them now pursued me quite determinedly. Later, Elizabeth told me that my popularity was inspired by my continuing public devotion to Katerina, the German girlfriend who had recently dumped me after I returned to America for college. But perhaps my advertising this exploitable weakness was only her reason for noticing me.

Liz drifted back into dorm life some time in the middle of

the fall semester, when she began going to movies with a regular group that included Christine Kim and me. On the surface there seemed nothing inevitable about our slow convergence. Yet the two of us often found ourselves walking side by side to the student-run campus theater, and afterward we usually became absorbed in discussions of the finer points of cinematic technique.

In the course of November 1984, Elizabeth and I started seeing each other almost every day, not just twice a week after our dorm group's excursion to the cinema. The Tree House, a campus snack bar near our dorm, became our regular meeting place. At closing time we were often still deep in conversation, and for a while we became something of an institution there. If anyone needed to find us, he or she only had to go to the Tree House. Friends would come by for a chat, and afterward we two would pick up our private discussions where we had left off.

Liz regaled me with countless tales of her travels in Europe, after running away from England. She made it all sound like so much fun: sleeping on the beach in Italy with Melissa; cracking open pay telephones to finance their heroin addiction; moving into a Hare Krishna shelter near Rome when the money ran out; living on lentils and curds and chanting Buddhist prayers at dawn; and running away again, this time to Berlin, to a commune near the old Reichstag and the Wall. If Charles Dickens had lived in the twentieth century, he would have sent his Oliver Twist on adventures like Liz's.

But many of her stories were far from amusing. While attending an elementary boarding school in Switzerland, Elizabeth had been raped in a particularly brutal manner. Her whole life had been altered by this trauma, she told me. Soon after the rape she began abusing drugs and seeking physical affection from other girls at her single-sex boarding schools. Naturally, she found it impossible to trust others, especially men.

Even more painful was the attitude of her parents, she said. Elizabeth felt that they did not comfort her sufficiently after her rape but instead shunted her from one English boarding school to another while they stayed in distant Canada. Now, after her capture in Berlin and her return to Lynchburg, her mother and father kept her on an unbearably tight leash.

I listened with awe to Liz's outpourings in the Tree House. No one I knew had suffered the sickening tragedy of rape. A few of my high-school friends had smoked marijuana regularly, but none of them had experienced anything like the terrors of cold-turkey heroin withdrawal, as Elizabeth had. The loneliness of seeking love in bars, the cold isolation engendered by reflexive mistrust, the desperation that drove her to run away to Europe—such unhappiness had never touched my placid existence.

Yet in spite of these horrors, Elizabeth had made her life a success, winning awards in high school and making A's in college. Sometimes she even joked about her past! I could not help but see her as a saint, elevated to greatness by passing through hellish suffering.

And Liz was also an excellent listener at a time when I truly needed a friendly ear. Throughout the fall semester I was slipping deeper and deeper into the dreaded Freshman Identity Crisis, a common phenomenon among preppies suddenly removed from the safe confines of parental homes. The goals I had cherished in high school now appeared empty, and the process of finding new dreams was painful and confusing.

I had come to college with the intention of studying psychology as a major. But the University of Virginia's psychology department had little room for my favorite, Freud, or personality psychology in general. Instead, the professors here expected eager students to pay their dues by drilling holes into thousands of rats' skulls, attaching electrodes, and watching which way the poor rodents jumped when the current was turned on. Psychobiology was too bloodthirsty for me. I would have to look for a different major.

Another of my main interests from high school, journalism, was also fading fast during the fall semester. In ninth grade I was suspended from my school's newspaper for one year because I wrote an article about cancer-causing artificial colorings in the imitation orange drink served with lunch. But parents who read my article forced the school to bring back pure orange juice, so I was instantly hooked by the power of the written word. When my suspension was over, I worked hard until I became the paper's editor-in-chief in twelfth grade.

But the overwhelming poverty I saw during a vacation in Mexico in the summer of 1984 shattered my faith in the powers of journalism. Traveling from the beautiful, wealthy districts of Mexico City to the Aztec pyramids in the countryside, my hosts and I had to pass through miles of shantytowns. Here, enormous chemical factories vomited green smoke on unprotected workers' huts while half-naked children played among dried human feces because sewers did not exist. There was no ignoring the deprivation; even with eyes closed, the stench seeped through the car's air conditioner. And it seemed endless, endless, endless.

For the first time in my life I noticed how incredibly privileged and sheltered my life was. On the way home from Mexico I glided through the airport undisturbed, just by waving my German diplomatic passport with its large U.S. diplomatic visa. The other travelers had to wait patiently in line for immigration control, and they were the lucky ones. Most people on the planet saw airplanes only from underneath, from those rows of cardboard-and-mud hovels.

I could not imagine how those people lived. And I certainly could not imagine how I could help them by writing editorials for some newspaper. I began to question the whole direction of my education so far: my bilingual upbringing in German and English, my five years of French classes and two of Latin. What good did my talent for languages do if words could not change anything?

Elizabeth listened patiently as I pondered these weighty questions in the Tree House. My obsession with my Freshman

Identity Crisis was so complete that I never wondered why she seemed to take me as seriously as I took myself. To me, Liz was an older and wiser mentor, and nothing more. Meanwhile, I continued to take girls from our dorm to dances and parties, and she presumably attended exotic drug orgies with sexually fluid art-history majors.

So I was completely flabbergasted by Elizabeth's reaction when I joked one day that we seemed like an old married couple, since we spent so much time talking. Liz stared at me—and then she announced that she had loved me from afar for two months!

But that was not all. She wanted to sleep with me, *immediately.* This of course was far too much for my virgin nerves to handle. I sent Elizabeth to her room and went to mine alone, almost faint from the shock.

It took Liz four hard days of persuading until we finally ended up in the same bed. Naturally, it was a complete disaster. The second time things worked, but only just. Two weeks later, I was enjoying myself so much that I failed my psychobiology exam, dropping my final grade from the perfect A I had maintained so far down to a flat B.

During the first half of December 1984, Elizabeth left this letter in my college dorm room:

> *Jens, I am writing this down because I am a writer not a thinker or speaker—writing is the only way in which I can communicate with any depth; also I need to talk to you now, and you must not be disturbed. So with all of that please forgive the elementary school notion of passing notes.*
>
> *First of all: I love you. I love you selfishly and I love you with pain.*
>
> *I can envisage writing long lists of how desperately I love you, but I have written too much already. Fatigue*

and weariness of affection will drive you to indifference and boredom. (You just left; how hard it is not to cling to you.) Our talk this evening struck me to the whites of my toes. I was shaking so much I could hardly speak. I am glad you realize that I have never physically touched a man the way I touch you, but how can I make you understand that no woman could ever take your place?

    Two months is a long time. It is a longer time when you feel a wheezing pain of loneliness. It is a time long enough to discover one's own mind. During this period I tested every aspect of my devotion. I even tempted my devotion: I pulled and twisted it into multiple amoebas of contortion. I studied as the Jesuits do and still it held fast. The night I went to the gay bar, I was picked up. She was very attractive, amusing, confident and very seductive. For a moment I thought I was rid of the pangs. But as lovely as she was, sitting there, staring at me with enormous blue eyes, tempting, teasing, daring me, she didn't spark any desire. The only thought which passed was a trickling rivulet of giggles that I could still attract the most beautiful girl in the room. A vanity, a small conceit which left a blinding void. Yes, I would have enjoyed dancing with her, feeling the sensuous delight and dangerous thrills of a female companion, but I didn't want her companionship. I wanted her for show. Melissa was for show. There is a special deliciousness in possessing the most desired person in the community. For them to want you and for you not to feel anything. It is an intricate and exotic game. It is a forbidden game. These things made it appealing to me in the past. The difference now is that I want to feel. I want to enjoy the tortuous, wrenching tides which batter me. It has very little to do with genitals. Girls attract me because they are forbidden. The uncertainty, the isolation;

it fascinates me. I enjoy defying the values I'm instilled with. If men have physically tormented me, girls have too, because one is so vulnerable in a lesbian affair.

I'm rambling excuse me.

Joe B.[1] is sleeping in my bed.

I could have fallen in love with a girl. I didn't. I fell in love with you.

When I'm with a woman I long for a man. When I'm with a man I long for the forbidden thrill of a woman.

When I'm with you I feel only longing for all of you and to possess the sweet and equally forbidden fruit of love.

Love has always been forbidden to me. Not for a daisy's whisper I have cared for someone [sic]. They passed through my life if I enjoyed them, and when they bored me I abandoned them. Yes, I have been very cruel. I revelled in being a stone. No one affected my life very much.

I hated my love for you for a long time. I hated myself for discovering vulnerability, but as the weeks passed I began to understand. I had always believed that I made men fall in love with me so that I could take out all the hatred I felt for them by humiliating them. I despised their cheap lust and easy passions. And in the end I made them hate themselves for loving me and the torture I inflicted. I would make a man humiliate himself to obtain me, then I would give him the best fuck he's ever likely to get and then walk out. Then I searched and discovered that the supposed relief and comfort I found in women was exactly the same. I treated them the same way, except I was kinder. It had nothing to do with genitals it was me. For ten years I've been despising myself, and you changed

---

1 Joe B.'s last name has been deleted to protect his privacy.

that. You cared without lust, and you made me feel like a young girl again who had the sun in her eyes and not just a moon between her legs. You were always caring—just caring. I have known (sounds like grandpa) many people, and simple, straightforward caring is a rare thing. One other person in my life cared—she always picked up the pieces—but I never loved her.

That is why I love you (not only because you care, but against all odds being male you care) and that is why I continued in almost peace a sort of turbulent peace to love you for two months and why I want it to go on forever. (At this stage I feel that I can afford to be naive and optimistic.) My mind is full of grandiose expressions which I will spare you—this has all been quite enough.

Looking over it, it is as feebly expressed as anything I have ever said, and even more confused. So it shall suffice to say that I love you, and it may alter in intensity and direction from time to time, but I will always love you with a part of me which no one else will be able to snatch. Elizabeth

So much of our bond was reflected in this letter, so much of my own future could be read in these very lines. If only I had paid attention.

During those long discussions in the Tree House I had come to doubt the power of words. What a fool I was! I should have used my expensive private schooling, with its emphasis on languages, and examined the words in Liz's letter: "I would give him the best fuck he's ever likely to get [. . .] . And in the end I made them hate themselves for loving me and the torture I inflicted." Like the DANGER! HIGH VOLTAGE! signs on our excursion to the summit of Observatory Hill, this letter was a warning. And because I ignored it, two lives were ended and two more were destroyed.

Over the years, I have had much time to pace my cell at night and ask myself, *Why?* Why did I not refuse Liz's attentions? Why did I not choose one of the other girls in our dorm who asked me to dances and parties? Why was I drawn to Elizabeth Roxanne Haysom? It was in 1991, I believe, that I happened to look at a photograph of Liz while passing time by torturing myself with these questions. Suddenly, after so many years buried, a memory returned: my very earliest recollection.

I can remember nothing before the age of two, when I was operated on for a suspected brain tumor. But now I recall waking after surgery in the German hospital to which I had been sent from my father's posting in Cyprus. In the ICU cot next to mine there was a small boy. He was a little older than me, with short blond hair, blue-gray-green eyes and porcelain-white skin: beautiful. I showed him the orange Ferrari with the battery-operated engine fire, which my maternal grandmother brought me. He showed me his white-and-blue river ferry with its little red cars.

I next remember him lying motionless under the bubble of a plastic oxygen tent. And then I remember his bed empty. He had gone to heaven, the nurse told me.

Through the mysterious logic of children I concluded that heaven was the terrifying blackness beyond the edge of my memory, before the operation—that void where sight, sound, taste, smell, and touch were meaningless.

My very earliest memory, thus, is of the death of my first friend, my comrade in adversity. As soon as I found him, I lost him again to that awful nothingness that I had just escaped. And there, in the photograph that had prompted the resurrection of this memory, was Elizabeth: a little older than me, with short blond hair, blue-gray-green eyes, and porcelain-white skin. Beautiful.

—2—

Letters of Love and Hate

"I have the ultimate 'weapon."

December 1984–January 1985

I RECALL THE Christmas holidays of 1984 as the emotional low point of my life thus far. By that time, my parents' marriage had been unhappy for more than ten years. I remember my mother and father arguing during family picnics on Cyprus as early as the beginning of the 1970s. One time, we visited the very beach where Aphrodite, the Greek goddess of love, stepped from the waves onto the shore. I managed to cover myself with sticky black tar from an oil spill that had washed up on the sand that day. Such mishaps upset my father terribly, and the air grew electric with tension. My younger brother and I wandered off into the dunes as soon as possible, leaving behind a heated dispute between my parents about whose fault it was that I had gotten dirty.

After our family moved to Bonn in 1973, I began to notice that my mother was allowing her health to deteriorate because of the frequent arguments. It was also in Germany that my brother Kai and I began to choose sides in the parental battles. Kai tended to support my father, while I sympathized with my mother. As a result, I increasingly became a secondary target of my father's outbursts.

Those years in Germany also marked the time that I was first consciously imbued with the notion that love meant sacrifice. My mother had told me very earnestly one day in Cyprus that she would stay with my father "in spite of everything" because she wanted my brother and me to have "a real family." At the time, I was too young to understand what she meant, but in Bonn I learned that many parents did not remain together forever. All around us in our apartment block, neighbors carried on marital disputes, sometimes very publicly.

My father strongly reinforced the concept that to love meant to sacrifice. He had been at the top of his class at the German Foreign Ministry's academy, and his promotions always came very early in the 1950s and 1960s. The best route to continuing his career advancement was to remain at the Foreign Ministry in Bonn. But my mother was unhappy in our relatively small apartment in Bonn's military district, so my father accepted a transfer to the consulate general in Atlanta, in 1977.

During our first few years there my parents' marriage seemed to improve. We had a large, beautiful house; diplomatic duties entailed an active and varied social life for my parents; and my brother and I attended a prestigious private school. But my father's tour of duty ended in 1980, and further promotions depended on his return to headquarters in Bonn. He decided, however, to forgo advancement for the sake of his family.

His next tour of duty ended in 1983, leaving me with one year of high school to complete. Many diplomats' children suffer greatly from constant changes of schools, and they sometimes even fail to qualify for university. To avoid such a fate for Kai and myself, my father took the unusual step of arranging a third tour of duty in America, though he had to transfer to the consulate general in Detroit. For my sake the family even split up. My father and brother moved north in 1983, while my mother and I stayed in Atlanta until my graduation in June 1984.

When I returned to our new house in Detroit in the second half of December 1984, I found that the atmosphere at home had not improved during my absence at college. But if my family had not changed in those four months, I felt that I had. For the first time in my life I had spent four continuous months out of the pressure cooker, and I could not readjust now.

Many of my friends were in open conflict with their parents because of similar family problems. But I always remained aware of the sacrifices my mother and father had made to raise my brother and me properly. They had given us everything we had wanted, and more. Every angry argument was, in fact, a reminder that my parents stayed married primarily "for the sake of the children." So, unlike my friends, I found it difficult to be angry with my parents. Instead, I felt torn and unhappy and guilty.

Unfortunately, I could not find even temporary relief from the stress of Christmas vacation at home. All my high-school friends were in Atlanta, and all my college friends were in Virginia.

If that were not enough, my dreaded Freshman Identity Crisis flared up again. The Soering family's boy-genius scholarship winner had returned from his first semester at university. But all I could tell my parents was that my old career plans, psychology and journalism, had imploded under the pressure of reality.

So I became deeply, deeply depressed.

Of course, all teenagers sooner or later must suffer through the depths of despair, the crushing anxiety of self-doubt, the existential angst that comes with hormonal changes and an overabundance of pimples. My mistake was to write about my feelings. When Elizabeth sent me a letter from her parents' retirement cottage in Lynchburg, I responded with a thirty-four-page, single-space, typed collection of diary-letters full of loneliness, boredom, and gloom. Sixteen months later, after Liz and I were arrested in London, the police found these letters in our luggage. What Elizabeth and I had written seemed so suspicious to them that they traced our movements all the way back to Virginia and alerted investigators there. If Elizabeth and I had thrown away those letters, we would have been released after serving short sentences for the check-fraud charges on which we had originally been arrested in London. And we would now be free.

From the point of view of the policemen, many parts of my diary-letters certainly appeared sinister. My own lawyer told me years later that, when he read the first of my letters, he thought it could serve as a basis of an insanity defense because it was so bizarre. But at the time I wrote the letter, I had merely been trying to lift my depression by having a little fun. The first few pages were an experiment with a stream-of-consciousness technique, where I scribbled down every thought fragment that entered my mind without organizing or editing anything: the crazier, the better. Earlier, I had received a telephone call from Liz, so I wrote something about a psychedelic "Ma Bell." Next, I professed my love for Elizabeth in the weirdest, most outrageous terms I could imagine, involving an astronomical phenomenon explained in a sketch. Wildness was the effect I aimed for, and the policemen and my lawyer's reactions much later confirmed that I succeeded all too well.

Soon after the stream-of-consciousness experiment, however, my depressed mood reasserted itself. I proceeded to wallow in self-hatred by means of a *Selbstgespraech*, a written conversation with myself about my many terrible failings. These faults included playing electric guitar less than perfectly and maintaining no more than an A-minus grade-point average. The remaining thirty or so pages of my diary-letters contained no further stylistic experiments of this type, but thematically they never strayed far from such insecure navel-gazing.

Looking back now at those decades-old letters and the person I was then, I am struck by how self-absorbed that eighteen-year-old Jens was. Not only did I spend an inordinate amount of time mulling over my own problems, but I also seemed to blame myself for everything that seemed wrong with my life. My general attitude was straight out of a Linda Ronstadt song that was popular then, but has meanwhile been mercifully forgotten: "Poor, Poor Pitiful Me."

Yet what did I really have to be depressed about? By any reasonable standard my life was blessed: I had parents who loved me (even if they didn't love each other); an international childhood (with summers spent sailing off the Outer Banks, horseback riding in northern Germany, or hiking the Swiss Alps); an academic scholarship to a "top ten" university (at least U.Va. was in the "top ten" in the mid-1980s); and a working knowledge of basic three-chord rock 'n' roll (which everyone knows is the true key to happiness and even wisdom). So my self-pity, self-doubt, and self-hatred had no objective, external justification. In reality, I should have been humming another pop song from the 1980s: "My future's so bright, I gotta wear shades."

Elizabeth, by contrast, really did have reasons to be depressed . . . or so I believed. At the time, it never occurred to me to question the veracity of her many tragic tales. Why would anyone lie about being sexually assaulted, for instance?

Take the story Liz told me in the Tree House about being orally raped by three men while attending boarding school in Switzerland. There were so many graphic and gruesome details that it simply had to be true. Even her description of the reconstructive jaw surgery after the attack was compelling, as if she were reliving the pain even as she was remembering it.

At Elizabeth's 1987 sentencing hearing, however, one of her half-brothers testified that there had been no sexual assault at the Swiss boarding school. There might have been a case of indecent exposure, but that was all. So, in fact, she had invented just about the whole story of the rape. And as I came to discover later, she told similar lies about everyone and everything that she disliked.

Item: boarding school. Liz told police in 1986 that she deeply resented being sent away from home to boarding school, and the story of the attack in Switzerland was her expression of that resentment. Item: Melissa. After running away to Europe, Elizabeth needed a scapegoat to share some of the blame, so she accused her lover of being the sexual aggressor in that relationship and of plying her with lesbian pornography; at least, that is what Colonel Harrington, the U.S. Army Intelligence officer who caught her in Berlin, wrote Elizabeth's mother in a letter.

Item: prison guards. Although all inmates hate correctional officers, only Liz went to the extreme of telling a representative of the German Embassy in 1986 that one guard had been suspended for sexually assaulting her. Item: Mrs. Massie. Before her sentencing hearing, Elizabeth learned that her mother's best friend planned to testify that, in her opinion, Liz had physically participated in the murders of her parents; so Elizabeth told authorities that, years earlier, Mrs. Massie had made a pass at her and stroked her breast. Item: Jens Soering. As her 1987 sentencing hearing approached, Liz told police officers and her American psychiatrist three different versions of how I had raped her on the night of her parents' funeral. First she was drunk, next on tranquilizers, and finally asleep. I also could not become sexually aroused without hard-core sadistic pornography, and I fantasized about stocking a basement with torture equipment so I could maltreat Elizabeth with a soldering iron. Last but not least, I repeatedly beat her, and I attacked our pet cat with a knife.

The most detailed and troubling accusations of this type that Elizabeth made were the ones concerning her parents. During our long conversations in the Tree House, she told me that, after her rape in Switzerland, her mother, Nancy, had begun to blame her for provoking the attack. The rape had occurred in a bar while Liz was playing hooky from school. Going to a bar, even in staid old Switzerland, was tantamount to soliciting sexual advances, so she had asked for it. Elizabeth was a whore, and crying rape afterward was only her way of making excuses. These were the sorts of accusations Mrs. Haysom supposedly made when she was drunk, and Liz had had to suffer such emotional cruelty throughout the years after the rape.

But she was not only forced to listen to hurtful words, Elizabeth told me. When she was in her drunken rages, Mrs. Haysom reasoned that, since her daughter was a whore anyway, she would not mind having sex with her mother. So every time Liz returned home from school or holidays, Mrs. Haysom would eventually find an occasion for sexually fondling and touching her daughter. Soon these episodes progressed to outright molestation, in which Elizabeth was forced to perform sexual acts. She did not elaborate when telling me this in the Tree House, and I certainly did not press her, since she seemed close to tears.

Unfortunately, there was more. In later years, Elizabeth said, her mother developed a sexual ritual for herself and her daughter, based on them bathing and then sleeping together. Finally, the abuse even involved Mrs. Haysom's hobby of photography. She took nude pictures of Elizabeth, often in the garden outside their house, and then deliberately humiliated her daughter by showing these photos to friends like Mrs. Massie. This degradation was supposed to prove that Liz really was a whore.

Her father Derek, meanwhile, did nothing to protect his daughter from her mother. Elizabeth told me that she had gone to him repeatedly in earlier years, but his only response had been to stare as if frozen until his daughter left the room. She did not even know if her father disbelieved her, or if he did not care. He simply did not want to get involved. His marriage to Elizabeth's mother had become an emotionless formality and his daughter was a misfit, so why should he bother with what the two of them were doing? Mr. Haysom was only interested in his work and, after retirement, in his hobby of shortwave radio.

In the months before her sentencing hearing in 1987, Liz repeated a version of these accusations to police and her American psychiatrist, but at the actual hearing itself she withdrew all her charges under intense cross-examination by the prosecutor. In those days, when child molestation was still taboo and little understood, lawyers often launched oral attacks on victims of sex crimes in open court; nowadays, such behavior would not be countenanced. As we shall see, local law enforcement, including the prosecutor, had been subjected to intense pressure by Derek and Nancy Haysom's relatives to protect the family's reputation. Forcing Elizabeth to recant her sexual-abuse allegations on the stand was, unfortunately, far from the only instance of official deference to the Haysom name.

What made the prosecutor's in-court attack on Liz all the more surprising was that he had strong evidence to support her allegations—much stronger than is usual in sex-crime cases. First of all, he had the actual photographs. Secondly, Mrs. Massie testified that Mrs. Haysom had shown her and other friends these nude photos of her daughter, explaining them as artistic studies for her hobby of painting watercolors. (However, no watercolor paintings of Elizabeth in the nude were discovered in the Haysom residence.) Thirdly, the well-known local psychiatrist Dr. Robert Showalter testified at the hearing and submitted a detailed written report, according to which he stated that there "definitely" existed what he called a "sexual relationship" between Nancy and Elizabeth Haysom. In Bedford County and across the world, prosecutors win convictions with far less evidence than that.

But this case is different, of course. At Elizabeth's 1987 sentencing hearing, the judge placed both the nude photographs and the psychiatrist's report under seal, so that no one to this day may look at them. (As we shall see later, the judge was and remains a good friend of Nancy Haysom's brother.) In 2008, an assistant producer for the Discovery Channel told me that the transcripts of Liz's sentencing hearing had disappeared from the courthouse. (I still have an official, notarized copy of those transcripts—possibly the only copy in existence.) To any student of the legal records, therefore, there is now no evidence at all that Nancy Haysom sexually abused her daughter. Quite amazing.

I recount these details here because, looking back, I have come to conclude that this pattern of covering up Elizabeth's sexual-abuse allegations is indirect evidence of their truth. If these stories were simply lies, why put so much effort into making the photographs, the psychiatrist's report, and even the transcripts vanish?

Over the last thirty years, I have read a great deal about child molestation, in an effort to understand Liz and her motives. Experts agree that, in virtually all cases, other family members know that abuse is happening. So, in my judgment, it is very likely that some of Derek and Nancy Haysom's relatives were aware of the "sexual relationship" between mother and daughter. And at least conceivably, some of these relatives felt guilty, after the murders, that they had not intervened earlier to stop the abuse. Certainly, I felt and continue to feel intense guilt over this precise issue, as I will explain later; so perhaps they did, too.

If some of the Haysom family members indeed felt guilt over not intervening to stop the molestation, that would explain the great efforts to cover up all evidence of sexual abuse. It would also explain why some relatives seem to hate me so intensely.

I understand that my continuing to bring up this subject must be very painful for the victims' family, and I am truly sorry for that. But what else can I do? I am innocent! It was Liz who killed her parents—and the underlying, fundamental reason was the sexual abuse. So I cannot keep silent about this.

The murders were incredibly violent: dozens of stab wounds, throats slashed all the way to the backbone. Whoever committed this crime was in the grip of overwhelming rage—as well as mentally unbalanced and probably on drugs, too. What can explain such rage? Sexual abuse.

Sexual abuse would also explain much else about Elizabeth. As we shall see in this chapter, she was diagnosed as having borderline personality disorder, which is very frequently associated with a history of sexual victimization. Using drugs and running away from home (or, in Liz's case, boarding school) are also common among abuse victims. Even her pathological lying (with which she was diagnosed, too) as well as her frequent mixing of fantasy and reality make sense, if one sees them as defense mechanisms.

The theme of sexual violence in Elizabeth's tall tales, outlined above, also becomes understandable if she was, in fact, abused by her mother. On some level, Liz probably experienced every real or imagined threat as being sexual in nature. As strange as this may sound, psychologically or subjectively she may have been telling "the truth" as she saw or felt it.

Of course, this is only my view now, after literally decades of reading and studying and puzzling these things out. Back in 1984, however, I simply accepted Elizabeth's allegations of being molested as fact, and this explains why I was not shocked by her Christmas 1984 diary-letter containing fantasies of killing her parents. Given the supposed fact that her father had abandoned her to the sexual perversions of her mother, I sympathized with the feelings Elizabeth expressed. My only concern was to give her any comfort and support I could.

Unlike my own diary-letters, Elizabeth's letter was not neatly typed but scribbled almost illegibly, with lines wandering across the page at drooping angles. After we fell in love, Liz had promised me that she would stop using drugs, but just from the appearance of her writing I suspected that she had not been able to keep her promise. I did not blame her because I accepted her excuse that she needed drugs to cope with the horrors of life at home.

Elizabeth began her letter by telling me that she and Jim Farmer, the son of a local Lynchburg judge, had gone out with his lover to buy some marijuana. Then she included some sketches representing herself and her parents. One particularly striking picture was composed as an inverted triangle, with her mother and father hovering above her. The style of the portraits was similar to Edvard Munch's *The Scream*; her mother and father were drawn as evil, threatening beings while she suffered below in howling agony. Most of Liz's diary-letter was simply a written version of the same theme. She graphically articulated her profound resentment of her parents, describing them as drunken, hateful people who wanted to control her every move. In one passage she wondered:

> *Would it be possible to hypnotise my parents, do voodoo on them, will them to death? It seems my concentration on their death is causing them problems. My father nearly drove over a cliff at lunch, he nearly got squashed by a tree when he got home (and he keeps falling over), and my mother (drunk) fell into the fire. I think I shall seriously take up black magic. . . .*
>
> *We can either wait till we graduate and then leave them behind, or we can get rid of them soon. My mother said today that if some accident befell them, she knew I would become a worthless adventurer. More maternal acumen.*

When I read those words, my only reaction was an overwhelming feeling of pity for Elizabeth. How deep was her suffering, that she expressed it in such terms! I also believed I had a deeper, semi-professional insight into Liz's personality because, throughout high school, I had read widely in the field of psychology. With all the wisdom of my eighteen years, I concluded that Elizabeth's fantasy of doing voodoo on her parents was her way of using humor to gain emotional distance from her anger. Freud had explained all that, it was obvious! Why else would she have chosen something as ridiculous and unrealistic as voodoo? After all, everyone knew that so-called voodoo only happened among uneducated Haitians who believed so firmly in their witch doctor's powers that they gave up on living and died. The psychology books I had read called this phenomenon *autosuggestion*.

So I responded to Elizabeth's apparently humorous voodoo fantasy by playing along with her joke. I thought it best to encourage this form of venting her frustration and anger; the alternative was for her to smoke marijuana with Jim Farmer. Also, by indulging her I could let Liz know that I sympathized with her, that she was not alone in her suffering. Since "voodoo" was to be the theme of her running joke I answered by quoting every Wolf Man, Dracula, and Frankenstein movie ever made: "Strange things are happening within me," after which the full moon rose and Lon Chaney Jr. turned into a werewolf. True, this was not side-splittingly funny. But I was feeling depressed myself, and her life did not seem very humorous either. The entire passage in which I responded to Elizabeth's voodoo fantasy reads as follows:

> By the way, were I to meet your parents, I have the ulti-
> mate "weapon." Strange things are happening within
> me. I'm turning more and more into a Christ-figure (a
> small imitation, anyway), I think. I believe I could either
> make them completely lose their wits, get heart attacks,
> or they would become lovers (in an agape kind of way) of
> the rest of the world.

Years later, the police attempted to use my choice of the word *weapon* in this passage as evidence that I had been planning murder. This always seemed far-fetched to me. Did anyone really think that I had been plotting to kill my girlfriend's parents through psychical-ly induced heart attacks? Moreover, I had deliberately enclosed the word *weapon* in a second set of quotation marks: ". . . the ultimate 'weapon.' Strange things. . . ." As any English schoolbook explains, the grammatical significance of that second set of quotation marks was to indicate that I had meant not a real but a metaphorical weapon. And a few lines later I had explicitly written that "love is [. . .] the ultimate 'weapon' 'against' your parents." The additional quotation marks around the word *against* again indicated that the metaphorical weapon of love could not really be used "against" anyone.

In fact, I had only expressed my faith in the power of "love" to overcome any problems. This was my admittedly feeble attempt to take up Liz's dark voodoo fantasy, to play along with it to comfort her, and then to turn it into something positive. I was harking back to the theme of Elizabeth's letter quoted in chapter 1, reminding her that she now had a weapon against the suffering at home, a force for the good: our love.

My diary-letters contained only one more reference to Liz's letter: ". . . 'voodoo,' etc., is possible." Again, I used quotation marks to indicate that, whereas real voodoo did not exist, the associated phenomenon of autosuggestion certainly was possible. In total, I spent perhaps half a page of my thirty-four-page-long diary-letters responding to Elizabeth's fantasy of killing her parents. Most importantly, nowhere in my letters or hers were there any plans to commit homicide four months later.

But our correspondence about willing the Haysoms to death through voodoo clearly was evidence that our relationship and our thoughts were abnormal as early as the Christmas holidays of 1984. In Liz's case there were some clues in her biography that she was disturbed in some way: running away to Europe, abusing drugs including heroin, forming unhealthy relationships. But what explanation could there be for me, a Jefferson Scholar who had virtually no contact with drugs and, until recently, had been a virgin?

Some answers may be discovered in the findings of two prominent English forensic psychiatrists, Dr. John Hamilton and Dr. Henrietta Bullard, who examined both Elizabeth and me in our separate prisons shortly after our arrest in London. The doctors acted as neutral "friends of the court"; unlike the American system,

English judges appoint expert witnesses whose findings are accepted by both prosecution and defense. Since the police had provided
the psychiatrists with transcripts of our interrogations, they spent
little time questioning us about the killings. Instead, we had to
discuss our relationship in enormous detail.

By December 1986, the English doctors' reports were
complete. Liz was diagnosed as a borderline schizophrenic and a
pathological liar, whereas I was found to be suffering from a mental
condition called *folie à deux*. The American Psychiatric Association
in its *Diagnostic and Statistical Manual of Mental Disorders* has
abandoned the term *borderline schizophrenia* in favor of a range of
personality disorders:

> 301.83 Borderline Personality Disorder. . . .
> Frequently this disorder is accompanied by many
> features of other Personality Disorders such as
> Schizotypal, Histrionic, Narcissistic, and Antisocial
> Personality Disorders. In many cases more than one
> diagnosis is warranted. Quite often social contrari-
> ness and a generally pessimistic outlook are seen.
> Alternation between dependency and self-assertion
> is common. During periods of extreme stress tran-
> sient psychotic symptoms of insufficient severity or
> duration to warrant additional diagnosis may occur.
> At least five of the following are required:
> (1) impulsivity or unpredictability in at least two
>   areas that are potentially self-damaging, e.g.,
>   spending, sex, gambling, drug abuse, shoplift-
>   ing, overeating, physically self-damaging acts;
> (2) a pattern of unstable and intense interper-
>   sonal relationships, e.g., marked shifts of atti-
>   tude, idealization, devaluation, manipulation
>   (consistently using others for one's own ends);

(3)   inappropriate, intense anger or lack of control of anger, e.g., frequent displays of temper, constant anger;

(4)   identity disturbance manifested by uncertainty about several issues relating to identity, such as self-image, friendship patterns, values, and loyalties, e.g., "Who am I?", "I feel like I am my sister when I am good";

(5)   affective instability: marked shifts from normal mood to depression, irritability, or anxiety, usually lasting a few hours and only rarely more than a few days, with a return to normal mood;

(6)   intolerance of being alone, e.g., frantic efforts to avoid being alone, depressed when alone;

(7)   physically self-damaging acts, e.g., suicidal gestures, self-mutilation, recurrent accidents or physical fights;

(8)   chronic feelings of emptiness or boredom.[2]

Not even one year after Dr. Hamilton and Dr. Bullard diagnosed Elizabeth as a borderline schizophrenic, Dr. Showalter confirmed their diagnosis at her October 1987 sentencing hearing. He testified that Liz had the most severe case of borderline personality disorder that he had seen in his entire career. According to Dr. Showalter, the only symptom she did not exhibit was . . . physical violence. I nearly fell off my chair with laughter when I read this in the court transcript. As pathological liars go, Elizabeth must surely be one of the greatest in history.

Dr. Showalter never met or diagnosed me, but Dr. Hamilton

---

2 *Diagnostic and Statistical Manual of Mental Disorders*, third edition, American Psychiatric Association, 1980.

and Dr. Bullard found that I suffered from a folie à deux. The American Psychiatric Association describes this condition as follows:

> 297.30 Shared Paranoid Disorder. The essential feature is a persecutory delusional system that develops as a result of a close relationship with another person who already has a disorder with persecutory delusions. The delusions are at least partially shared. Usually, if the relationship with the other person is interrupted, the delusional beliefs will diminish or disappear. In the past this disorder has been termed *folie à deux*, although in rare cases, more than two persons may be involved.[3]

By the time the psychiatrists had made these diagnoses I had recovered sufficiently to accept their findings. However, I disagreed in one respect and told the doctors so. Before the homicides of March 30, 1985, I had been able to recognize that Liz occasionally stretched the truth. In a note I wrote to her in March 1985, I even made a joke of her exaggerations, dubbing them "perversions of truth" or "POTS." These POTS did not make her a liar in my view; I believed she had the wild, unrestrained imagination of a creative artist, and I loved her for that, too. But the doctors told me that my willingness to overlook Elizabeth's lies was itself a precursor to the folie à deux. I still find that explanation hard to accept, perhaps because it indicates just how far out of control I was.

In the endless years since 1986, I have had time not just to ruminate over my folie à deux but also to reread Shakespeare, whom I had loved so deeply in high school. One of his sonnets

3 *Ibid.*

casts an interesting light on my ambivalent and complex relationship to Liz's deceptions:

> *When my love swears that she is made of truth,*
> *I do believe her, though I know she lies;*
> *That she might think me some untutor'd youth,*
> *Unlearned in the world's false subtleties.*

That stanza describes the folie à deux as well as anything that the American Psychiatric Association has written.

The Happiest Days of My Life

"Then all of you will disappear into me."

January 1985–March 1985

T HE FIRST TWO-AND-A-HALF months of the spring 1985 semester were the happiest of my life. Liz and I were deeply, passionately in love, but our relationship was not yet as obsessive as it became after the murders. We were simply boyfriend and girlfriend: young, innocent, and joyously filled with life and lust.

At least, that is how our love seemed to me then. I was happy, often deliriously so, but my happiness was based on a web of Elizabeth's lies, which grew and grew until I was wrapped up like the spider's meal in a little cocoon, ready for consumption. But I remained blissfully unaware of the deception and the danger, and if anyone had tried to warn me I would not have listened. In fact, looking back, I think I was often more than just "blissfully unaware," more than just an innocent fly caught in an evil spider's web. On some level, I surely must have realized that our affair was literally too good to be true. But, like an alcoholic or a drug addict, I wanted the "high" that Elizabeth gave me because it made me feel so good. The "high" became more important than the truth, more important than anything.

And that is what hurts most now, even after all these years in prison. I just cannot remember a happier time in my life than the first three months of 1985, even though I now know everything was false. My first eighteen years, before Elizabeth, were comfortable but joyless; and all the years after our arrest have been hell. So that counterfeit love of Liz's, that poisonous fruit, really was the best of times for me. And the worst of times, too.

Was there any aspect of our relationship that was genuine, or was it all manipulative lies on her part and blind infatuation on mine? I do not think I can answer that question for either myself or Elizabeth. In prison in London, I asked the English forensic psychiatrists who examined us; one said that "some of it might have been real," but both also told me that borderline schizophrenics are unable to love others.

Some clue to Liz's feelings for me may be found in a letter she wrote to a mutual friend at U.Va. during the Christmas holidays of 1984, around the same time she sent me the diary-letter with the voodoo fantasy. After we returned to college in January 1985, this friend showed me the letter. I am not sure of his motives; like so many of the naive boys in our honors student dormitory he, too, had a crush on Elizabeth. Perhaps he hoped the letter's contents would cause me to leave her, giving him renewed hope. Perhaps he sincerely wanted to warn me.

Liz's written comments about me were not overtly sinister, but they revealed much about her underlying attitude. Although claiming to see some potential for greatness in me, she emphasized that I seemed to lack the courage to create. So far, her efforts to free me from my self-imposed shackles had been fruitless, and she was not certain she could ever overcome my cowardice.

Was I outraged by the condescension implicit in Elizabeth's description of me? Was I concerned that she saw her role in our relationship as a combination of schoolmistress, spiritual guide, and agent provocateur? No. I asked the mutual friend to whom she had written this letter whether I could photocopy it so I could

study Liz's remarks and learn from them. Living up to her expectations of me seemed the highest possible goal in life. Elizabeth truly
had me well in hand.

I loved being in her hand; oh, it was a downright turn-on! I still
have to smile when recalling the shock of her hand on my crotch as
we sat drinking wine in O'Halloran's, the blood rushing to my face
and loins. Pushing my glasses back up my nose, I peered around
the bar to see if we had been noticed. Simultaneously, I reached
under the table and tried to pull Liz away, but she refused to let
go! A public wrestling match over my penis was even worse than
her surreptitious groping, so I gave up. Instead, I asked her politely
to relinquish her hold on my member. I demanded; I cajoled; I
begged; I pleaded. But Elizabeth just smiled and smiled.

She stopped before the episode became messy, and we both
laughed about it long afterward. This incident was paradigmatic
of our relationship and a perfect illustration of why I loved her
so much. Liz had encouraged this first visit to O'Halloran's, a
well-known bar and restaurant on "the corner" diagonally across
from the U.Va. hallmark rotunda. It was the mild whiff of danger
surrounding the excursion that finally persuaded me to go. At that
time, Virginia licensing laws still permitted a twenty-year-old like
Elizabeth to purchase alcohol at the bar, but she was certainly not
supposed to bring a glass to me in the restaurant section of the
establishment. Having enticed me into becoming her accomplice
in this minor misdeed, Liz had to push on and risk public embarrassment and possibly worse. Of course, that risk was all mine, but
I did not mind. Quite the opposite: I loved it; wanted more and
more of it. I was growing addicted to the thrill of the unexpected,
the danger Elizabeth brought into my life.

The sex, whether public or private, had me hooked, too. Our
roommates came to dread our late-night appearances, hand-in-
hand at the door. Inevitably, we would ask one of them to leave for
a couple of hours, earning us the nickname, "the rabbits."

She wrote me a letter that encapsulates her excessiveness, her manipulative exoticism, and how completely beyond any kind of prior experience she was for me. This letter, which you may choose to skip given its pornographic nature, was made a part of the court record:

> *First I want to pull you close to me, just standing, feeling your breath on my neck, feeling my juices, feeling your hardness pressing against my belly, feeling my nipples growing hard, so hard they hurt, pressing them into your chest. My hand is on the nape of your neck. Pulling your head down to me, down to my mouth. Just a light kiss, a light, wet kiss. My lips pressed into you, and my tongue licking your lips, your teeth, sucking on your tongue, holding it, biting it, sucking your breath away and filling you with lust.*
>
> *And then on the bed, you on top of me, my hips raised, my legs splayed wide open, you're looking down at me, my lips full and red, so wet, aching for you, my nipples standing up to meet you, and you touch my naked body, on my thigh. I shudder and pull you down, your hardness sinking into my lips. I tremble, I shudder, my muscles are so tight, holding you, sucking on you, pulling on you. I can hear your breath, my back is arched to hold all of you. I grind myself into you.*
>
> *I want to fuck you till I bleed, and then, when we can barely move with exhaustion, I want to do it again, sooo slowly. I will rub you with my juices and nuzzle your balls with my nose. I want to lick you, to suck you, to nibble on the edge of your head. And then I will sit on you, rocking on you. My eyes are closed and I can feel your finger on my pussy. I will rock on you till I almost feel those huge rumblings in my aching hole. Then you*

will flip me over and plunge into me, long and slow, your hands clasping my outstretched buttocks. My hard nipples rubbing against the sheet, I will scream my love and pleasure for you.

We sleep in each other's arms. Our red faces cooling in the sweet breath of the other, our bodies intertwined, moist with the heat of our sex. And we sleep, a dreamless, peaceful, so deep sleep.

And when we awake, I will raise my lips to your lips. Your lips will tease and tantalize my huge wet need. Your nose will rub deep into every crevice, your finger will slip in and out, around and about the edges of my oozing hole. Your finger will slip between my buttocks and I will whimper and moan with abandon, in a tense anxiety. I will plead for you, I will beg for you, arching my body out to reach you, to cling to you. I will feel my head disappearing, my legs will strain to part further. I will grab your head and force you to release me, my own fingers will reach down to spread my lips further so that your probing, enquiring tongue can push further and further. And release will come, huge, brilliant, painful colors will rack through me, torturing me with their exquisite pleasure.

My eyes will slowly open, and I will see you smiling up at me from between my thighs. Your wet sweet face encased in my flesh, and I will smile back at you and pull you towards me. My fingers will reach for your hardness and hold it. Hold it and clasp it, rubbing it, pulling it, coaxing it to want me, and I will slip it in.

And when you tell me you are hungry, I will come and sit on your face, and you will eat your fill, and I will wiggle with ecstasy. And when I am hungry I will kneel before you and slip my face into your groin. I will knead

*your buttocks and slip my finger past your hole, touch its
wetness and feel its warmth. My lips will cover your head,
and it will ease its growth into my sucking, slithering
mouth. I will tug at you, wanting all of you, cuddling
your balls. My nose and lips, my fingers will explore the
hard ridge between your legs, your sacks of seed and your
hair. My finger will slip again to your hole and my mouth
will cover you. Then all of you will disappear into me.*

*O god, o god, o god I've gone on too long. But I
want you so bad your head in my lap. I'm going to wank
tonight. I will imagine you licking me. I will imagine you
lying beside me naked, our bodies arched towards each
other but not quite touching, your breath on my breast,
you touching my skin so lightly with your fingers oh, oh,
oh. STOP.*

Of course I did not want to stop. And perhaps I could not have
stopped even if I had wanted to. Elizabeth's overwhelming presence in my life, combined with my raging hormones and the sudden
induction into sex for someone whose sheltered life had been the
essence of control and responsibility, made her literally irresistible.

Having had no experience with other girls, I cannot judge
whether Elizabeth enjoyed sex with me or only employed it as a
carrot, a training tool for when I was a good boy. But I do know
that she deliberately used a very effective stick to make me behave:
my own feelings of guilt.

One evening during those first three months of 1985 I
returned from the library to Watson dorm and, as was my habit,
immediately went to Liz's room. She was squatting barefoot on
her mattress, with her face hidden between her arms as she hugged
her knees. The room was dark, and all I could glimpse in the pale
light of the street lamps outside was the tousled spikes of her short
blond hair.

I entered the room, flipped the light switch, and called Elizabeth's name. Not even using her middle name, Roxanne, elicited the usual reaction—a disdainful snort. Liz remained tightly curled in her egg. Stepping closer, I put my hand on her shoulder to stroke her, and finally she responded.

Slowly and very dramatically, her left arm straightened and turned, until I could see the inside of the elbow. There, on that beautiful porcelain-white skin, was a red needle-puncture mark topped with a tiny scab.

From the inside of her protective ball, Liz spoke a few short sentences in a low, raspy voice. She knew that she had promised. But I had not come to her room that afternoon before leaving for the library. She had thought I was getting bored with her. And then one of Jim Farmer's friends had come by. So she had gone along, and she had fallen off the wagon, and she had taken some heroin. She knew she had promised, she knew! She was sorry. She guessed I would not want her anymore now. She accepted that. Would I please leave her? She was not feeling too well.

I told her I loved her and kissed the top of her head, since no other surface was available for kissing. But when I tried to put my arms around her shoulders, Elizabeth shook me off weakly. She was sorry, so sorry, but she had to be alone. The heroin. . . . Would I please go?

So I left and spent a sleepless night alone in my dorm room. This was all my fault, mine alone! If only I had not been so thought-less, if only I had been more worthy of Elizabeth's love, then she would not have been forced to resort to drugs. Why, oh why, did I always think of myself first, instead of her, the most wonderful woman in the world? From then on, I made sure I informed Liz of my every move, lest worrying over me drove her to heroin again.

But she not only wanted to know my day-to-day schedule. As we resumed our night-long discussions in the Tree House, Elizabeth also took the lead in designing long-term career goals and strategies for both of us. It seemed natural to plan far into our joint futures, even though we had been in love for only a few weeks; after all, we were soul mates.

Liz's soul was that of an artist of course, and she told me much of how her talent would have to be nurtured and supported. The essence of creativity was risk-taking, Elizabeth explained. She needed to seek the new, the different, the dangerous, so she could transmute these experiences into art. This made her and all artists unsuitable for normal jobs requiring regular hours and stability, which explained why so many creative geniuses starved in garrets. In past centuries there had been a tradition of aristocratic patrons supporting artists to free them from financial worries, but nowadays the only option was to sell out, to prostitute one's talents in the service of Hollywood and Madison Avenue. Only very few artists were lucky enough to find a soul mate, someone who would provide for fiscal and physical needs while allowing the space and freedom required for creative risk-taking. Maybe she would get lucky, Liz joked, or else she would have to return to that commune in Berlin and crack open pay telephones again.

I shuddered at the thought of Elizabeth starving in a garret, just because she was a genius. Life was so unfair! And she was such a loving and considerate person. Not only did she share her most private thoughts on art and creativity with me, but she also asked me about my own plans for the future. What, for instance, did I plan to do with my scholarship?

This was a question I found almost impossible to answer. My Freshman Identity Crisis was only superficially in remission because of our love, and I still had no idea what new major might suit me. As far as my scholarship was concerned, I had not thought about it at all. So far, my attitude toward it had been almost entirely emotional: I resented it deeply.

In my last two years of high school I had worked deliberately on a plan to return to Germany as quickly as possible. The many advanced placement (A.P.) tests I took would have permitted me to attend a German university after only one more year at any American college. But in my senior year of high school I had unexpectedly won one of those sixteen academic scholarships in U.Va.'s national Jefferson Scholars competition. My school made an enormous fuss, and my parents took the view that this scholarship had retroactively justified their decision to split up the family so I could finish my senior year in Atlanta while my brother went to Detroit. No one considered the possibility that I might prefer going to Germany in one year instead of spending the next four in Virginia.

The day I received the telephone call with the "good news," I was interning with a law firm in Atlanta. I remember my mother's excitement; and I also remember my own complete absence of joy. Of course, I was proud to have beaten some incredibly talented competitors, but I also felt trapped. Later that afternoon, the lawyer supervising my week-long internship took me to a courtroom for a brief procedural appearance. As we waited for his turn, a wild-eyed young man with shaggy hair was brought in for a bail hearing. He stood accused of killing his father with an ax.

If that was another warning, I ignored it as well. I accepted the scholarship to U.Va., but I resented the college for delaying my return to Germany for four years. Most of all, I resented myself, for not having the courage to set my own dreams above my school and family's expectations. That was why I nearly shriveled with envy when I heard of Elizabeth's audacious decision to refuse her scholarship to Cambridge.

Liz burst into loud laughter when I finished my narrative in the Tree House. I had made my bed, she told me, so I might as well enjoy lying in it. Who had ever heard of anything as ridiculous as my feeling resentment over a plum like the Jefferson Scholarship? If only I were to look at it sensibly, I would realize that I had been given a wonderful opportunity.

As I listened to Elizabeth explain her views on my scholarship,

I felt surprised and obviously impressed that her mind had such a practical and even Machiavellian bent, especially for someone who considered herself an artist. The first thing she pointed out to me was that the U.Va. Alumni Association had not awarded me a scholarship then worth $32,000 out of pure generosity. The sponsors wanted highly talented seed corn for its many-tentacled old boys' network of alumni. Long after graduation, the former scholarship recipients and the Alumni Association would continue to open doors for one another, to the benefit of both. And not just any doors; the sponsors wanted us to rise as high as possible. Each semester, the scholarship winners were required to attend several field trips organized by the Alumni Association. Most recently, we had been bused to a U.Va. Alumni Reunion on Capitol Hill in Washington, where we were introduced to staffers, officials, and congressmen, including Senator Ted Kennedy. Building on these opportunities was an obligation I owed not only to the scholarship sponsors but also myself, Liz told me.

I was always yammering on about how I wanted to help people, how I wanted to save the world; but writing newspaper articles would not feed hungry Mexicans, and drilling holes into rats' skulls would not contribute to an understanding of the psyche. So why, she asked, did I not open my eyes to see the obvious solution in front of me or, more precisely, just across campus?

The U.Va. history department had a special program affiliated with the United States State Department, to provide training for applicants to the American diplomatic service. This was perfectly suited to my needs. If I were really smart, I would follow up on my B.A. here by transferring to Georgetown University's graduate-level program in international relations, which was also closely allied to the U.S. State Department. Throughout my studies, I should spend as much time as possible taking advantage of U.Va.'s strong connections in Washington, building a network of contacts in government and politics. That was what the Alumni Association wanted all the scholarship winners to do, and they would help me in any way they could. By the time I returned home, I would be virtually indispensable to the German Foreign Service, since America would always be my country's most important ally. My rise to the top of the German diplomatic service would be astonishingly fast, and if I joined the right political party I might even make a successful transition into politics.

I was born to join the Foreign Service, Elizabeth argued. I had grown up as a diplomat's child, I already spoke three modern languages, and I could always study a few more. If I wanted to help people and save the world, this was the way to do it.

I remember sitting in our booth in the Tree House and feeling stunned at the breadth and depth of Liz's vision for my life and career. She must have spent a great deal of time thinking about me! Until now, I had never systematically planned my own future, and I certainly had never thought in terms of networking and politics. Of course, others had told me that excellent test scores alone would not guarantee my success, but in practice my thinking had not progressed beyond that naive level. Clearly, I had much to learn from Elizabeth in this regard, as in so many others.

Although I was not sure I wanted to dedicate my life to diplomacy, I did have one comment on Liz's lecture that I shared with her straight away, to show I had been paying attention and also thinking of her. She, I suggested, would make an ideal companion in such a career—that is, if she really wanted me. Having grown up in many different countries, Elizabeth was accustomed to the migratory diplomatic lifestyle; she clearly had a talent for politicking and partying, the two main requirements for diplomats' spouses; and her career as an artist would be easily compatible with mine. In fact, since she required the new, the different, the dangerous to stimulate her creativity, frequent transfers to strange countries might be ideal for her: that is, if she wanted me.

Liz nodded sagely. Naturally, she had already thought of that, but she had wanted the suggestion to come from me so I would not feel she was pressuring me. The fact that I had arrived at the same conclusion so quickly just proved that we really *were* soul mates.

From the vantage point of my dingy prison cell I cannot help but smile at that tinsel dream of success, Elizabeth-style. She was no doubt right; theoretically, her career plan for me had been quite achievable. It also goes without saying that I would have been pleased to lick politicians' boots forever so long as this supported the extravagant international lifestyle a creative genius like Liz required.

Apart from supplying Elizabeth with raw material for her fantasies of networking me into the post of German Foreign Minister, the Jefferson Scholarship also provided us with some tangible benefits in the form of a generous amount of "spending money." Instead of using this for textbooks, which I let my parents buy, I paid for virtually all our frequent restaurant meals, cinema tickets, and so forth. Liz always offered to pay her own way, and likewise I always refused—except for once a week, when I allowed her to treat me. What she did with all the money that she saved through my scholarship never puzzled me, though I now have my suspicions.

At the time, however, Elizabeth had grandiose purchasing plans. She wanted to buy a genuine black London cab, which we had spotted in a used-car lot on the way to a movie theater. She would not be able to afford it by herself, but maybe. . . ? I had to let her down; even the Jefferson Scholarship spending money would not stretch to a London cab. Liz took the disappointment well, and we laughed at the idea. Her riding to classes in a lugubrious London cab with the steering wheel on the wrong side—that would have been a sight worth seeing! Quintessential Elizabeth: flamboyant, outrageous, and above all different, as distinct and separate as possible from the common herd.

Having become her lover and appendage, I found myself increasingly separated from the other students in our dormitory.

In part, this was simply the consequence of spending almost all my spare time with Liz instead of the other friends I had made during the first semester. But outright hostility by Elizabeth's former lovers, as well as some intentional maneuvers of her own, also contributed to my growing isolation.

Most of my male friends and acquaintances in Watson dorm found Liz as fascinating as I did, and when she chose me as her boyfriend at the end of the autumn semester, they were all disappointed to a greater or lesser degree. Some remained on relatively good terms with both of us, though a few of them had a habit of dropping by Elizabeth's room when I was elsewhere. Joe B., who was asleep on Liz's bed while she wrote the letter quoted in chapter 1, coped less well with losing the competition for her favor; he went into a depression marked by crying fits, which required Elizabeth's attendance at his bedside. How could she prefer a bookish type like me to him, a body-building athlete whose dorm walls were decorated with posters of bare-breasted girls wielding Uzi submachine guns? He discussed this mystery with me, too, and to his credit he tried hard to hide his disdain for me. Perhaps he assumed that there must have been some substance to me somewhere, since Liz would not have chosen a complete loser over him.

There were several other boys in our dorm whose relationships with me grew strained after Elizabeth and I became lovers. Only John H., an American of Egyptian extraction, maintained the same carefree, if not close friendship we had shared during the first semester. In February or March he even invited me to spend a weekend at his family's house in Washington. It was not long afterward, however, that his true feelings burned through the facade of friendliness. Since arriving at U.Va., John had developed the habit of drinking himself into a stupor twice a week. This time, he stopped before actually passing out, and when I entered his dorm room, he staggered towards me with a half-full bottle of alcohol and his cigarette lighter blazing. If I did not stop seeing his Liz, he yelled, he would pour the Scotch all over me and set me on fire. *And now I should get out!*

John's threat was not too credible, but the intensity of his feelings certainly was genuine. There were others who literally hated me because Elizabeth had chosen me over them. Another Jefferson Scholar in his third year at U.Va. made a point of glowering at me and demonstratively storming out of rooms whenever we happened to meet. Like the other older students who had frequently visited Liz's dorm room in the fall, he was convinced that she would soon leave me. Her rightful place was with their trendy clique of artists, gays, and drug users. How dare a boring little nobody like me come in and steal Elizabeth away from them!

That question was hurled at me one night by a fourth-year girl whom Liz and I met on our way home from the movies. I would have laughed at her if I had not first seen the abject worship in her eyes as she looked at Elizabeth, and the despairing misery when she turned to me. How well did I know that feeling of adoration, and how well could I imagine that pain if Liz ever left me! Later, Elizabeth told me that this girl had cut her hair short and dyed it blond in imitation of the object of her obsession. That might have been another one of her POTs, but I doubt it. So many young men and women at U.Va. burned with fanatical devotion for Liz. But she loved only me; no wonder I was ostracized.

If the antipathy of Elizabeth's disciples were not enough to isolate me, Liz herself slowly separated me from the normal social life of other students. The spring semester was supposed to see the birth of a new rock band led by me and the drummer of my second band in high school, who now attended the U.Va. school of architecture. We had purchased a new PA system, and part of the line-up was already set: Jonah Warn on drums, Jens Soering on electric guitar, and Elizabeth Roxanne Haysom on saxophone. But as week upon week of the spring semester passed by, Liz could still not find a saxophone, either bought or rented. Jonah and I suggested she look for a synthesizer, since she had also been an accomplished pianist in high school. No, this too was impossible, since that spiritless electronic sound would not permit the full expression of her artistic emotions. Perhaps, Elizabeth suggested, Jonah and I should form a band without her, though that would mean that she and I would be spending less time together. . . .

This was out of the question, of course! By the middle of the spring semester, Jonah had bought out my half of our new PA and was looking for other partners for his rock band. I did not miss him or my beautiful Les Paul, which was gathering dust under the bed in my dorm room. Who needed music when I had Liz?

For a little while there even seemed a chance that the band project would be reborn, this time as an acoustic ensemble. Christine Kim, Elizabeth's roommate, would play cello, Liz would play a real piano, and I could have my acoustic Yamaha guitar sent down from Detroit. Elizabeth and Christine could even switch up once in a while, I proposed, since Christine had studied piano and Liz was also a cellist.

But that idea did not receive Elizabeth's endorsement. A few weeks prior, Christine had heard someone play the cello beautifully as she walked past Watson dorm, yet she had not been able to discover the musician's identity when she asked around later. Liz now revealed to me that she had been the mystery cellist; she had used Christine's instrument without her permission. In fact, Christine did not even know that her roommate could play the cello. If we three now formed an acoustic ensemble, Christine would have to be told all this sooner or later, and that might rupture their friendship. Perhaps it would be best if we did not form an acoustic band, either. Also, would I please promise not to mention the cello episode to Christine?

Naturally, I promised. It seemed like such a small request. This was, however, the first secret of Elizabeth's that she made me keep, and lies—even lies of omission or silence—have an insidious effect.

From then on, I could not fully trust myself around Christine, lest I accidentally reveal Liz's secret, and Christine undoubtedly noticed my distance, even if she could not guess its reason. The lie always stood between us, separating us. As I became Elizabeth's accomplice in other, much greater lies, I would find myself isolated completely from the world. By then, it was too late.

The same air of conspiracy also infected my one and only meeting with Mr. and Mrs. Haysom. So far as I knew, Liz and I had no particular secret to keep from her parents, but as our lunch date approached, her extreme nervousness spread to me as well. Derek and Nancy Haysom were child abusers, as she had told me in shocking detail in the Tree House, and I would have to watch my every word lest it be turned against Elizabeth somehow.

Once the four of us had completed our introductions and found our table at O'Halloran's, I turned on my best bright-young-scholarship-winner-and-diplomat's-son behavior. The Haysoms were a little surprised, I think, that their troublesome daughter was dating such a clean-cut boy; pseudo-artistic drug users were more her style. But as I continued to call them *sir* and *ma'am* and used the correct fork for the salad course, Liz's parents began to relax and even stopped grilling me quite so intensely on my family background. Their interest in my social standing and history was the only mildly unusual aspect of our conversation, as if they too were thinking of me as a future son-in-law. Only the fact that I was two years younger than their daughter seemed to worry them a little.

Otherwise, we spent a relatively pleasant half-hour together. Mrs. Haysom had brought her Nikon, and since I had also been a hobby photographer, we discussed technique. My modesty about my achievements seemed to impress Mr. Haysom, though that did not excuse my ignorance about his hobby of shortwave radio. Elizabeth, meanwhile, remained almost entirely silent throughout lunch. Her face was pinched, and whenever I looked across to her I felt she disapproved of how well I got along with her parents.

Toward the end of our luncheon, however, a certain coolness returned to the Haysoms' manner. They dropped me off at Watson dorm so they could have a private discussion with their daughter about "family business." Perhaps that was the reason for Liz's nervousness during the meal, but I do not recall her explaining the "family business" to me afterward.

Since I met Mr. and Mrs. Haysom only on this one occasion I knew virtually nothing of who they really were. What I have learned later has come from obituaries and newspaper articles, and given the media's outrageous inventions about me, I do not trust those sources of information either. But some details about their lives must be included here.

Derek William Reginald Haysom was born in 1913 in South Africa, where he was raised in his grandfather's house. Liz told me that his father was a baronet, the younger son of an English baron, but Derek Haysom's grandfather was in fact a self-made man. Having emigrated to the English colony of South Africa in the 1800s, he started with nothing and built his own sugarcane plantation, Ilove Estates, through shrewd investments.

His grandson, Derek, earned engineering degrees in Durban and Manchester. During World War II he won medals fighting with the British Army against Rommel in North Africa, where his specialty was intelligence work. Press reports on his first wife conflicted; but she bore him three children after the war: Veryan, an attorney in later life; Julian, an engineer; and Fiona, a veterinarian.

Derek Haysom's second wife, née Nancy Astor Benedict, was born in 1932 in Arizona, where her father worked as a geologist. Her mother, Nancy Langhorne Gibbes, was the offspring of one of

Virginia's oldest families and a distant relative of the famous Lady Nancy Astor, the first woman elected to the House of Commons. Liz told me that Lady Astor was her godmother, but in fact this honor was her mother's.

Nancy Benedict and her brothers grew up in Lynchburg while their father worked in Alaska and elsewhere. Some media reports of her high-school activities indicate that she displayed the sort of talents that Elizabeth later claimed for herself, including state-wide honors for playing three musical instruments. In 1949, the family relocated to South Africa to join Nancy Benedict's geologist father. There she soon entered a marriage to an Englishman, which, however, did not last. Her first son, Howard, later studied medicine, whereas the second, Richard, grew up to be an architect.

Derek Haysom married Nancy in 1960 and settled his new family in Salisbury, Rhodesia, where he was manager of a steel mill. Although they were separated by a nineteen-year age difference and already had five children between them, they decided to have one more love child together, Elizabeth Roxanne. Not long after her birth in 1964 the family was forced to flee Rhodesia because of the unstable political situation. Between 1965 and 1968 Derek Haysom worked in Switzerland, Luxembourg, and New York before settling in Nova Scotia, where he again managed a steel mill. The media reported that his retirement was clouded by a dispute with a union over an investment in a cruise ship. By 1982, the Haysoms had bought a small cottage in Boonsboro, just outside Lynchburg, to spend their remaining years where Nancy Haysom had grown up.

On two occasions, I myself visited Loose Chippings, as Mr. and Mrs. Haysom called their new home. Liz and I used my scholarship spending money to rent cars on two weekends in February and March when her parents were out of town, so we could make love all day without worrying about college roommates.

Hidden behind high hedges and trees, the cottage was set well back from the quiet semirural road. Another small house shared the same gravel driveway and a large backyard, which sloped away to a valley with a beautiful view of the Blue Ridge Mountains in the distance. From the outside, Loose Chippings struck me as unprepossessing but comfortable, with stone walls for the first floor and a high roof with dormers for the second.

Inside, I was surprised by the Haysoms' unusually simple lifestyle. The front door opened onto a large living room with wood paneling, but there were no antiques like those that filled my parents' home. Derek and Nancy Haysom did not even own a color TV or modern stereo. Only the liquor cabinet was well and expensively stocked.

To the left of the living room was a small dining room with a stone floor and a plain slab of a table, which, Elizabeth joked, her father had nailed together himself. In the kitchen beyond we found little more than half a tube of imported English mustard, so there was no need to coax the aging stove into life.

On the other side of the house was the master bedroom and bathroom, while Liz's small bedroom and bathroom were upstairs under the steeply gabled roof. Her mattress lay on the floor without a bed frame, but Elizabeth claimed this was by choice, an interior-design statement. Otherwise, the second floor consisted only of a half-finished room, which Mrs. Haysom used as a painting studio, and an unfinished space under bare rafters where Mr. Haysom had set up his homemade shortwave-radio equipment.

As Liz showed me around she took pains to explain her parents' genteel poverty to me. After Zimbabwe achieved independence in 1980, all of the Haysom properties there had been nationalized by the new socialist government. Her mother's old and distinguished family had also fallen on hard times. True, the Astor branch still had extensive real-estate holdings in England, but those were tied up in trusts administered by obstreperous boards.

I smiled compassionately and did my best to pay attention as Elizabeth rambled on, but it was no use. My hormonally inflamed mind kept returning to the mattress in her bedroom and the sexual athletics it would soon see. Who cared whether the Haysoms were rich or poor? Only our love, only its consummation on that mattress upstairs, mattered; it made everything whole and solved all problems.

But Liz had other priorities at that moment. She led me to a wooden cabinet in the living room, to the left of the front door as one entered, and pulled open a drawer. I seem to recall us sitting on the living-room floor as she opened the envelope and handed me the photos—the nude photos of herself that her mother had taken. As noted, Elizabeth had told me about them already, during our long conversations in the Tree House in the fall. But this was the first and only occasion on which I saw them.

Looking back, I now wonder if showing me those photographs might not have been Liz's main purpose for that weekend at her parents' cottage. I say this because she acted differently on this occasion, as we sat on the floor and I leafed through the pictures. At any other time, Elizabeth was always talking, weaving stories, using her charm to dominate her listeners. But not now. She handed me the photos, reminded me who had taken them, and then turned strangely silent. When I asked Liz a few questions, she responded only briefly—totally unlike her usual demeanor.

It may all have been just another act; with Elizabeth, one can never know. The photographs were real, however, so there is some chance that her reticence on this occasion may not have been fake. Perhaps she was reaching out for help to the first person she trusted even a little bit.

If that was what Liz was doing, then I let her down completely. I interpreted her unusual reluctance to speak as embarrassment, as a sign that she would prefer to change the topic. And since I was embarrassed by those awful pictures, too, I gladly followed what I thought was Elizabeth's lead and put the photos back in the envelope. That was the past; we could and even should move on.

But from my current viewpoint, I can see that I simply gave

in to my cowardice and maybe even my lust. I wanted to have fun that weekend, which mostly meant having sex. Looking at those photographs and having to see the terrible expression on Liz's face, the pain in her eyes—that made me feel uncomfortable. And it certainly was no fun at all. So the easiest thing to do was to shove the pictures back in the envelope, and to pretend to myself that I was being "sensitive" to my girlfriend's embarrassment.

One thing is certain: Whether or not Elizabeth was in fact reaching out to me for help by showing me the photos, I missed an opportunity here to alter the course of events. Regardless of her motives, I could have taken the envelope to a counselor at U.Va. and told him or her about the sexual abuse. That act would have broken the chain of events that led to Derek and Nancy Haysom's murders roughly two months later. So, if I had shown more courage, more genuine love on that weekend trip to Loose Chippings, they would still be alive, and Liz and I would not be in prison. I had a chance to prevent this crime—and I blew it.

Had I really loved Elizabeth, instead of just wanting to get her on that mattress upstairs, I would have focused on helping her. But I was lost in the romance, the fantasy of love, the delicious feeling it gave me. I wanted to be in love, not to do the hard work of actually loving someone.

When I look back now to the first three months of that spring semester, I remember Liz and I returning to college from one of our stays at Loose Chippings. We had chosen to drive along the Skyline Drive, the scenic route that runs along the very summits of the Blue Ridge Mountains. It was warm for February, and the sun was beginning to set. We pulled over at one of the picnic spots, sat on the hood of the car, and shared half a bottle of warm, flat Coke. Below us in the far distance lay a highway with miniature people rushing back and forth in toy cars. Elizabeth's pullover was scratchy against my skin, and her hair smelled sweet and clean when I kissed it. There was no sound but for the wind playing in the grass.

We did not tear off our clothes and have wild, noisy sex al fresco on the hood of the rental Toyota. We simply sat quietly, experiencing the grace of love. I remember feeling blessed: blessed to be loved by a girl as wonderful as Elizabeth, and blessed to be allowed to love her.

Through our love, my teenage awkwardness and angst had been banished. The abject depression and feverish self-hatred of my Christmas diary-letters seemed not two months but two life-times away. Even some of my remaining friends in the dormitory told me that I had become a much happier, more secure person since I had started dating Liz. Sitting on the hood of that car with her I finally felt at home in this world. For so many years before Elizabeth, I had been a stranger.

The last time I felt comfortably a part of the mainstream of my peers was in Germany from 1973 to 1977. There I did not have the social stigma of excelling academically, since I achieved no more than a B average. When the neighborhood boys met for the daily soccer game I was neither the first nor the last to be picked when teams were chosen. If anything distinguished me at all, it was that I was the first boy in my class to take a girl to an ice-cream parlor, a daring venture for a ten-year-old.

But as soon as I arrived in Atlanta on my eleventh birthday, I became an outsider. My first day at that exclusive prep school began with my classmates shouting, "Nazi, Nazi!" Re-runs of the *Hogan's Heroes* had persuaded these children that all Germans were Nazis, including the new arrival, me. I tried to ignore the unending taunts until eighth grade, when I had the one and only schoolyard fight of my life. The other boy and I managed to land one punch each before being hauled off to the principal's office.

Once my class entered high school, the Nazi teasing stopped, but that particular chip never left my shoulder. I became known for my sarcastic sense of humor, especially on subjects like Southern hospitality, and I remained extraordinarily defensive about my

German heritage. At the slightest provocation I would launch into long, boring speeches arguing that post-1945 Germany was a paragon of liberal virtue compared with the militaristic, reactionary America of the Reagan era. Of course, my left-wing politics did not help me gain acceptance with my preppy schoolmates either.

Looking back, I realize that these difficulties were and perhaps still are not that uncommon; many Germans have found their country's past similarly burdensome. Since World War II, German politicians, the media, and the educational system have conducted a massive campaign to keep alive the warning memory of the Holocaust. All schoolchildren must attend class trips to concentration camps, and public TV stations broadcast a steady stream of documentaries. No one is allowed to forget that the worst form of murder is the killing of a citizen by his or her government.

But Germans in Germany at least are not alone. Everyone there shares the same awful heritage; everyone nurses a guilty conscience, even if some youngsters rebel against it by shaving their heads and yelling fascist slogans. I, on the other hand, was the only German in my school class in America. So it became my personal responsibility to prove that Germans had learned from their Nazi past, that they were now practically perfect in every way. My defensiveness about my nationality even influenced me in decisions such as refusing to join the high-school ritual of getting drunk after every Friday football game. As a good German I could not allow myself to participate in anything so crassly American.

Even at college my heritage continued to stigmatize me. While visiting Germany in early 1985, President Reagan joined Chancellor Kohl at a wreath-laying ceremony at Bitburg Cemetery, where a few young Waffen-SS soldiers were buried in one corner. Paroxysms of outrage immediately swept through the American media, and all day long acquaintances and even strangers insisted that I explain the German point of view on this scandal.

The Bitburg Cemetery episode was, needless to say, only one of the countless, constant reminders throughout my childhood and youth that I was not truly at home anywhere in the world. In America I would always be a stranger from the perpetually dishonored nation of Germany. Yet if I were now to transfer to the University of Bonn, I would still not fit in because I had spent almost my entire life outside my country. Even my parents' house was not a home but, instead, the altar on which they sacrificed their happiness to the ideal of family life.

Certainly, I could win my parents' or my American and German peers' approval as long as I kept delivering all those awards and scholarships. But no one seemed to like me very much; nowhere was I truly wanted—until Elizabeth rescued me.

I remember feeling joyous amazement as I sat on the hood of that Toyota in the Blue Ridge Mountains in February of 1985: She loved me! She really loved me!

Me, Jens Soering, the German outsider, the cause of my parents' endless, unhappy sacrificing! She really loved me!

She loved me: not just accepted me; not just liked me; but loved me! No, not just loved, she *desired* me. She wanted to "tug at [me], wanting all of [me], cuddling [my] balls," as she wrote in that erotic letter. How could a lonely young German resist that siren call?

Separating from Liz, even if only for the nine days of spring break in March, seemed too painful to contemplate. But we had no choice: I had to catch up on all the schoolwork I had neglected, and she had commitments with her family. As soon as Elizabeth left, I threw myself into work, convinced that this was the only cure for the agony of being without my love.

My main project was to complete two-thirds of a film script for my creative-writing course. To get into a suitably artistic mood, I took the method-acting approach to writing: I sat at my typewriter late at night in my underwear, ate cold pizza for breakfast, and even tried to smoke a cigarette to complete the image. Now I just needed to supply a corpse for my script's hero, a detective who used the philosophy of Zen to solve crimes. Dozens of devilishly ingenious plans for the perfect murder landed in my trash can before I finally settled on a slow poison made from the skin of a tropical fish or frog found in the Far East. Naturally, my Zen detective missed none of the tiny, important clues that cleared him and pointed to the real murderer. This was a movie, after all, not reality.

Liz meanwhile was skiing in Colorado with her half-brothers from her mother's previous marriage, Howard and Richard. On Ramada Inn stationery she wrote me a long letter complaining bitterly about her parents. They had prevented her from inheriting a mansion in London left to her by Lady Astor; they were not giving her the additional spending money they had promised for kicking her heroin habit; they would never give her the money she felt she deserved since they wanted to control every aspect of her life. The only solution, Elizabeth wrote, was to run away again, to cut her ties with her family completely. If necessary, she would resort to stealing her mother's jewelry. At great length, she then begged my forgiveness for lying to me and not telling me these things earlier.

When Liz returned from Colorado we hardly discussed this letter. I saw no need, since it was obviously just an exasperated outburst without anything like firm plans for running away. There was certainly no hint of murder. Love would solve all our problems; it was the weapon that would overcome any obstacles raised by her parents, as I had written her in my Christmas diary-letters. An insufficient allowance was hardly a genuine problem, anyway, compared with the one facing me. I had rented a hotel room so we could celebrate Elizabeth's return to college with a night of wild sex; but since there had been a delay in her travel plans, I had lost the room. No sex, after nine days of abstinence during spring break—now that really was a disaster!

The passage in Liz's letter, in which she asked forgiveness for lying to me, seemed no more important to me than her worries about spending money. By now I was well used to her POTS, and since she had promised not to lie again, that issue seemed to have been resolved.

On the weekend of March 23–24, Elizabeth went to Lynchburg by herself to celebrate her father's birthday at home. She returned ecstatic: contrary to her expectations, her parents were going to reward her for straightening herself out. They had even begun to set up an account at the Bank of Bermuda with a small sum as a gift for her upcoming birthday on April 15. Everything was going to be all right.

The next weekend, Liz and I drove to Washington for a mini-vacation. We had been in love for three-and-a-half months.

—*4*—

Murder and Cover-up

"It is a far, far better thing that I do, . . . "

March 30–March 31, 1985

O N THE AFTERNOON of Friday, March 29, 1985, Elizabeth and I drove north from our college dorm in the gray Chevette she had rented. There was nothing unusual about our mini-vacation. In the two-and-a-half months since our separate Christmas holidays, we had used my scholarship's spending money on two sleepless nights in motel rooms off campus, as well as the two trips to Loose Chippings.

But this weekend was supposed to be Liz's treat, and she had made all the arrangements and reservations. She even paid in cash when we checked into the downtown Marriott Hotel at about 7 P.M. Needless to say, we immediately rushed upstairs to make love; I had my priorities for this weekend.

When we decided around 8:30 to go to a movie, Elizabeth and I discovered that we might not have enough ready cash for all our plans for Friday, Saturday, and Sunday. So on our way out of the hotel, I paid for our room with my father's VISA card, and Liz received back her $95. We drove around Georgetown and eventually saw the film *Porky's Revenge* at a huge mall at the northern end of Wisconsin Avenue. Normally, we would have considered

Porky's Revenge beneath us, but since this was a vacation we decided to drop our intellectual pretensions for once.

The next morning Elizabeth and I spent making love and eating breakfast in bed. Eleven o'clock had passed before we were ready to get dressed and face the world. What a blissful, perfect, lazy day this was promising to be! Even the weather seemed to cooperate, the sun beaming down on the beautiful residential district of Georgetown as we circled looking for a parking space.

For the rest of the morning and the early afternoon Liz and I window-shopped. I remember passing an importer of Thai silk, a reminder of my place of birth transported halfway across the world. To make up for the lowbrow movie of the previous night we decided to reestablish our credentials as connoisseurs of pomposity by purchasing a white-sleeved LP by the Art Ensemble of Chicago. Later, we got back into our car and drove north on Wisconsin Avenue again, past the ugly German Embassy building on our right.

It was about 3:30 p.m. when Elizabeth and I decided to park and have a late lunch. The restaurant where we stopped was decorated with a train motif: there were trains painted on the walls, drawn on the menus, and printed on the napkins.

Freud would have had a fit over all that phallic imagery, I joked. We had a pleasant, if unremarkable meal and afterward relaxed over a couple of soft drinks.

The conversation began as so many others had before: *Jens, I have a small confession to make. . . .*

I was neither shocked nor worried. In the time we had been in love, Liz already had to confess quite a lot to me. Both of us saw my forgiveness as a foregone conclusion, I am sure.

Elizabeth's newest little confession in the restaurant was that she was still using heroin. Two months earlier, after she had shown me the needle mark on her arm, she had promised me that she would stop. Naturally, Liz apologized profusely for her lying and her continuing addiction. She was throwing herself completely on my mercy, she said, but if I sent her away now she would understand. She knew she did not deserve me, but she would continue to love me from afar.

In fact, Elizabeth gave me almost exactly the same speech now that she had written me three weeks earlier in the letter from her spring skiing vacation in Colorado:

> *Hate me, shout at me, torture me, make me rob the Federal Reserve whatever but please hug me when we meet. I will do anything to compensate. You're the only person I've ever loved, and you're the only person who has ever really loved me. You are my life. To have any deception remaining in my life would be unbearable. It is time to risk all for the truth may some fate, god, realize that the horror of this truth and confession and all that it entails is more than equal to all my scheming deception in the past.*
>
> *You know the whole truth, nobody else on this planet has a glimmer of the whole truth of Elizabeth Roxanne Haysom, for I have deceived them all to a lesser or greater degree please don't create the greatest irony of my life. All my defenses are down there is nothing left but raw flesh love in its real form is a truly revolutionary thing. I love you, and no matter what your judgment I will always love you.*

I forgave Liz for the lies she had confessed in that letter. And three weeks later in the restaurant in Washington, I forgave her again for lying about her drug addiction.

I begged Elizabeth to stop apologizing and reassured her that I loved her. She could hardly blame herself for her heroin addiction, since that dependency was a disease, not a sin. A member of my own family had problems with alcohol, so I knew what a terrible psychological toll such an addiction took. If anything, I should apologize to her for not having noticed, for not having won her trust so that she could have sought my help sooner. Anything I could do now to help her kick her habit, I would do. She only had to say the word.

Liz thanked me for my understanding and concern. She swore that she had now resolved to break her addiction for good. Unfortunately, there was just one little problem: she had run up a debt with her dealer, Jim Farmer.

I knew Jim because he had received a Jefferson Scholarship from the U.Va. Alumni Association two years before me. We had met again outside Alumni Association functions because he was one of the many older, pseudo-artistic drug users who frequently dropped by Elizabeth's dorm room in the fall semester of 1984.

Liz had met Jim through her parents. Jim's father was a local Lynchburg judge and thus moved in the same social circles as Mr. and Mrs. Haysom. In her Christmas diary-letter Elizabeth had written me that Jim had given her some joints and asked her to join a menage à trois with his male lover.

Of course, I offered to pay Liz's debt to Jim. I thought it could only amount to a few hundred dollars, and her freedom from her addiction was worth much more than that to me.

Again Elizabeth thanked me profusely, and again she raised a new problem. She had already arranged to pay off her debts to Jim by picking up a large shipment of drugs in Washington this weekend and bringing it back to U.Va. when we returned on Sunday. Since the whole thing had already been set up, she could not back out now. Jim was no longer interested in money but only in her courier run.

Telling him to get lost was no option either, Liz explained. If she did not fulfill her promise to transport the drugs, Jim would snitch to her parents. He would tell them that, contrary to her claims and promises, Elizabeth was still using drugs, as on that certain weekend she had spent in Washington with her new boyfriend, Jens, without asking her parents' permission.

Mr. and Mrs. Haysom would believe Jim's story. He was a scholarship winner, a judge's son, practically an old friend of the family. Jim had never been suspected of drug use, much less drug dealing.

Liz, on the other hand, had a reputation for lying and had even run away to Europe to live as a junkie and tramp. Even worse, she would not be able to deny making our trip to Washington without her parents' permission; the Haysoms could easily confirm that part of Jim's story. And once they caught her in one lie, they would immediately assume that Jim's accusations of drug use were also true.

Elizabeth's explanation made sense to me. She would have to transport the drugs. I insisted that I accompany her when she went to pick up the shipment from the dealer in Washington. I had no illusions about my intimidating anyone, but it seemed obvious that I could not let her go alone.

Liz, however, objected once again. Jim had arranged for her to pick up the drugs alone, and if two people suddenly showed up the dealer would get nervous. Who knew what might happen then? Also, I was so obviously not a drug-user that the dealer would refuse to do business around me for fear of being arrested. Elizabeth thus not only had to pick up the drugs, but she would have to do so without me.

In any case, there was no time for further conversation. The last part of Liz's little confession was that she was scheduled to pick up the drug shipment soon. She had to leave more or less straight away, and she wanted to know where she could drop me off.

Finally, I objected a little more strenuously. I needed to think this over. What, for instance, would stop Jim from blackmailing her again and again into making courier runs?

I am not sure, but I think I remember relief passing across

Elizabeth's face when I asked this question. She certainly had an answer ready. While she was picking up the drugs, I should go to a movie and purchase two tickets as an alibi.

Then, if Jim snitched to her parents, she would admit to having been in Washington with her boyfriend without their permission. Confessing that much would establish a little credibility. But after a great show of digging through her various pockets, Liz could fish out a pair of ticket stubs. A set of two tickets would help support her claim that she had been with me the whole weekend, and no one could possibly suspect Jens Soering of abusing drugs.

This alibi would surely be enough to protect her from at least some of her parents' wrath, Elizabeth told me. Right now, however, there was no more time. She had to leave without further delay, and she needed to know if she could trust me and rely on me, *please?*

The pressure for an immediate decision and Liz's puppy-dog pleading silenced my internal alarm bells. The alibi was hare-brained but not actually harmful; I would go along with it to calm her today and to end her addiction to heroin later. We climbed into the car and discussed this so-called alibi further on the short drive to the nearest movie theater. She dropped me off around 4:30, and I watched the 5:05 showing of *Witness* with two ticket stubs in my pocket.

When I arrived by taxi back at the hotel at about 7:30, I cashed a personal check at the front desk. After I had paid for the room with my father's VISA card the previous evening, Elizabeth had put the entire refund into her wallet. In the rush to meet her drug dealer she had driven off with all the money, leaving me with only a few dollars in cash. On the back of my check, the hotel cashier noted details from my driver's license, took an imprint of the VISA card, asked me to sign again, and initialed and dated the whole thing.

I went to our room and waited. Liz had told me that picking up the drugs would take at least two hours, so she should be returning soon. I turned on the TV and flipped through the channels, unable to concentrate because of my fear for Elizabeth's safety. I got up and paced about. I sat back down. The whole foolish, dangerous mess would blow up in our faces, I was sure of it.

But it was too late to turn back now. Liz was relying on me and this stupid alibi. The nonsense with the two tickets was unnecessary and unworkable, of course, but I had given my word. Perhaps it would all work out.

Finally, I ordered room service for two, another part of the alibi that Elizabeth and I had discussed before her departure. If she turned up soon, we could at least have a snack before going out again. I definitely remember the hors d'oeuvres of pink shrimp fanned atop lettuce leaves on glass plates, but I simply cannot recall the entrées: Welsh rarebit, or something simple like that. I signed the room-service bill and was given a small, torn-off receipt.

But Liz did not arrive. So around 9:30 that evening I gave up waiting and proceeded to the final stage of the so-called alibi. I took a taxi to a small movie theater and bought two tickets for the 10:15 showing of *Stranger than Paradise*. Screamin' Jay Hawkins' rendition of "I Put a Spell on You," the film's theme music, seemed an appropriately ironic comment on my nervous wait for Elizabeth. I chuckled to myself and hoped she was safe.

As soon as the movie ended I rushed to the nearest pay telephone on Wisconsin Avenue to call our hotel room. No one answered. I had almost expected the endless ringing and finally lost my temper. The whole evening, half of our weekend in Washington, had been a complete waste of time and money. I was sick and tired of waiting around for Liz and her stupid drug deal, and I was sick and tired of this wasteful idiocy of buying tickets and meals for two.

Angrily, I stomped onto Wisconsin Avenue and waved down a taxi. I was going to see the special midnight showing of *The Rocky Horror Picture Show* at a small theater in the heart of Georgetown and with only one ticket, too. Whenever Elizabeth deigned to carry her precious behind back to the hotel, she could wait for me for once.

I arrived at the Marriott around 2 A.M. in a huff, fully expecting Liz to be waiting for me. But our room key was still at the front desk. In the room I began pacing again, sitting down to flip some channels on the TV, and pacing some more. Something had gone wrong; I just knew it! I started to regret my anger at Elizabeth. She was not late; she was in trouble. And I had no idea how to find her or help her. I should have refused to go along with this drug deal, or I should have at least accompanied Liz.

Suddenly there is a knock at the door, and I rush to open it. Elizabeth is standing in front of me, and with one glance I know there has been serious trouble. Her face is white and tense, her eyes wide. She is wearing different jeans from those she wore when she left Washington; this is the baggy pair with the big pockets on the legs. Her blouse looks different, too, somehow.

Liz pushes past me without saying a word and sits down on the end of the bed, hunched over with her elbows on her knees. I sit down next to her and turn to my left toward her.

Elizabeth speaks in a monotone while staring at the floor in front of her. Over and over she repeats variations of the same phrases: *I've killed my parents! I've killed my parents! But it wasn't me, it was the drugs that made me do it, the drugs did it, not me. They deserved it anyway, my whole bloody childhood, always sending me away, and now they want to control every little thing, it serves them right, they deserved it. If you don't help me, they'll kill me; you have to help me or I'll go to the electric chair; you have to help me or they'll kill me!*

None of this sinks in immediately of course. My mind is blank during Liz's recitation. I simply sit and listen. Is there a punch line coming? Is this some new mind game, a new POT?

I look to my left at Elizabeth's profile as she speaks. No, that mixture of shock and anxiety is still in her face. Why is she wearing different jeans, a different blouse? I look past her to the table with the leftovers from the room service: the little bowl of garishly red sauce for the shrimp. Then I look at her exposed forearms resting on her knees. Her hands are clean, but there are dry reddish-brown smears on the arms.

I continue listening, and she keeps repeating the same phrases in that flat, quiet monotone. The phrases start to sink in. I begin to believe her. She has killed her parents. The drugs made her do it. They deserved it anyway. I have to help her, or they'll kill her in the electric chair. The phrases sink in. I believe her. But *what. . .* ?

Then a new sentence enters her litany and slowly awakens me from my stupor. *I've been with you the whole evening; you have to say I've been with you; you have to be my alibi, you have the movie tickets, you have the alibi!*

My mind begins to stir. Something about the alibi, there is something about the alibi.

I interrupt Liz's flow: *It will never work. They'll never believe me. I am the boyfriend, and no one believes husbands and boyfriends. The tickets prove nothing. It will never work.*

At last, Elizabeth is silent. She looks into my eyes, and I look into hers. In the background someone on TV is trying to sell a food processor with fifteen amazing attachments and a lifetime guarantee.

I cannot think. I cannot think about Derek and Nancy Haysom lying dead in their home in Lynchburg. I dare not think of that horror. I cannot think about Liz's actions. I dare not think of how that blood got onto her forearms. I cannot, I dare not think of my own guilt: if I had not agreed to create an alibi, she might not have. . . . No, I cannot think, I dare not think, I must not think! I am only looking at Elizabeth, just looking.

What do I see when I look into her eyes? I do not see a cold-blooded, heartless butcher sitting beside me on that hotel bed. On TV, murderers always look like monsters, inhuman; but this person looks like Liz, the same girl I love more than anyone in the world. She looks not like a vicious reptile but like . . . a victim, silent with shock, her blue-gray-green eyes staring wide, her porcelain skin now gray, her shoulders almost quivering. She looks the way she did in those nude photographs her mother took. She looks the way she did a couple of months ago, when she showed me the photographs and refused to answer when I asked if her mother had abused her. She looks the way she did at the Tree House, telling me little but hinting at the fondling, the bathing, and all the rest. She looks frightened, heartbreakingly lonely and helpless. That is what I see.

She has killed her parents. The drugs made her do it. They deserved it anyway.

I do not think about options or morality or legal consequences. I do not think about the victims or their killer or myself. I can bring myself to think about only one question: *How do I stop them from frying Liz?*

Sending her off to go on the run by herself is impossible. Elizabeth's passport is at Loose Chippings, and she is in no condition to travel anyway. How do I stop them from frying Liz? How do I stop them? How?

And then, somehow, I have my brilliant idea.

I did it! Whenever the police arrest us and that's got to be soon I'll just tell them that I did it. You are the accomplice, not me. We'll switch roles! Heck, it's been done before. Think about Sydney Carton in *A Tale of Two Cities*, or those Los Angeles street gangs you see on TV. I've heard it's part of their initiation ritual for underage kids to take the rap for older gang members, because minors get less time. If those guys can make it work, so can we. You'll be out after a few years; everyone will feel sorry for you. And you won't have to go to the electric chair. And me, I'll get diplomatic immunity, at least partially. I'm a diplomat's son, right? I've got a German diplomatic passport with a U.S. diplomatic visa. They'll arrest me and ship me back to Germany and put me on trial there. That's what they did with the Japanese Consul General in Atlanta during my senior year of high school, when he was caught for drunk driving or hit-and-run: they just shipped him back to Japan. Of course, they'll have to put me on trial for the murders once I get to Germany, because there's no more full-diplomatic immunity. But eighteen-year-olds like me can't get more than ten years under German law; I read that in the newspaper. They'll let me out on parole after five. We'll probably get out at the same time. It'll work! It'll work! The police will believe me because only guilty people confess to murder. And the police will believe you because only guilty people confess to arranging an alibi for the killer of their parents. It'll work!

Elizabeth did not hesitate. She accepted my "sacrifice," as she called this plan in the letter she wrote me shortly after her parents' funeral. Now Liz and I only needed a theatrical paradigm on which we could model our performances. We chose Shakespeare's *Macbeth*, of course: Elizabeth would play the part of the instigator, Lady Macbeth, while I should play the Thane of Cawdor, the murderer Macbeth. During the remaining early morning hours we fleshed out our version of Shakespeare's plotline. I told Liz what I had done, so she could confess convincingly how she arranged the alibi. Then Elizabeth described the scene of the crime, and I tried to imagine how I might have been driven to kill her parents. She did not tell me why she had driven to Lynchburg or what had actually happened at Loose Chippings, and I did not want to know. We never mentioned the murders directly to one another again.

In July 1986, shortly after we had been interrogated about the murders, Liz wrote me that the detectives "made it quite clear how they perceive the situation, and believe me, you're a 'poor boy' and I am an 'evil' Lady Macbeth creature who used sex and emotional blackmail to get what I wanted." That Shakespearean allusion was intended to remind me of the plan we had made on the evening of the homicides, a plan that was spectacularly successful. Later, when I had come to regret the success of our plan, I turned again and again to *Macbeth* to study the relationship between the driven, bloodthirsty Lady Macbeth and the weak but murderous Macbeth himself. Could she have pushed Macbeth to kill if he had not had slaughter on his mind already as he returned from a hard-fought battle? And how would Lady Macbeth have satisfied her ambitions if her husband had not been a great warrior, but a courtier or a diplomat unused to swords? Would she then have grasped the knife herself? In act 1 of the play it is Lady Macbeth, not her husband, who calls out,

> *Come, you spirits*
> *That tend on mortal thoughts, unsex me here,*
> *And fill me, from the crown to the toe, top-full*
> *Of direst cruelty! . . .*
> *Come, thick night,*
> *And pall thee in the dunnest smoke of hell,*
> *That my keen knife see not the wound it makes,*
> *Nor heaven peep through the blanket of the dark*
> *To cry "Hold, hold!"*

—5—

The Investigation Begins

"A woman or a small man or boy"

April 1985–May 1985

PROUDLY CALLING ITSELF the "hill city" after its location straddling the James River, Lynchburg in 1985 exuded the self-satisfied air so typical of the false prosperity of the Reagan years. Its 100,000 inhabitants worked in a foundry fed on fat defense contracts, in the Reverend Jerry Falwell's expanding religious empire, and in a collection of terribly expensive and terribly exclusive private girls' colleges. Back then, the future seemed forever golden with Ronald Reagan's promise that "the sun [was] rising on America."

Blue-gold shimmered the high summits of the Blue Ridge Mountains as the first rays of sunlight kissed them at dawn, and brown-gold gleamed the tobacco plants in the gently rolling foothills outside Lynchburg as the morning mist burned away. From colonial times until today, this crop, grown in sight of those majestic blue peaks, had been the very foundation of Virginia's wealth. Only recently, the fields had begun giving way to spreading retirement communities, but tobacco farmers who sold out to developers were considered traitors to tradition even by those retirees who now lived here.

Green-gold shone the fairways of the Oakland Country Club,

where the all-white membership gathered in the bar to escape the midday heat. Forty years earlier, in the 1940s, Nancy Haysom had grown up in nearby Peakland Place, the wealthiest suburb, and nothing had changed since then. When public pressure finally forced the club to offer membership to an African-American, he wisely declined; old times there were not forgotten by either race.

Red-gold glowed the evening sun through the stained glass of the white-columned churches lining upper Rivermont Avenue, halfway to the town's center. The Methodists, the Episcopalians, the Presbyterians all worshiped the same God side by side, but among the denominations and within each congregation a strict hierarchy ruled. Which church's membership indicated higher status, and whose bloodline entitled him or her to sit closer to the altar—these were nuances jealously preserved by Lynchburg's leading families, who attended every service to ensure that the social order was not violated.

The Massies were one such old and respected family, less famous but no different from the Langhornes and Gibbes from whom Nancy Haysom had descended. To Mrs. Massie, Nancy Haysom's best friend, "tradition" was not a synonym for folklore, but an active way of life today. Whether the traditions were large or small, it was her duty to protect them, as they protected her and her family's status. In tradition lay order and safety.

So when a minor tradition was violated, Mrs. Massie naturally set out to investigate. She and two friends drove to Loose Chippings to discover why the Haysoms had not attended the regular Wednesday meeting of the bridge club and why they had not answered the phone. At the house, they discovered Derek Haysom's BMW and Nancy's Dodge van in the driveway, but their knocks on the door were met only with silence. Now worried, Mrs. Massie decided to use her spare key. One look inside, however, was enough to know that her friends were beyond her help.

Directly to the left of the front door, across the doorway to the dining room, lay the body of Derek Haysom, nearly decapitated and covered in dozens of stab wounds. In the kitchen on the far side of the dining room, Mrs. Massie could glimpse the corpse of Nancy Haysom, whose throat had also been slashed. The floor and even some of the walls in this part of the house were covered in blood so thick that in places it had formed a crust. Over everything hung the cloying, thickly sweet smell of death and decay.

From a pay telephone at a nearby convenience store, Mrs. Massie called a man who was the very embodiment of the traditional order and safety in that part of the state: Bedford County Sheriff Carl Wells. While the Haysoms conducted their limited social life in Lynchburg, Loose Chippings actually lay just beyond city limits in the Boonsboro district of the county of Bedford. A hulking bear of a man, Carl Wells had been the sheriff there for as long as anyone cared to remember, and he ran his county as if it were his personal fief. This paternal attitude helped ensure public safety, but it also led to some difficulties for Sheriff Wells later. In the early 1990s, according to press reports, a special prosecutor was appointed to investigate why, for decades, the sheriff had skimmed the interest off a bank account holding his deputies' payroll. The county eventually sued Sheriff Wells to recover those thousands of dollars; he considered the money his, just like all of Bedford. No charges were ever filed.

The sheriff's partner in the administration of law and order in the county was Commonwealth's Attorney James Updike. Over six-feet tall, red-haired and slim, Prosecutor Updike liked wearing flashy, all-white suits and winning his cases with courtroom theatrics. His political ambitions first became evident in the unusually high number of capital-murder cases he brought and won. So many of Virginia's Death Row inmates came from Bedford that no one dared oppose his reelection. Later, when the state approved a pilot project for televising trials, Commonwealth's Attorney Updike made sure that Bedford's small circuit court was one of the two experimental courtrooms with cameras. My own trial of 1990 was to become his greatest TV triumph: to launch his 1993 campaign for the office of attorney general at the State Democratic Party Annual Convention, he played a videotape of his cross-examination of me.

On April 3, 1985, the day Mrs. Massie called in to report a double murder, Sheriff Wells and Prosecutor Updike were the two men charged with bringing to justice Derek and Nancy Haysom's killer or killers. But beyond that immediate problem of law enforcement loomed the much more daunting task of restoring the public's sense of security. How could Lynchburg ever feel safe again when two of its leading citizens had been brutally murdered in their own home? Only if this awful mystery was solved, only if the culprits were found soon, could the good people of the hill city resume their calm, structured, quiet lives.

Sheriff Wells and Commonwealth's Attorney Updike understood their community's craving for a speedy return of the old, familiar order and security. They also understood that they could not satisfy this craving through quick arrests. The crime had clearly occurred several days before Mrs. Massie made her gruesome discovery at Loose Chippings, and the murderers' trail was growing colder by the minute. But something had to be done to make the public feel safe, so the sheriff and the prosecutor organized an enormous and widely televised manhunt throughout Boonsboro, Bedford, Lynchburg, and all of central Virginia. Eventually, their regional task force even extended the search to California, where fingerprints from Loose Chippings were compared to those of the infamous "hillside strangler."

Interestingly—in view of my own subsequent conviction as the sole perpetrator of this crime—the Bedford County Sheriff's Department began their search for the killer(s) by issuing an "all points bulletin" for two men with a "buck" or hunting-type knife. This made a lot of sense, given the evidence at Loose Chippings. Even a layman could see that the attack had begun in the dining room and then spread in two different directions: the kitchen, where Nancy Haysom's body was found; and the living room, where lay Derek Haysom's body. Both the kitchen and the living room had doors leading to the outside of the house. So if there had been only one attacker, assaulting either victim, the other victim would have had ample opportunity to escape, or to arm him- or herself with a kitchen knife or fireplace poker (depending on his or her location). But that clearly did not happen. Instead, Derek and Nancy Haysom were killed simultaneously, by two different attackers. And hence the APB for two men armed with a knife.

In the following weeks, the working theory of two murderers was further confirmed by the state's pathologist and serologist. The pathologist found two distinct types of knife wounds: extremely shallow stab wounds (only one was deeper than an inch) and extremely deep cutting or slashing wounds to the victims' throats (in one case, down to the backbone). The serologist found all four blood types: the victims' A and AB, as well as tiny quantities of O and B. What else could this mean but that there were two killers?

Unfortunately, the search for these killers produced no results. In spite of scores of detectives earning hundreds of hours of overtime, the investigation yielded no arrests, and as the days passed, the yearning for answers became almost hysterical. Rumors spread through town, multiplying and growing more extravagant at each retelling. Did the ANC (African National Congress) order the murders as revenge for some possible misdeed of Mr. Haysom's branch of the family in the former racist state of Rhodesia? Perhaps fanatical union members from his Canadian steel company had finally avenged a lost contract dispute. Or maybe it was the daughter of a local Lynchburg judge; she was reported to be mentally unstable and supposedly blamed the Haysoms for preventing her marriage to one of Elizabeth's half-brothers. No matter how outrageous the rumors became, they at least provided some explanation of the unknown, some answers to the questions that still puzzled Sheriff Wells, Prosecutor Updike, and their detectives.

But the people of central Virginia were not the only ones to be racked by nervous speculation and rising fear. Liz and I experienced those emotions even more sharply, though for different reasons. Every siren in the distance, every knock on the door, made us flinch and shiver. When would we be arrested? It had to be soon. Since most murders are committed by the victims' families or friends, the police logically would begin their investigation with Elizabeth, the only relative of Derek and Nancy Haysom in this state. Her drug use, her running away to Europe, her troubled relationship with her parents—these were all common knowledge among the Haysoms' friends, and the detectives would soon know, too. First she would be questioned, and then me. We would try to tell the police we had both been in Washington, but they would not believe us. And, eventually, I would have to fulfill my promise to save Liz's life by "confessing" to the murders. If only the detectives would finally come and end this grinding uncertainty.

Even though it was Elizabeth who, but for my promise, faced the electric chair, I suffered much more from the stress and fear. In fact, I can recollect very little of the weeks immediately after the killings, as if my memory were still clouded by the same haze of terror and tiredness that numbed my mind then. Some disjointed, almost surreal episodes are all that remain.

I remember Mrs. Massie's husband driving us south from U.Va. to Lynchburg, the lights of the cars in the opposite lane dipping up and down, up and down, while Dr. Massie asked me about BMWs because I was German. I remember the Laura Ashley bedsheets on the four-poster bed in Mrs. Massie's guest bedroom; Christine Kim and Liz stayed in a room together upstairs. I remember a ray of sunlight making the dust in the air sparkle as one of Nancy Haysom's relatives announced, in a voice that sounded drunk, that he was glad she was dead. I remember going to a movie with Christine Kim and the wife of one of Elizabeth's half-brothers, and getting lost on the way. I remember Liz telling me that she would pretend not to be able to park her mother's van, so she could ask one of her brothers for help and thus make him feel useful.

None of it made any sense. What was I doing here, an accomplice to murder, attending the victims' funeral reception? And where were the police? Why had we not been arrested yet? It made no sense, no sense at all.

My greatest crisis, and the one I can recollect most clearly, was witnessing the two sets of siblings from Derek and Nancy Haysom's previous marriages meet in a hotel room. Their grief and their love for their parents were so deeply felt that I nearly broke down. So much pain, so many tears, and I was the cause. If only I had somehow protected Elizabeth from her monstrous parents, then she would not have felt driven to kill. If only I had not agreed to arrange that ludicrous attempt at an alibi, then she would not have thought she could get away with the murders. If only I had earned Liz's full trust, then she would have come to me and we could have found some other way. But I had failed, failed her and myself, and failed the Haysoms' other five offspring who now cried forlornly as they hugged each other in the hotel room. Only my fear for Elizabeth's life kept my emotions in check.

I left the room as soon as I could and went to the hotel bar, where I once again contemplated suicide. The police would then have a convenient and penitent murderer, Liz would be safe, and I would have kept my promise to her, though by a different method from the sacrifice we had planned together. Above all my agony would be over, and my failures would be atoned for.

But I could not kill myself. Even if I left a suicide note claiming responsibility for the murders, no one would believe that I killed the Haysoms. I was too much of a "wimp," as Elizabeth called me at her sentencing hearing in 1987. To save her life I would have "to confess" live and in person; killing myself now would only throw more suspicion on Liz.

Frightened by the possibility of losing her fall-guy through suicide, Elizabeth wrote me a letter that I now consider her absolute masterpiece of manipulation. Only once did she slip and let her real intentions show, when she described my thoughts of killing myself as a "threat" to herself. Otherwise, her technique was perfect.

First she applied the carrot by telling me, at great and flowery length, how much she loved me. Then came the stick. She chastised me for asking her to pay her share of the VISA bill from our Washington vacation, and she accused me of wanting part of her father's inheritance. (In fact, it was generally known that the Haysoms' estate was small, just enough to finance Liz's college education.) After the carrot and the stick came the embrace: "We did it"; we were equally involved; it was us against the world. My "sacrifice" would only become a "burden" to us if I thought she was now "obligated" to me, she warned.

Looking back to those early April days after the murders, I almost sympathize with Liz's need to bring me to heel with that letter. I nearly spoiled our plan, while she remained icily calm throughout our stay at Mrs. Massie's house. Only twice did she show any signs of weakness. During the funeral service, held in an old stone church atop one of Lynchburg's hills, Elizabeth cried as she listened to her half-brother's eulogy, and I believe that at least some of her tears really were for her parents. It was the only occasion I ever saw Liz cry in all the time I knew her.

That night we stayed in the house of other family friends who had left town on vacation. I came to Elizabeth's room to talk, to share the burden of the terror we both felt. Because Christine Kim was in a nearby bedroom we had to whisper, so I climbed onto Liz's bed. At first, we only held each other in the dark room, afraid that we were about to lose each other forever. Tonight, tomorrow, or the day after the detectives would come and arrest us; it was only a matter of time. We did not want to let go. So we held each other as tightly as we could.

With the wisdom of hindsight I am not surprised that Elizabeth later chose this particular night, when she showed her frail humanity, as the basis of one of her worst lies. I did not rape her as she claimed in 1987. Reaching out for one another through the fear, we made love without desire and, even retrospectively, with a wistful beauty.

But Liz always hated any weakness in herself, and during April 1985 she certainly needed all her strength. I remember her half-brothers calling a meeting at Mrs. Massie's house to announce that police considered her the prime suspect in her parents' murders. The next day they would hire one of the top local attorneys to persuade the Bedford County Sheriff's Department to drop this line of inquiry. Though I am not sure, I believe I also remember the Haysom siblings discussing how to use the media in order to maximize the pressure on law enforcement.

Sheriff Carl Wells and Commonwealth's Attorney James Updike quickly agreed to focus the investigation on someone other than Elizabeth. Their job was to restore the public's sense of security, to make Lynchburg's citizens feel that order had returned to their town. It was bad enough that two members of one of central Virginia's oldest and most distinguished families had been murdered; but if another member of that ancient bloodline, the victims' own daughter, were now accused, all the old certainties of life would be toppled. The family tree that had produced all those famous Langhornes and Gibbes and Astors simply could not produce a murderess! The suspect's half-brothers and a prominent local attorney had staked their reputations that she was not involved, and she apparently had some sort of alibi about being in Washington with her boyfriend. It seemed safest and best for the town to drop Elizabeth Roxanne Haysom as prime suspect.

In the end, Sheriff Wells and Prosecutor Updike's detectives did not even bother to check Liz's alibi by interviewing me. Only two explanations are possible for this investigative lapse: monumental stupidity or undue deference to the bloodline. In either case, the Bedford County Sheriff's Department missed its chance to solve the crimes quickly since I undoubtedly would have lost my nerve and told the police the truth if I had been questioned in April 1985. Fifteen months later, when a Bedford detective interrogated me in London, I had lived with my lie so long that it was comparatively easy to "confess" to killing the Haysoms.

Failing to check Liz's alibi with me was only one of many oversights by Sheriff Wells and Commonwealth's Attorney Updike's investigators. Some of the mistakes were minor but revealing. When police asked Elizabeth during an informal interview shortly after the murders what her father's favorite food was, she blurted out "ice cream," and then she stammered until she repeated, "ice cream." Liz realized she had made a mistake because ice cream was the late night snack her father had been eating at the dinner table where the murderous knife fight had begun. Crime-scene specialists found the half-consumed bowl still sitting on the table at Loose Chippings, and the other half of the bowl's contents in Mr. Haysom's stomach. In spite of the stammer that betrayed her during questioning, however, the detectives did not press Elizabeth further on how she could have known such a telling detail of the scene of the crime.

Even more strangely, Bedford County investigators also failed to follow up on three forensic reports incriminating Liz, which they received in the following days and weeks. First, crime-lab scientists discovered her fingerprints on a half-empty vodka bottle on the front row of the liquor cabinet in the living room, three steps from her father's body. This location was significant because the alcohol levels of both victims were .22, more than twice the legal limit for drunk driving. Elizabeth's fingerprints were on the extreme opposite ends of the bottle, with the intervening space wiped clean.

The second forensic report revealed that a drop of type-B blood (Liz's type) had been found on a damp washcloth hung on the front of the washing machine, only one step from her mother's corpse. Diluted blood spatters in the kitchen sink directly above the washing machine indicated that the attacker or attackers had washed off blood there, and the dampness of the washcloth implied that it must have been hung on the washing machine only a few days before the discovery of the murders.

Finally, a third report, dated April 8, 1985, determined that a bloody sneaker-print found in the living room (now called LR2) was left by "a woman or a small man or boy." Most likely, it was a New Balance, "a 6½ or 7 shoe." That just happened to be Elizabeth's approximate size, and of course she was a woman. (By contrast, I am a man, neither large nor small, and wear a size 8½ to 9.)

Sheriff Wells and Prosecutor Updike knew this evidence alone was insufficient to convict Elizabeth. The sneaker-print LR2 could have been left by any woman wearing that approximate-size shoe, and theoretically she could have left those fingerprints on the vodka bottle when she visited her parents' cottage on the weekend before the murders. Also, since the spot of blood on the washcloth was too small to be subtyped, it could arguably belong to any of the ten percent of the population that has type-B blood. If Liz were brought to trial, her lawyer might even claim that the blood test had malfunctioned, so that Nancy Haysom's AB type or Derek Haysom's A type were incorrectly registered as B type.

Such arguments by the defense could easily be countered. The Haysoms were known to have been such heavy drinkers that Elizabeth's fingerprints would not have remained undisturbed for a whole week on half a bottle of vodka, and there could hardly be an innocent explanation for wiping the middle of the bottle clean. As far as the accuracy of the blood-typing tests was concerned, it would be easy to show that their history was nearly error-free and that they had not failed in any other sample from Loose Chippings.

Still, Liz's half-brothers had already hired one of the best local attorneys, and he might persuade a jury to believe anything.

But even if the fingerprints, the blood drop, and the shoe print by themselves would not guarantee Elizabeth's conviction, this evidence could be used to try to shock her into confessing. That was police procedure so common, in fact, that the U.S. Supreme Court allowed interrogators to lie to suspects about forensic evidence. If the suspect were guilty, he or she might believe that a fingerprint had been found, give up hope, and confess; and if the suspect were innocent, a policeman's lie about a fingerprint would not matter. But Sheriff Wells' and Commonwealth's Attorney Updike's detectives decided not to follow normal police procedure by confronting Liz with the vodka bottle, the washcloth, and the sneaker-print. Perhaps they were still in shock from the April visit by the Haysom brothers' attorney, who had bullied them into focusing the investigation away from their half-sister. Or perhaps they had honestly convinced themselves that a scion of one of the oldest and most respected families of Lynchburg could not commit murder.

Because of the Bedford police's overabundant respect for Elizabeth's family tree, she and I learned nothing of these developments in the manhunt for the Haysoms' killer or killers. As April 1985 passed into May, we worried less and less about being arrested and having to persuade the police that I, not she, had killed her parents. Instead, we concentrated on catching up with our schoolwork at U.Va. and playing the roles of the grieving daughter and her supportive boyfriend. So persuasive was my performance, that one of the girls whom I had dated in fall 1984 complimented me on my devotion and, on the verge of tears, asked me to call on her if I should ever grow tired of Liz. As I looked into this girl's eyes, I felt physically ill for a moment. What would she think of me if she knew? But the hollow cramp in my stomach quickly passed, and such revolts of my conscience grew fewer. I was becoming a practiced liar, completely enveloped in the folie à deux.

While Elizabeth's small deceptions had begun to separate me from my friends during the first few months of 1985, our shared great lie now isolated us completely in the second half of the spring semester. Staying apart from our peers was partially intentional, to protect us from giving ourselves away. And perhaps some of our remaining friends also shunned us because they did not know how to comfort Liz in her supposed mourning. But I now believe most of our isolation was an unconscious withdrawal by both of us, some awareness deep within that we had set ourselves outside of society through our acts on March 30 and 31. We did not believe that we were wrong, of course, but we knew we were forever different.

When I look back to that second half of the spring semester of 1985, I remember waking one morning next to Elizabeth after a long night's lovemaking. We had slept in the back of her mother's old Dodge van, one of the very few items Liz inherited from her parents. Stripped down to bare metal and loose wires on the inside, the van at least had a flat cargo floor on which we had placed a few old sofa cushions as a mattress.

The sound of many shoes slapping the ground woke me that particular morning. Our sleeping breath had condensed on all the windows, so I could see nothing of what lay outside. I wiped a small spot on the fogged glass.

The sun shone into my eyes from high above Observatory Hill in the distance, where Elizabeth and I had met. Around us a long-distance race was in progress. Joggers in numbered shirts passed directly beside the van, and down the street stood a few spectators.

I had heard nothing about a big race planned for that day, nothing at all. Liz and I were safe and happy in our bubble.

6

Going on the Run

"The case is about to be solved."

May 1985–November 1985

O UR SENSE OF safety from the police was a dangerous illusion. In fact, the last few days of May 1985 were a turning point in Sheriff Wells and Commonwealth's Attorney Updike's hunt for Derek and Nancy Haysom's murderer or murderers.

At the end of the spring semester, I returned to my family's home in Detroit while Liz went to Lynchburg to prepare Loose Chippings for sale. Commercial cleaning companies had refused the job of removing all the blood smeared on the floors and walls of the cottage, so Elizabeth, some of her half-brothers, and Mrs. Massie were forced to do this gruesome work themselves. I remember Liz later showing me a snapshot of her brothers holding mops in the front yard, as though everyone were engaged in some pleasant family project. But if cleaning up her hated parents' blood was a happy task for Elizabeth, other members of the group were occupied with serious thoughts and apparently decided to watch Liz carefully.

Their wary vigilance was soon rewarded. During a break in the work when Elizabeth believed herself unobserved, she took off her shoe and compared her bare foot to several smeared sockprints on the blood-encrusted living-room floor. Clearly, she was worried that her feet might betray her. The two members of the cleanup crew who witnessed Liz's suspicious behavior decided to inform law-enforcement as soon as possible.

Until then, Bedford County investigators had paid relatively little attention to the two bloody sockprints, designated LR3 and LR5, and the one bloody sneaker-print, labeled LR2, which they had found at Loose Chippings. All three had been photographed, of course, and in the case of LR5 the piece of wooden floorboard bearing the print was even removed and preserved. But the sock impressions in particular were smeared and faint, while the imprint of the shoe sole was not sufficiently detailed to identify the specific sneaker that made it—only the brand. When the detectives learned of Liz's incriminating footwork while cleaning Loose Chippings, however, they decided to examine the sock- and shoe-prints more carefully.

During the summer of 1985, forensic examiner Rick Johnson sent two reports to the Bedford County investigators. In the first, dated June 7, he determined that the bloody sockprint LR3 was left by "a man's size 5 to 6 . . . or a woman's size 6½ to 7½" foot. The second report, dated August 29, stated that one of Elizabeth's half-brothers could not be eliminated from the investigation on the basis of his footprints, because ink samples that he provided to police contained too many similarities to the LR3 sockprint at the scene of crime. What Johnson could not say at that time was whether Elizabeth could have left the bloody sockprints, because detectives had not yet asked her to make sample footprints in ink for a scientific comparison.

(As an aside, it is worth noting that these forensic reports by Rick Johnson are the only analyses of the sockprints conducted before Liz and I went on the run in October and thereby officially became suspects. That makes Johnson's findings the only truly "blind" and therefore unbiased scientific evidence regarding LR3 and LR5. So it is surely significant that these reports eliminate me as a potential contributor of those sockprints, since I had a man's size 8½–9 foot. Elizabeth, on the other hand, had a woman's size 7½–8 foot.)

In the summer of 1985, however, Liz and I knew nothing of the police's interest in footprints generally and her suspicious comparison of her feet to the bloody sockprints at Loose Chippings specifically. So safe did we believe ourselves that we left the U.S. at the end of June to tour Europe in a rented Ford Fiesta, supposedly to help her overcome her grief.

Our vacation seemed heavenly then. During the week we spent in West Berlin, Elizabeth taught me how to drive a stick shift on an empty lot next to Checkpoint Charlie, and we had cherry-pit spitting contests in the ornate gardens of the Charlottenburg Palace. On our way south we danced away our single night in Prague, to the sounds of a three-accordion combo playing covers of Western disco music. Mozart's *Magic Flute* at the Staatsoper was the high point of the seven days in Vienna, though we nearly fainted from the smell of the unwashed French schoolchildren in the seats around us. For two weeks, Liz and I loafed around and made love on the balcony of my maternal grandmother's chalet atop the picture-postcard mountains that leap to the skies around Lake Geneva. Thousands of feet below us floated tiny toy boats, while on the other side of the water were the French Alps, their summits level with ours. On rainy days, Elizabeth and I could look onto the tops of the clouds above the lake.

Our vacation indeed seemed heavenly then. But when I look back now, I believe we traveled through Europe like two ghosts, invisible to others and unable to make contact with anyone beyond our self-contained world. Apart from border guards and waiters, I do not recall Liz and me speaking with other people. We did not engage East Berliners in conversation to learn about life under Communist rule. Shaggy-bearded environmentalists tried to chat with us in Vienna, but Elizabeth and I rebuffed them. High in the Swiss Alps we drove past backwoods characters on small lonely roads without stopping to offer them a lift. Liz and I kept ourselves completely apart, alone.

And we did not mix any more with others once we returned to America. I spent a few days with my family in Detroit while Elizabeth visited relatives in New York, and then we joined up at summer school. Again, we isolated ourselves from our fellow students, who enjoyed the relaxed summer atmosphere by having one long, continuous party.

Liz and I instead spent a considerable amount of time meeting with professors and department heads to develop a special double-major program in business and Mandarin. At that time, popular magazines were advising America's youth that this combination of skills was the surest way to breathtaking success, since China was at that time opening up to the West. Our plan was in fact a variation of Elizabeth's spring semester daydream about propelling me into the upper echelons of international diplomacy. But bringing capitalism to Beijing promised to be far more profitable than working for any government foreign service.

When Liz and I began the fall semester of 1985 we practically never left each other's side during the day, since we were taking almost exactly the same classes for this double major. All my nights were spent with Elizabeth, too, after I moved into the large house she shared with three other girls and our cat. Before the murders, I had arranged to share a dormitory-style apartment with some friends, but now I only kept a few clothes there.

Liz and I led quiet lives and worked hard for our many difficult classes. The murders were banished to a far-distant past that no longer concerned us, and when we mentioned them at all we called them "our little nasty." Nothing seemed to threaten the happiness of our shared future.

Nothing, that is, except those bloody sockprints at Loose

Chippings. In mid-September, Bedford County investigators contacted Elizabeth to obtain samples of her footprints, for comparison to the LR3 and LR5 prints at the scene of crime. It was only a formality, they told her.

Liz was scared when she returned from the sheriff's office. After taking ink samples of her footprints, the detectives had asked her awkward, hostile questions about a discrepancy in the mileage of the car she had rented for our Washington vacation. Yet they seemed reluctant to accuse her directly, perhaps because of the Haysom brothers' pressure not to besmirch the family name. Were the authorities closing in on us? Or were they just fishing for information?

Looking back, I now believe that Sheriff Wells' detectives must have been almost as unhappy as Elizabeth and I were at the direction in which the investigation was headed. For six months they had tried to protect the reputation of one of Virginia's oldest families by focusing on suspects other than Liz. But if the LR3 and LR5 prints from the crime scene turned out to be hers, their tact and discretion would become very embarrassing.

Although I do not know exactly what the police did with Elizabeth's ink samples in 1985, it seems clear that they did not compare them to the bloody sockprints.

Before my 1990 trial, my lawyers combed the prosecution's files without finding any report analyzing Liz's feet. Even more strangely, Commonwealth's Attorney Updike did not call his forensic expert from 1985, Rick Johnson, to testify at my trial.

In late September 1985, a few days after Liz provided detectives with ink footprint samples, the police called me and asked if I would agree to be questioned. I drove to Bedford County one weekend and denied all knowledge of the murders. My feeble attempts to explain away the incriminating mileage discrepancy undoubtedly raised the investigators' suspicions even further. Not only did the miles noted on the rental-car bill correspond perfectly to Elizabeth's murderous round-trip to Lynchburg, but I kept blushing when the detectives pointed out that a Jefferson Scholar was unlikely to get lost on the drive from Washington to U.Va.

During the interview, Investigator Ricky Gardner told me that he had "probable cause." Probable cause for *what* I cannot now recall, but as far as I was concerned at that time I had just been given the final warning. Liz and I would have to go on the run. "Confessing" now was the only alternative, and I saw no need to take that ultimate step to protect Elizabeth until we were actually arrested.

Having made this decision, I immediately stopped cooperating with the investigators. When they asked me to provide my fingerprints, I stalled them with a lame excuse about calling my father and the German Embassy. My fingerprints could be used to trace me on the run, after all. Even if I assumed a different identity I might be arrested years from now for some minor offense like drunk driving. The police would feed my fingerprints into a computer and discover that I was not John Doe but Jens Soering, America's Most Wanted. I became so worried about being traced that I even wiped all my fingerprints from my apartment before fleeing.

But fingerprints were only one of many areas in which Liz and I tried to outwit the police. We withdrew all the money from our college bank accounts on a Friday afternoon, hoping that the weekend rush would leave the Bedford detectives insufficient time to learn of our imminent departure. To mislead the investigators further we booked our airplane tickets in false names, left on different days, and did not fly directly to our final destination.

On Saturday, October 12, 1985, I embarked on a "People Express" flight from D.C. to Brussels, and then took a train to Paris. But in the haste of departure I forgot my collection of Elizabeth's love letters to me. So I called Liz from the airport and asked her to go to my apartment to pick up those letters, as well as my own Christmas 1984 diary-letters.

That telephone call was one of the most unfortunate of my life. When Elizabeth and I were arrested for check fraud in London a few months later, the suspicious passages in those letters prompted the English police to trace us back to Virginia. And if that were not enough misfortune, Liz then claimed in 1987 that I had used these incriminating letters to blackmail her into following me to Europe. The truth is recorded in our travel diary and in the transcript of Elizabeth's police interrogation of April 1986.

My phone call from the airport was Liz's excuse for leaving U.Va. She pretended to her roommates that I had asked her to join me for another vacation in Washington. Instead, she took the same circuitous route to Paris one day after me.

Our complicated departure from Virginia had an epilogue that illustrates the depths of Elizabeth's manipulativeness and my obsessiveness. About a month after fleeing the U.S., Liz and I began keeping a diary of our travels. Both of us were compulsive writers, and recording daily events was a cheap form of entertainment. At first, Elizabeth did the writing—until I discovered that her overactive imagination had led her away from strictly factual recording. As so often, she was mixing fantasy and reality.

In the first four diary pages, covering our escape from Virginia, Liz included six POTS. She began by writing about a laser operation for a brain tumor, which I knew was nonsense. Another passage mentioned a friend in the Irish Republican Army who could get us false passports. He was also fictional. In 1987, Elizabeth admitted that an entry about a telephone call from her brother was untrue, as was the description of her flight from the U.S. to Europe.

A little later in the diary she described one of our hotels as a "white slave transfer point," another instance of the theme of sexual violence that troubled her imagination.

These inventions, however, did not bother me nearly as much as this passage: "The case is about to be solved. Perhaps fingerprints on coffee mug used by Jens in Bedford interview gave him away."

This remark made no sense, since Liz and I both knew that my fingerprints could not have been found at the scene of crime. (What we did not know then, but what is surely significant, is that her fingerprints were found at her parents' cottage, in a very incriminating position, too.) Even though this diary entry made no sense, one thing was clear: it incriminated me.

When I confronted Elizabeth about the laser surgery, the fingerprints, and the other fictional passages, she gave me the same excuse she gave the English police in April 1986: her portion of the diary was full of "lies" and "fantasy" because the journal was intended as the basis of an "adventure book." Strangely enough, the English police accepted this explanation in 1986. But in 1985, I pointed out to Liz that we could not publish a book about our travels since we were on the run.

Elizabeth eventually admitted the truth to me. The passage about my fingerprints had been intended as insurance, in case we were arrested. Because Liz would again be the prime suspect after our escape to Europe, she wanted to ensure that there would be seemingly objective evidence that pointed to me as the killer.

My fear of being traced on the run through my fingerprints had given her the idea to include a paragraph about leaving fingerprints on the Bedford police coffee mug.

The normal reaction to such a deception would be anger, I suppose, but I only felt guilt. Somehow, I must have given Elizabeth reason to doubt me. Somehow, she had come to believe that I might let her go to the electric chair: Liz, the love of my life! There had never been any doubt in my mind that I would accept responsibility for the murders.

So I apologized profusely to Elizabeth and assured her that of course I would admit killing her parents if we were caught. As proof of my willingness to "confess," I even agreed to leave the passage about my fingerprints in the diary. But from then on I wrote all the entries, so our journal would be purely factual.

Such was the nature of the folie à deux. For the first time, I had absolute proof that Liz's POTS were not just fictionalized yarns about her past, but that she lied intentionally to create traps in complex schemes affecting both our lives. Yet I did not suddenly recognize her for what she was. Instead, I made a groveling apology for forcing her to scheme against me.

A few days after my fingerprints on the coffee mug supposedly forced me to flee to Europe, I woke up alone in one of Paris' cheapest hotels. It was Tuesday, October 15, the day I was to rendezvous with Elizabeth below the Arc de Triomphe. Being apart from the love of my life for forty-eight hours left me extraordinarily tense and more than a little frightened. At first, I did not even recognize her because she had dyed her hair red this time. But then we fell into each other's arms, elated to be united again.

That evening we had a terrible meal at a Rive Gauche restaurant and thus learned one of the eternal truths that Paris teaches all visitors: without plenty of money, one quickly ends in those infamously odorous French sewers. Although Liz and I had safely escaped the Bedford police, we now faced the rest of our lives alone, short on funds, and on the run.

Our first attempt to find some sort of safe haven failed miserably. Before leaving Virginia, Elizabeth and I had discussed the possibility of fleeing to Africa and laying low as aid workers, at least for a while. But the Zimbabwean Embassy in Paris was uninterested in a couple of unqualified youths. When we tried the Botswanan Embassy in Brussels two days later, we were turned down again.

The weekend was approaching, so Liz and I decided to change countries again. We took the train south from Belgium to the tiny village of Ettelbruck in Luxembourg.

Ettelbruck was perfect: cheap by West European standards, and so obscure that not even James Bond could have traced us there. We stayed at a modern inn and took long walks in the freezing, wind-blasted, Luxembourgeois countryside. We looked at the sheep, and the sheep stared back at us. The sheep went back to grazing, but Elizabeth and I had to figure out just how we would support ourselves for the rest of our lives on the run.

On Monday, October 21, 1985, we returned to the city of Luxembourg and set up our HQ at the local post office, with its banks of telephone booths. First, we called airlines to inquire about ticket prices for flights to Thailand. Since we could not go to Zimbabwe, the country of Liz's birth, perhaps the country of my birth would oblige us with new passports to obscure our pasts.

But even Pakistan International Airways turned out to be too expensive for our limited means. So we fell back on plan number two: stealing a car and driving as far east as possible, at least to Turkey and perhaps to India. There was a continuous land route, and we phoned most of the embassies of the countries we would have to cross. Starting from Luxembourg, there was France, Switzerland, Italy, Yugoslavia, Bulgaria, Turkey, Iran, Pakistan, and India, with only three wars along the way! If we did not make it to India, we could always sell the car in Turkey and try to fly to Thailand on the proceeds.

Because Elizabeth and I knew nothing about stealing cars, we simply rented one with my father's VISA card. Unfortunately, we had to settle for a four-door Fiat Regatta, since the agency refused to give us a Mercedes 190.

Driving south on Tuesday along the French–German border, we soon reached Bern, and checked into the hotel that Liz later described as the "white slave transfer point" of our diary. In town we acquired an international driver's license for Elizabeth and then proceeded to obtain transit visas from the embassies of the countries we needed to cross on our way to India.

The Yugoslavs and Bulgarians had already told us on the phone in Luxembourg that we could get tourist visas at their border checkpoints. An information officer at the Turkish Embassy gave

us a very long and very loud lecture about Turkey's friendship with
Germany and Canada, which obviated the need for visas. Finally, we
went to the Iranian Embassy. The triple security gates and machine
gun–toting guards were more than a little intimidating, but the
Ayatollah's diplomats treated us politely. I will never forget their
hilarious propaganda posters: FILTHY REAGAN IS PIG-FLESH-EATING,
BABY-MURDERING SATAN!

Liz and I drove south again on Thursday, October 24, passing
through the long tunnels of the Swiss Alps into Italy and traveling
on the Autostrada east past Genoa to Trieste. Late in the evening
we crossed into the Slovenian republic of Yugoslavia and spent the
night sleeping in our car at a truck stop near Zagreb in the Croatian
republic.

The following day's weather should have warned us that
trouble of the most surreal kind lay ahead. The plains of Croatia,
Bosnia, and Serbia were covered by a fog of such astonishing
density that we saw virtually nothing of the countryside. Through
the mist we could barely discern small, huddled figures in colorless
rags doing some futile chore on the desolate turnip fields.

A policeman in a Yugo squad car pulled Elizabeth over for
rashly exceeding the 40 MPH speed limit. I gave him some deutsche
marks, and he suddenly discovered that he had been mistaken. By
midday we'd reached Belgrade and made a quick tour of the wide
empty avenues lined by unbelievably hideous concrete high-rises.
No doubt the architecture was supposed to convince visitors of the
virtues of socialism; the city's planners succeeded, though not quite
as they had intended.

In the afternoon, Liz and I drove through the southeastern
regions of Serbia near Macedonia. The countryside here became
less darkly Central European, more dustily Mediterranean. As
the sun began setting we passed through ragged, wildly beautiful
mountains onto arid plains enlivened only by a few army barracks.

It was nighttime when the Bulgarian border guards told us

that we had to drive all the way back to Belgrade to get transit visas from the Bulgarian Embassy there.

The information we had been given over the phone in Luxembourg was wrong, after all.

Elizabeth turned around and drove back through the pit of liquid disinfectant that all cars entering Bulgaria had to pass through. I think there was a moon overhead, and the Fiat's radio was playing that summer's Yugoslav number one hit: "Daggy-da, daggy-da, daggy-daggy-daggy-da!"

And then Liz very nearly killed us both.

7

Changing Identities in Bangkok

"Minimum order one hundred!"

November 1985–December 1985

O N THE OPPOSITE side of our two-lane road a constant stream of cars was heading southeast toward the border checkpoint that Elizabeth and I had just left. Suddenly, one of the oncoming Yugoslav drivers decided that he could wait no longer for the excitement Bulgaria had to offer. He sheared into our lane to overtake another car without so much as a warning honk of his horn.

Liz jerked the steering wheel to the right, and we slewed onto the gravelly shoulder of the road. The Pirelli tire on the front right wheel exploded instantly, sending us left again across the road. My last memory was of the fierce yellow headlights of an oncoming Yugo.

I awoke to see the roof of the Fiat, which now sloped downward to touch the dashboard in front of me. Elizabeth was shouting in my ear to find out if I were hurt, and we slowly checked each other for injuries. Because we had worn seat belts, Liz suffered no more than a bruise, while I sustained several deep cuts on the head and hands.

We crawled out of the wreck, and Elizabeth told me what had happened. After crossing the road we had hit the embankment, rolled once, and landed on our wheels. Unfortunately, the Fiat had still been in gear and thus started moving again. We crossed the road once more, only to be hit in the rear quarter by another car.

Around us was a major traffic jam, and heading in our direction was one clearly angry Yugoslav car owner whose automotive pride and joy had just disintegrated upon impact with our sturdier Western car. He ranted and raved incomprehensibly until he noticed that I could hardly see him through the blood running into my eyes, much less understand him. Together, we managed to push the Fiat off the road, took out our suitcases, and waited for the police.

The officers from the nearby town of Pirot handled the situation in an exemplary fashion. Arriving in force soon after the accident, the police immediately separated Liz and me to prevent us from cooking up some sort of story. She was put in the warm squad car with our luggage, while the driver of the other car and I were questioned on the roadside.

A tow truck arrived to move what was left of the Fiat, and the other driver and I were taken to the Pirot police station. Both of us had to repeat our stories to make sure the details had not changed. Since none of the officers spoke English, German, or French, I drew a series of sketches to explain what had happened.

It took quite a while to make the police understand that Elizabeth, not I, had been driving the car. This revelation was a source of some astonishment to the locals; Serbian machismo precluded a woman behind the steering wheel. The male was supposed to be active and aggressive—*just the type to cause a car wreck*—whereas the female was supposed to be passive and gentle. And I was the one covered in blood; so I must have been the driver.

Finally, the officers accepted that in the decadent, capitalist West, even women could drive cars and cause crashes. Once the paperwork was completed, the tow-truck driver took Liz and me to a large hospital, where a young doctor with a smattering of French gave me various injections and sewed up my still-bleeding head wound.

Elizabeth and I spent the next day-and-a-half in the company of the translator–spy supplied by the Pirot police. Like so much else in Yugoslavia, he seemed almost a caricature of himself: a black-bereted veteran of World War II Balkan campaigns, he was one-eyed, red-nosed, dark, squat, and permanently drunk. But the translator–spy actually spoke a few words of German and, more importantly, always got us a table at one of the two local restaurants. Whenever Liz and I tried to eat by ourselves, the doormen inevitably managed to communicate that a wedding party was in progress. We only learned much later that this was East European code for "Give me a bribe."

Our translator introduced us to the only entertainment available in the dusty little backwater of Pirot: drinking Slivovitz and eating oily stuffed paprika. While he drank and we ate, the tow-truck driver dropped by to inform us that he would make a fortune from gutting our Fiat for parts but we had better pay him a bribe anyway.

Our trial took place on Saturday, October 26. The judge, our translator, the driver of the other car, and Elizabeth and I all crowded into a small office in the local courthouse.

Fortunately, the judge and I immediately struck up a friendly conversation. He was eager to practice his excellent German, and I was relieved to find one person in Pirot who could actually understand what I was saying.

Soon, it was time for the trial to begin. The judge straightened in his chair and put on a serious face. During the official proceedings, he told me, we could only communicate through the official translator, who was provided for such official purposes.

After the driver of the Yugoslav car had testified, it was Liz's turn. The judge asked a question in Serbian, the translator would pass it on to me in pidgin German, I would translate it to English for Elizabeth, and then the answer would return.

I could see the judge's face growing redder and tenser, and I began fearing the worst. Finally, he could stand it no more. He leapt from his chair and bellowed what must have been the most devastating and elaborate Serbian curses. The translator shrank against the wall, quivering with fear and Slivovitz. Apparently, he'd mistranslated one of my responses, and the judge had caught him on his error.

Of course, we could not dispense with the official translator, who was provided for such official purposes. So, for the next hour, the judge would listen to my answer in German, then listen to the translator's Serbian version, and finally proceed to explain to the translator what he had translated incorrectly. The same happened in reverse. If the judge's Serbian question did not reach me in perfect German the translator would have to try again and again and again.

Finally, the trial was over. The judge leaned back in his chair, glowered at us over his steepled fingers, and pronounced the verdict: guilty of reckless driving and sentenced to a fine of 50,000 dinars . . . I think.

Liz and I looked at each other, blanching for a moment. If we could not pay the fine, the judge might send us to the fog-shrouded plains of Croatia to pick turnips on a Yugoslav chain gang! But then we realized that 50,000 Dinars amounted to something like $7.50.

We took the train to Belgrade the next day. To avenge his humiliation at the trial, our translator helped us buy tickets, which only sufficed to take us to the next town, though we paid the price for the full trip to Belgrade. But deutsche marks persuaded the train's ticket collector to allow us to continue on our journey.

Elizabeth and I took our seats in a half-full compartment next to a young man from Bulgaria. Using hand signals, grunts, and his few words of German, he told us that he was a mechanic and held up his slender, clean hands with long pinkie nails and gold rings. He grinned and winked significantly. Clearly "mechanic" was East European code for a man of influence, a man who could oil the wheels of Communist bureaucracy.

During the long trip to Belgrade, Liz and I watched this mechanic in action. He had set his heart on winning the favors of a rather ugly Yugoslav girl in our compartment, so he spent a half-hour in deep discussion with the girl's male companion. Bulgarian brandy changed hands, and so did the girl.

Our mechanic celebrated his successful transaction by passing around an enormous bottle of Slivovitz. For the rest of the slow train ride the five of us shared that bottle, giggling and grinning mutely at one another with the warm love felt by one drunk for another.

The night train from Belgrade brought us to the Italian town of Trieste on the border between the two countries. I will never forget the beautiful Renaissance center of Trieste, which encircles a small blue-green Adriatic bay. And I will never forget the courage of the town's bus drivers, who steered their vehicles along impossibly narrow roads up the steep mountains surrounding the bay. On top of one of these mountains was a public bathhouse where Elizabeth and I washed off the unhappy memories of Yugoslavia. We ate pizza in town and prepared for the night train north, back through the Alps and on to Vienna.

Liz and I spent a week recovering from Yugoslavia and revisiting some of our favorite Viennese haunts from the summer vacation only a few months earlier. How long ago that seemed now! We attended Strauss' *Rosenkavalier* at the Staatsoper and went hiking in Grinzing's foggy mountaintop woods. In the evenings, we had a few glasses of wine at a bar near Sigmund Freud's house. But our excursions only filled us with melancholy, for we were planning on leaving Europe forever.

Before we could depart, however, Elizabeth and I had to take care of some medical problems. First, I had my stitches removed from my head wound. And then we had to rid ourselves of the crabs we had caught from the unwashed sheets at our hotel in Pirot.

On our way to the coin laundry a dive-bombing pigeon managed to deposit droppings on my head—a good omen, according to Central European tradition. The next day, we left by train for Salzburg on the border of Germany. There we spent an entire day making cash withdrawals with my father's VISA card to replenish our ebbing travel funds. Liz and I hoped this trail of VISA bills from Vienna westward to Salzburg would lead the pursuing police forces to search for us in Germany or points west.

Meanwhile, we doubled back to Vienna that evening and caught an incredibly cheap L.O.T. Polish Airlines flight east to Warsaw. Thence L.O.T. took us to Bangkok, via Tashkent in the Uzbek Republic of the Soviet Union.

When Elizabeth and I arrived in Thailand on November 6, 1985, we immediately fell in love with the country. Bangkok looked at first glance much like metropolitan areas in Western nations. There were skyscrapers and wide highways and traffic jams and functioning telephones and air conditioning. But around every corner there lay uniquely Thai surprises.

The shiny glass-and-chrome shopping malls had the same goods as their European or American counterparts and then some. A young store clerk explained to us the logos on Thai T-shirts like FUZZY ORANGE SUPER-COUP EATS BANANA. According to the clerk, Thais considered the meaning of the words irrelevant and simply admired the shape and arrangement of the foreign letters.

Everywhere and every day the Thais found ways to weave Western influences into the fabric of their own culture. On Bangkok's back streets, Liz and I saw elephants used as living forklifts to unload boxes of consumer electronics or clothes. And after a hard day's work, extended families sat together to eat the painfully spicy local food in instant restaurants that sprang up on the city sidewalks while traffic roared all around.

On the streets, the best method for travel was the tuk-tuk taxi, a Vespa motor scooter converted into a colorfully painted three-wheeler. As in a rickshaw, the passenger sat behind the driver on a two-person-and-one-piglet bench with a flimsy sunshade. These vehicles were owned by Chinese merchants who rented them to poor Thai drivers from the bamboo shantytowns.

Elizabeth and I first stayed at a hotel that had been famous in the 1960s for its regular hippie customers who sought enlightenment in opium. But after some friendly advice from a Thai engineer who had lived in the U.S., we moved to a small hostel that cost the equivalent of $2.50 or so per night.

Three white, two-story bungalows for the guests and the owner's residence surrounded a rectangular courtyard full of palm trees and other tropical plants. The interior of the guest bungalows was typically Southeast Asian: the top quarter of the rooms' walls was mosquito screening, which allowed the ceiling fans to cross-circulate the hot air. A simple wooden frame bed with thin but cool mattresses filled most of the room, and everyone had to share a bathroom down the hall. But the place was spotlessly clean and cheerful.

Our days began at the neighborhood Dunkin' Donuts, where Liz and I rested our aching tongues from the fiery Thai cuisine with some wonderfully bland Western food. Then we set out on our errands, crisscrossing the city under the hot sun of the November–December dry season. All around us, Thais were preparing for Christmas. Bing Crosby holiday classics blared from radios, and storefronts were decorated with Santas of all races and colors.

Since our entertainment budget was limited, we spent most of our evenings making hot, sweaty love while enormous blood-crazed mosquitoes hurled themselves against the window netting. It was at this point, as I recall, that Elizabeth and I started keeping the travel diary—in my case, out of sheer boredom; and in hers, perhaps with an ulterior motive. Occasionally, as a special treat, we indulged ourselves with a couple of hours of air conditioning in a theater. Before every movie the entire audience had to stand at attention, listen to the national anthem, and watch a film clip of Thailand's living God-King Bhumipol.

Using the hostel as a base of operations, Elizabeth and I made genuine attempts to establish ourselves as legitimate citizens. I visited the German Embassy to track down a copy of my Thai birth certificate from 1966, the first step to acquiring Thai nationality. We learned, however, that the birth certificate was untraceable and that the Thais were reluctant to naturalize *farangs*, as they called foreigners.

Next, we tried to find work. Bangkok had two newspapers published in a pidgin-dialect meant to be English, and hiring Liz and me as sub-editors would have transformed these publications from laughable to near-respectable. But the Thais were proud people who did not appreciate *farangs* correcting their grammar.

Elizabeth and I also tried to find work teaching English. But once we found the British–American Language School in an apparently abandoned high rise, we immediately sensed that something very strange was going on there. A dark-haired, thin white gentleman in his thirties emerged from an office after a long wait. Behind him we caught a glimpse of a large bed with colorful silk sheets, under which lay an obviously middle-aged Thai lady. This place clearly was the feminists' revenge for Thailand's infamous sex-tourism industry. Since older white men bought young Thai girls, older Thai women were now buying younger white men.

In fact, the truth may be even stranger. Several months after my arrest in London, English newspapers reported the expulsion of a youngish white man from Thailand on charges of espionage. He had seduced the wives of high-ranking Thai military officers using the cover of a language school.

Since we could not make money honestly in Thailand, Liz and I turned our minds to crime. Looking for inspiration, we wrote dozens of letters to small companies advertising in the back of the *International Herald Tribune*, *Soldier of Fortune*, and *Venture Capital*. Every day, we hopped on a tuk-tuk, shouted "*Praekanesang*," and rattled across town to check for responses at the main post office. There may still be *poste restante* letters waiting for us there.

In the hostel we met a suspiciously slim, middle-aged woman with a well-bred British accent who told us that she imported carpets from Thailand to England. I agreed with Elizabeth that, like so many Westerners in Bangkok, this woman was probably involved in the smuggling of heroin from the Golden Triangle of Burma, Laos, and Thailand. I did not, however, agree with Liz's idea that we, too, should make money from drugs. Her previous addiction to heroin and the Draconian Thai punishments made smuggling a most dangerous proposition.

Another one of Elizabeth's brilliant ideas was to rob foreign tourists with the aid of a stun gun. Who would ever suspect that the perpetrators were not desperate? I nixed that plan as well.

Looking back, I can see now that our relationship began to change subtly during this period. Up to this point, Liz had clearly been the dominant partner. But when we failed to establish legitimate lives in Thailand, and her ideas for moneymaking crimes turned out to be useless, I was more or less pushed into taking on more leadership responsibilities. Eventually, I would come up with a scheme to generate some income for us, and that fact put me into the metaphorical driver's seat, at least as far as many of our day-to-day decisions were concerned. Of course, Elizabeth was a more than active back-seat driver—by no means did she suddenly become passive—but over the following months she was no longer initiating actions, but merely influencing plans and decisions made by me.

I find this significant because, as mentioned in earlier chapters, I have had time to study borderline personality disorders and associated psychological conditions and illnesses. According to the therapeutic literature I have read, people like Liz go through stages in their relationships with significant others—usually ending in a traumatic and dramatic break. Killing the significant other is, of course, an extremely unusual form of engineering such a break, but Elizabeth had proved herself capable of this already. So I now wonder what might have happened if we had not been caught by the police on April 30, 1986.

Our relationship was already beginning to shift as early as the end of 1985, with me assuming more and more of a leadership role. What if this shift had continued? What if Liz and I had cycled through the remaining stages of a borderline personality disorder? How would she have engineered the traumatic and dramatic ending of the relationship with me? Would Elizabeth have killed me, too?

Idle speculation, perhaps—or maybe not so idle. She was seriously contemplating the pros and cons of stun-gunning and robbing tourists in Thailand. Such a stun gun could have been used on someone other than a tourist, eventually.

In any case, in late 1985 I rejected Liz's plans for armed robbery. Instead, I went to Bangkok's well-stocked English bookstores and learned as much as I could about the English banking system. One of Elizabeth's stories of her adventures as a runaway had given me an idea for a bank fraud. Researching in magazines and bookstores was, for me, the natural place to start my career as a criminal. Similarly, I had read up on tropical fish poisons when planning the perfect murder for my Zen-detective movie script at U.Va. just nine short months before.

Whichever form of crime we eventually settled on, we would need plenty of false identification. English was the only language that both Liz and I spoke fluently, so we decided that I would be a Canadian like her. We bought drafting pencils and paper, and together designed a very attractive but completely fictitious driver's license for one of the Canadian provinces.

Nearly every commercial district in Bangkok had at least one tiny printing shop, usually run by diminutive Chinese gentlemen with lots of gold teeth. Elizabeth and I took our sample driver's license to one of the seedier-looking printing shops in the hope of finding an owner too desperate to worry about legal niceties like forgery laws. We crossed the store's threshold and stepped up to the counter.

The Chinese proprietor smiled at us, and we despaired. He had an unusually large number of gold teeth, so his store was doing better than the shabby exterior indicated. Liz and I swallowed hard and silently pushed our sample across the counter. Talking was pointless, since most commercial transactions between *farangs* and locals took place through gestures and pidgin English.

The owner examined our drawings, looked back at us, and still smiling spoke two words in almost accent-free English: *Driver's license?*

Instantly, my heart sank to my stomach, where it began making loud rumbling noises. Another part of our plan had gone wrong. The man knew exactly how illegal our request was.

I was ready to run when the Chinese gentleman's smile widened imperceptibly. No problem, he told us. Both Elizabeth and I sighed audibly with relief. Blubbering with gratitude I asked him whether he could possibly make three of the driver's licenses.

The owner's smile was suddenly gone. Pursing his lips he spat out the word, *Impossible!* Despair flowed through me again. But before I could lower my request to one or two false driver's licenses, the Chinese proprietor smiled again: *Minimum order one hundred, ready tomorrow. Twenty-four-hour service*, he added with pride.

The next day, Liz and I picked up four boxes with twenty-five crisp Canadian driver's licenses each. Over the following weeks, we also acquired one hundred blank Certificates of Citizenship, an ID-card that Canadians must produce during any contact with their government's agencies. For this document, we used Elizabeth's original as a sample and obtained nearly perfect forgeries. We had the front of the card produced at one shop, the back of the card at another, and the corresponding rubber stamps at a third.

Yet another store manufactured Canadian Embassy rubber stamps and forged, blank certified copies of Canadian passports. Here again, we used Liz's real passport as a sample for nearly perfect forgeries.

To complete these false IDs, Elizabeth and I had three sets of passport photographs taken, one set for each of the three kinds of documents. If someone inspected our identification papers carefully, he could see that our hairstyles and the photo backdrops differed on all three documents, just as they would if they were genuine. Details like these were critical if our forgeries were to pass as real.

Liz and I now only had to attach the photographs to the blank forms, type in false names and facts, certify the documents with our rubber stamps, and laminate the IDs in clear, hard plastic. Each false identity would thus be supported by three matching documents: a driver's license, a certificate of citizenship, and an embassy-certified copy of a passport. And since we had one hundred copies of each of the forged, blank IDs, Elizabeth and I could invent fifty fictitious aliases each. Best of all: the forgeries together cost us only $50.

Our money was beginning to run low, so Liz and I had to make definite plans for producing some income soon. We decided to attempt the con man's old standby, a traveler's check fraud. After Elizabeth bought several hundred dollars worth of American Express traveler's checks in Bangkok, we took a bus north to Chiang Mai, Thailand's second largest city.

Heroin is the only reason Chiang Mai exists. Northern Thailand is peopled by poor, ethnically separate Hmong tribes who lack advantages such as the large ruby mines of the country's east, the golden tourist beaches of the south, or the highly developed culture of classic Siam in Thailand's geographic center. After Mao Zedong's victory in China's Communist revolution of 1949, some of the beaten Nationalist soldiers of Jiang Jieshi (Chiang Kai-Shek) also settled in these northern Thai regions. The Chinese ex-soldiers subsisted on robbery until the CIA made them equal partners in the heroin trade, to finance America's undeclared war in Laos. Since then, the former Nationalist warlords have linked up with the Triads in Hong Kong, and Chiang Mai has become the capital of the Golden Triangle. By the 1980s, it had skyscrapers, superb French restaurants, and one of the largest DEA outposts in the world.

But Liz and I were not interested in heroin as we walked past the water buffalo and the stretched Mercedes, the orange-robed Buddhist monks and the desperate-eyed European heroin tourists. We were here to cash traveler's checks at small local banks, which, we hoped, would take a long time to process the paperwork.

Before returning to Bangkok we attended the Loi Krathong celebrations, one of the few genuine tourist attractions of Chiang Mai. Colorful processions noisily wound their way down the main streets to the canals, where ornamental rafts and tiny paper boats with candles were sent drifting into the darkness. A pickpocket reached for my wallet in the crush of the crowd, but he failed to get the money we had conned from the banks that day.

As soon as Elizabeth and I returned to Bangkok, we told the stern young woman at the local American Express office that thieves had stolen our checks during our trip to Chiang Mai. It was a common enough story. We immediately received new traveler's checks, thus doubling our assets.

That day and the next we cashed our refund checks and discovered to our consternation that the Thai bank clerks frequently wanted to photocopy Liz's passport. Our sob story about pickpockets in Chiang Mai might have been common, but so apparently was traveler's check fraud.

My research on banking and related subjects had not given me warning of such extraordinary precautions, and Elizabeth and I soon lost our nerve. We decided that this fraud would only be a test. Penitently, we returned to the American Express office with the excuse that we had now found the original checks that we had thought stolen.

It was clear that Liz and I had no future in Thailand. We had to return to a country where we could speak the language, where we could eat the food without getting diarrhea, and where the bank clerks were less suspicious of *farangs*. Since my father's VISA card had meanwhile been blocked, we would have to find a cheap method of travel, which, additionally, should include some false trails for the American detectives whom we believed to be pursuing us. So Elizabeth and I began making plans for our second great escape.

First we converted $900, nearly all our remaining cash, into American Express traveler's checks bought in my name. Then we purchased bus tickets for the thousand-mile trip from Bangkok through Malaysia to Singapore. Flights from Singapore were inexplicably cheap, and we hoped no pursuer would suspect us of leaving Thailand by this circuitous route. We packed our bags, made a final trip to the *"Praekanesang"* to check for mail, and on the evening of December 26, 1985, climbed aboard the bus south.

The journey did not begin auspiciously. On the outskirts of Bangkok, the bus suddenly pulled over to the side of the road and two policemen entered. The first barked a few orders to the driver, while the second walked slowly down the central aisle of the bus with a video camera to film all the passengers. Gripped by paranoia, Liz and I slid lower into our seats. I began coughing into my hand, and she bent down to tie a shoelace—anything to avoid having our faces recorded.

Once the officers left, we leaned across the aisle to ask a fat Australian backpacker why the Thai police should want to video all passengers of a tourist bus. We held our breath, expecting the worst.

But the cops were not conducting a nationwide search for a couple of young murder suspects from Virginia. Videotaping the passengers on buses headed south was a completely routine procedure, the Aussie told us. With the help of the tape, the police would be able to identify the charred bodies in the wreckage after the Communist guerrillas had blown up the bus.

What?

Had we not heard that the entire Thai panhandle to the south was infested with Thai and Malaysian Communist insurgents, some commanded by Japanese soldiers who had refused to surrender after World War II? Had we not heard about the tourist buses they blew up after robbing the passengers? Why did we think there was a police car in front of the bus and another behind, accompanying us on the hundreds of miles down the panhandle to the Malaysian border?

The Aussie grinned engagingly, and Elizabeth and I peered outside. The jungle seemed awfully dark and awfully close.

I spent a sleepless night on the bus, but not because of the guerrillas. The enormous long-distance Volvo bus had air conditioning, TV, a toilet, and very comfortable seats. But Thais are small of stature and thus install the rows of bus seats closer to one another than even an average-sized *farang* like me could bear. It felt wonderful to stretch my legs the next morning in Hat Yai, the last major Thai town before the Malaysian border.

Initially, Liz and I were surprised that Hat Yai should be so large. There was neither heroin nor ruby mining nor sex tourism for Europeans down here, so how did the locals finance the shiny modern hotels among the bamboo huts? We eventually figured it out. Malaysia is an Islamic country, so the Malays had to cross the border to the open-minded Thai Buddhists when they needed to indulge themselves with alcohol or prostitutes.

It took Elizabeth and me nearly an entire day to sort out our connecting tickets to Singapore. Finally, late in the afternoon of December 28, we were rolling south again on a Malaysian bus, which had air conditioning and TV but no bathroom. Every couple of hours the driver stopped at the Malaysian equivalent of a U.S. Interstate Howard Johnson's. Here fez-wearing Malays assaulted us with small wooden spears of mysterious meat, which they had charcoaled over an open roadside fire for the travelers. For once, Liz and I declined to try the local cuisine.

Most of Malaysia passed in the night, and we awoke the next morning at the border checkpoint to Singapore. Formerly a British colony and then briefly part of Malaysia, the tiny ethnically Chinese island-city of Singapore had been ruled by Lee Kuan Yew during the three decades since independence. Lee's friends called him autocratic, and his enemies all languished in his prisons. But no one could deny that Lee had brought his citizens economic success rivaling that of Japan.

Apart from money, Lee's other overwhelming obsession was the absolute cleanliness of his little realm. The street vendors, omnipresent in any other Southeast Asian city, had been banished to special indoor malls here. Spitting on the sidewalk was punishable by large fines, and bubble gum was illegal because of its messiness. Until recently, male tourists with shoulder-length hair even had to have it cut short at the border checkpoints before being allowed to enter the country.

Unfortunately, Elizabeth and I checked into the only Singaporean hotel that had escaped Mr. Lee's hygiene police. A few weeks later in England we discovered that, for a second time, we had caught the crabs from unwashed hotel bedsheets. But we were too tired to inspect our accommodations after two sleepless nights on buses.

On the morning of Monday, December 30, 1985, Liz and I set out to investigate Singapore. Our attention was focused on the many large international banks, where I cashed the $900 of American Express traveler's checks, purchased in Bangkok. Next, we went to the local Aeroflot Soviet Airlines office. Aeroflot was the cheapest airline on the planet, and flying with the Communists seemed perfect for throwing capitalist American investigators off our tracks. However, the two tickets to Zürich still took most of the $900.

That same evening we climbed aboard an Ilyushin 62 and flew west to Moscow via Bombay.

8

Kiting Checks in London

"Not even decent sex."

January 1986–April 1986

W HEN ELIZABETH AND I arrived in Moscow on the morning of December 31, 1985, we were informed that we would have to spend one night at the so-called Transit Hotel at Shermetyevo 2 Airport. The Aeroflot agent in Singapore had assured us that a layover would not be necessary, but delays and inconveniences seemed to be a natural part of the Soviet system.

Naturally, Liz and I would not be allowed to take our suitcases to the hotel. Naturally, we would wait patiently for hours with our beautiful Intourist guide until a bus became available to take us through the yard-deep snow.

Naturally, the nice young soldiers at every hotel exit could not allow us to be so foolish as to go for a walk.

Naturally, there was no plug for the bathtub. The battle against capitalist-imperialist aggressors inevitably led to such shortfalls in the production of consumer goods, and the homeless people in Western countries had neither bathtub plugs nor bathtubs.

Naturally, we would have to report our movements to the concierge guarding each hotel floor. Naturally, we would have to accept a couple of Pakistanis on camp beds in our room. The battle against capitalist-imperialist. . . . Oh, if we were on our honeymoon, then the Pakistanis would be put elsewhere. Russians understood love.

Naturally, we would eat only when we were summoned to the hotel's dining room, and naturally, we would eat what was put on the table.

Naturally, there was no coffee in the tiny hotel bar to keep us awake until midnight and the New Year.

Naturally, pink champagne from Soviet Georgia cost a bundle of hard currency deutsche marks.

But, naturally, there was plenty of vodka.

Elizabeth and I landed in Zürich on January 1, 1986, and as always we covered our tracks by moving on to another country immediately. But when we counted our remaining money the next morning in Stuttgart, we found that the trip from Bangkok had left us nearly broke. Our only assets were Liz's jewelry and the refund stubs from the American Express traveler's checks I had bought in Thailand and cashed in Singapore. There was no choice: we would have to risk the fraud.

The American Express office was located across from the train station in one of the many beautiful and incredibly expensive shopping arcades. I had passed through Stuttgart years earlier with my family on the way to pick up our Mercedes from the gigantic factory nearby. Back then the region's great wealth had impressed me as a manifestation of the new, successful, peaceful West Germany that had risen from the ashes of World War II. But now the sparkling sidewalks, the glittering stores, and the fur coats on the passers-by seemed almost threatening. If we failed to con American Express, Elizabeth and I would not be able to feed ourselves.

Work or welfare were unobtainable for us. In Germany, as in all European countries, everyone had to register his or her address and carry a government ID card in order to get a state pension or a job. But any contact with government agencies would have meant instant discovery and arrest for us. So we had to get those $900 in fraudulent traveler's check refunds.

Liz and I entered the American Express office on the morning of Thursday, January 2. Nervously, we explained to the lady at the service counter that my checks had been stolen in Thailand or Singapore.

As I filled out the refund form, the American Express agent picked up a telephone and dialed a number. In a loud voice she began asking questions about a certain Herr Scheering who had tried to defraud American Express with a story about stolen checks in Taiwan.

My hands began to sweat, but I pretended not to notice what the agent was saying. I listened carefully while I continued to write down details on the refund form. Yes, she kept saying "Scheering" not "Soering," and "Taiwan" not "Thailand." And she kept repeating herself, and her voice was unnecessarily loud.

Was she perhaps testing me? If I were innocent I would not be concerned about some Herr Scheering in Taiwan, but if I were a fraudster I might be panicked into running out of the office. That kind of scheme seemed too byzantine even for American Express. So perhaps she was on to us, or the New Year's holiday had not provided enough of a delay in data processing, or she already knew that we had cashed the allegedly stolen checks in Singapore.

However, Elizabeth and I needed this money desperately. So I controlled my fear and handed the completed refund form to the agent behind the counter. During our test run in Thailand we had been given new checks at this point in the process, but now I was told to return later that afternoon. My panic and dread intensified; this definitely smelled like a setup. The police would surely be waiting for us if I returned for the refund.

And the police were indeed waiting later that afternoon. Liz and I saw the green-and-white police car parked directly in front of the American Express office as soon as we turned the street corner.

Immediately, we circled the block and approached the office from the other side.

But the police car was still there, though twenty minutes had passed in the meantime. They had to be waiting for us! Elizabeth and I went into a bar and had a couple of beers while we thought things over.

Twenty minutes later the police car was still parked in front of the American Express office. But there seemed to be no one near, and the office would be closing soon. There was no choice. As casually as possible we sauntered down the opposite side of the street to reconnoiter. And then I saw it: a small sign next to the police car that read OFFICIAL POLICE CAR PARKING SPACE.

Laughing at myself and elated with relief, I ran across the street and into the office. Five minutes later, I was back outside with $900 worth of brand new refund traveler's checks. I hugged Liz, but she seemed stiff with shock. As soon as I had entered the office, she told me, the police had left. Seconds later, a police van had pulled into the parking space, and ten policemen in riot gear had stormed out of the vehicle and into the building directly adjoining the American Express office. Elizabeth had to assume that the raid was connected with us.

I took one look at the police van now in the parking space and decided to take no chances. We ran to the nearest streetcar stop and jumped aboard a trolley that was just leaving. At the next station we changed trains again, and only then did we begin to feel safe. Eventually, we found our way back to our bed-and-breakfast and had a decent meal nearby. We were not going to starve.

The next day we took a train south to Freiburg in the Black Forest, where Liz and I laid low over an extended holiday weekend. For the first time since our return from Thailand, we felt we could enjoy ourselves just a little. There was snow here, not the infernal heat of Christmas in Bangkok, the food did not scorch our tongues to numbness, and the people around us spoke a language which I shared fully and Elizabeth at least partially.

But $900 was only $900. We would have to leave Germany again, since our next frauds were designed specifically for English banks. So on Wednesday, January 8, Liz and I took a train north to the Belgian port of Oostende and from there a ferry to Dover.

My first impression of England was one of shabbiness. From the ship's railing, the White Cliffs looked gray, the ferry terminal and the train station were old and drafty, and the trains themselves looked like New York subway cars without the graffiti of the period but with extra layers of unspecifiable grime. Nothing I saw of England in the following months dispelled this impression of general shabbiness, yet the English people I met bore their lot with a wonderful mix of stoicism and humor.

Elizabeth and I took the train from Dover north in the direction of London and disembarked along the way in the small town of Canterbury. This region of southeast England had been spared the economic devastation inflicted upon the rest of the country. So of course greedy property developers had built particularly hideous shopping complexes almost in the shadow of Canterbury Cathedral, headquarters of the Anglican Church. But there was still a certain charm to the narrow streets and the old, whitewashed houses in the center of town.

On the outskirts lay the University of Kent, a large, modern college that was the reason for Liz's and my journey here. Once we had settled into a small bed-and-breakfast, we went to the nearest branch of Lloyds Bank to open a joint savings account and a joint checking account. We told the bank clerk that we were Timothy and Julia Holte, a couple of Canadian exchange students who had just arrived for the spring semester. Since we were from Canada, we could provide no English bank references. But we both had driver's licenses, certificates of citizenship, certified copies of passports, and several hundred English pounds to deposit, so the bank clerk trusted the charming young couple from Canada.

In fact, he did not even telephone the university to check

whether Tim and Julia were enrolled there. Our original plan had called for a specifically prepared set of Canadian documents using names we would have chosen from the university registrar's list of enrolled students, in order to provide at least that much as a reference. But Canterbury's shopping malls had no laminating machines to seal our forged papers, so Elizabeth and I were forced to use a set of identities that we had already prepared in Thailand: the Holtes.

Unfortunately, our initial deposit in our accounts was not large enough to persuade the bank clerk to immediately grant us the check-guarantee cards that we needed for the fraud. But if we operated our accounts responsibly for four to six weeks, the clerk assured us, then there should be no problem in issuing us the cards at that time.

Four to six weeks of waiting, four to six weeks of keeping a respectable balance in our accounts—it seemed impossible. The money we had left was nowhere near enough for four to six weeks of hotel room rates and restaurant meals. Living on the run was incredibly expensive, at least in Europe. To cut costs, Liz and I decided to leave the bed-and-breakfast and rent a room in the home of a Canterbury social worker. The house, located in a large residential project, was modern but sparsely furnished; it was obvious that the family needed the small additional income from letting a room to a couple of college students.

During the days, Tim and Julia had to go to classes, of course. So Elizabeth and I spent much time sitting in the warm local public library or wandering around town in the cold, damp snow. There was no money for entertainment in our budget now. We even economized on food by eating only the cheapest-possible canned foods at home in the evening.

Apart from letting us use their kitchen, our landlords were also kind enough to allow us to watch the TV in the children's playroom at night. This gave Liz and me a welcome respite from the stress of having to call each other Tim and Julia in the family's presence. Not once could we slip up. Even in bed we moaned our aliases at one another in case one of the children was eavesdropping on our lovemaking.

To raise additional cash, Elizabeth and I took the train to London, where we sold an expensive guitar and camera that I had bought in November in Salzburg for just such emergencies. Liz even sold her jewelry, some in Canterbury and some in Brighton. But her mother's watch, which she had stolen from Loose Chippings just before the murders, fetched a much lower price than expected because it was not a genuine Omega.

After three weeks in Canterbury, it was clear that Elizabeth and I would not be able to stretch our money for four to six weeks merely by cutting costs and selling jewelry. In desperation we converted almost all our remaining funds, £350, into American Express traveler's checks bought in the name of Melissa A. Taylor, another one of our previously prepared false identities.

On January 29 we took the ferry from Dover to Calais, and then the train to Brussels. Since our forged papers consisted only of a certified copy of a Canadian passport instead of a full passport, the Belgian American Express agent gave us our refund only with the greatest reluctance. Later in the day we also discovered that most banks were unwilling to cash Melissa Taylor's refund traveler's checks without a full passport. But eventually we managed to convert all the checks to cash at a slightly dubious bureau de change.

Using our well-established methodology of frequent changes of country to cover our tracks, Liz and I spent a weekend in Luxembourg-City. Both of us felt very low. Elizabeth had a severe cold, and I feared that we would never make enough money from American Express frauds to satisfy the Lloyds Bank clerk and obtain those check-guarantee cards. The entry in our travel diary for this weekend read, "Not even decent sex."

At four o'clock on Monday morning we left our Luxembourgeois hotel without paying. Liz headed for Paris, while I took a train to Amsterdam. Since we had such difficulties in Belgium cashing traveler's checks with our fake Canadian identity papers, we decided to use our real names in separate attempts.

We both failed. In Paris, Elizabeth was questioned by American Express agents about her transaction in Thailand, but since that test run had been aborted she was let go. I ran into more serious trouble in Amsterdam. The agent took my passport, typed my name into his computer, walked into a back room, and reappeared ten minutes later behind me in the waiting room. Sweating profusely, he told me to return in two hours to receive my passport and my refund checks.

Of course, it was a trap. I sprinted past the canals and the famous Amsterdam sex museum to the train station and was out of the country before the two hours were up. Though I had to leave behind my German diplomatic passport, I still had my regular travel passport.

When Liz and I counted our money in Canterbury, we discovered that we had made nearly no net profit from this excursion to the continent. In the following days, we tried to find semi-legitimate jobs that, we hoped, would not require us to register with the relevant governmental agencies. Elizabeth answered an ad for a housekeeper, and I called a pub looking for an assistant bartender. But every time we inquired, the positions had already been filled.

On February 13, Liz and I began preparations for a fraud that she had seen years earlier on an English TV show. We went to the local Canterbury offices of the Red Cross and the Royal Society for the Prevention of Cruelty to Animals and somehow managed to persuade them to give us coin-collection boxes with their charities' logos. Then we spent a whole day printing up one thousand raffle tickets with a small hand-printing kit we had purchased. Elizabeth and I even made Red Cross and RSPCA ID-badges for ourselves.

But when we made our rounds at the local housing project on February 17, I was soon stopped and questioned by a couple of Canterbury policemen. Clearly, one of my donors had seen the same TV program that had given Liz the idea for the fraud. With some fast talking, I was able to calm the officers' suspicions, but later that evening Elizabeth and I decided to give up this risky method of raising funds. The fraud was not very profitable anyway: Liz collected £35 and I only £5. And exploiting a donor's generosity was so despicable that I was glad to stop. This was, however, the last time my conscience stirred in revolt, at least until we were arrested.

Of all the crimes I committed, this is the one of which I am most ashamed. I can make up some sort of lame excuse or mitigation for just about everything else—but stealing from the Red Cross? That is beneath all contempt. Ten years later, in 1996, it was the memory of this crime in particular that prompted me to start tithing my prison paycheck to a charity called Feed the Children. I did that for more than seven years without missing even one monthly donation—several hundred dollars, all told. But that cannot make up for the £5 I stole in 1986.

By the second half of February 1986, the four-to-six-week wait for the Lloyds Bank check-guarantee cards was nearly up, but Elizabeth and I were also nearly out of money. Somehow, we had to come up with a major infusion of funds for our bank accounts. On February 19, we took out our old checkbooks from U.Va. and wrote two checks for five hundred dollars each from Elizabeth Haysom to Julia Holte. The Lloyds Bank clerk had told us earlier that it usually took three weeks to clear a check from a small American bank. With those two checks from Elizabeth Haysom, Tim and Julia's Canterbury account would appear to have a much higher balance for twenty-one days before Liz's check was returned from the U.S. for lack of funds.

When Elizabeth brought her two checks to the Holtes' bank branch, our clerk was very pleased. We had run our accounts responsibly during the entire four-to-six-week trial period, and now we were bringing him a couple of nice, fat checks from America. Of course, we could have our check-guarantee cards.

As she was leaving the bank, Liz asked the clerk offhandedly whether we could withdraw some of the money from the American checks before they had cleared. She expected to be told no, but the bank clerk gave her a major surprise: Lloyds would credit the Holtes' account with the full cash amount as soon as the checks were deposited, without waiting for clearance. I could hardly believe my ears when Elizabeth told me this. Though we were tempted, we decided not to push our luck with more checks from Liz to Julia.

The next day, the mailman brought us two check-guarantee cards and the additional two checkbooks we had ordered. Finally, after six weeks of waiting and economizing, Elizabeth and I were ready to proceed with the fraud.

English check-guarantee cards resembled American credit cards in size and shape. However, their sole function was to guarantee the check's recipient that the bank would honor the check, whether or not the account holder had the funds to cover it. When a customer made a purchase in a store, the cashier simply wrote down on the back of the check the code number on the card and compared the customer's signature on the card with the signature on the check. The check was now as good as cash up to a limit of £50 (about $75 then) per check.

Since Liz and I had a total of four checkbooks with thirty checks each, we could now spend £6,000 (about $9,000) in stores across Britain. After months of near-penury on the run, that sum seemed enormous to us.

Naturally, Elizabeth and I withdrew all but about £60 from the Holte accounts before spending our £6,000 of guaranteed checks. The remaining £60 ensured that at least one £50-limit check would be fully covered, in case a suspicious store cashier decided to double-check by phoning our bank. But no cashier ever bothered to double-check, since the cards guaranteed that our checks would be covered by the bank.

There was practically no way for us to be caught. Because we had opened the accounts ourselves using forged Canadian documents, Tim and Julia Holte did not report their checkbooks lost or stolen. We also did not have to forge Tim and Julia's signature, as in a common stolen-checkbook fraud, since Liz and I were the Holtes. Best of all, the financial damage would be done before the bank even realized that it had been defrauded: in 1986 a check spent in a London store on a Monday took until that Friday to reach the issuing bank branch. But Elizabeth and I could easily spend all 120 checks before Monday's first check bounced on Friday. Even if Lloyds could somehow alert every store in the country immediately, it would still be too late to catch Tim and Julia.

The stores did not suffer, because they were protected by the check-guarantee cards. Only the banks sustained a loss. But if each individual account were defrauded of less than £10,000 (about $15,000), then the bank would not report the fraud to the police. The banks knew that the police did not have sufficient manpower to pursue small-time con men, even if the banks were to bother with reporting frauds under five figures. So the banks simply absorbed the losses from small frauds. As long as Liz and I kept below the limit of £10,000 for each false identity and each bogus account, we were safe.

If someone suddenly decided to pursue the case of Tim and Julia Holte, the investigation would soon reach a dead end anyway. The bank did not photocopy our forged Canadian documents, so the police would have no pictures of us. Our names were fake, our Canadian addresses were nonexistent, and our English address was a bed-and-breakfast that we had left nearly two months earlier. The police had no place to start their search.

In fact, the only lead the police might have had for the Holte account was the pair of $500 checks from Elizabeth Haysom. But our ebbing funds had made this risk necessary. And even with the Haysom checks, the total loss from the Holte account would still be less than £10,000, so the bank should not report it to the police. Thus, no connection would be made between the Holtes and the murder investigation in Virginia.

As noted, the theft of £5 from the Red Cross is the crime of which I am most ashamed. I wish I could say I was equally ashamed of the check-fraud scheme, but that would be untrue. It goes without saying, I am ashamed of this crime, too, and I regret doing it: I exploited that bank clerk's trust dishonestly, with the specific intent to do something wrong (and illegal). Looking back, I am so angry with myself for sinking to such a low level. In addition to those emotions, however, some part of me is also a little proud.

My childhood had been as sheltered as one could possibly imagine; absolutely nothing had prepared me for having to survive on the streets, without any help at all. Yet survive I did. I landed on my feet, when most other diplomats' sons and private-school graduates would have tucked tail and run back to daddy. This little whiff of pride embarrasses me, but it exists.

Also, I am . . . if not proud, then at least relieved that the check fraud was completely nonviolent and that no individual suffered. These facts do not make this crime any less illegal, immoral, or stupid. But I have to live with an awful lot of guilt already, so I am thankful that the check frauds did not harm any person.

With the perspective of more than three decades, those months when I was on the lam with Elizabeth seem shockingly heedless. I'm not going to lie. Almost perpetual motion and necessary alertness to danger at every turn were like freebasing adrenaline. That said, if you, the reader, have just spent three chapters appalled at our apparent indifference to the murders and our revelry in defrauding others, then I entirely sympathize. I look back at myself and marvel how rapidly I descended into outright criminality, and how breaking the law became normal. It's hard for me to reconcile the image

I had of myself as a moral being, a hero, a real-life Sydney Carton, with the reality that I was a thief, a forger, and if not a murderer, then at least the protector of one.

Back in 1986, when my moral and ethical senses were as good as dead, Elizabeth and I left Canterbury as soon as we received our check-guarantee cards. On the weekend of February 22–23, we toured the sights of London: Tower Bridge, Parliament, Buckingham Palace, Hyde Park, Regent's Park Zoo, the West End, Leicester Square, Piccadilly Circus. There was none of the usual English shabbiness here; if only the rest of London and Britain could catch up.

Even a few steps beyond the West End, the squalor began again. Liz and I stayed at one of the many small bed-and-breakfasts near Paddington, one of London's enormous, grimy, Victorian train stations. The bright lights of Marble Arch at one end of Regent Street were almost within sight of our hotel. But in the ramshackle rooms around us, families on welfare argued all night, got drunk, and used drugs bought in the small park outside. We shuddered whenever we remembered how close we had come to being unable to afford even this much.

On Monday morning, Elizabeth and I began converting our checks to cash. Simply making cash withdrawals at other branches of Lloyds Bank was impossible, since every checkbook contained a small calendar that the bank teller stamped to let other tellers know that one check had already been cashed that day. So we had to go to Marks & Spencer, Britain's largest chain of clothing stores.

For ten hours each day, we took the underground from one Marks to the next. At each store we purchased a £49.95 leather jacket with a check and returned it at the next store for a cash refund. I saw little of London that week, except for the small areas around the catacomb-like underground stations and nearby Marks & Spencer stores.

It was in Knightsbridge, another small island of prosperity in London's sea of shabbiness, that I had my only moment of excitement in our check-fraud scheme. As always, I went to the refund counter and returned my bag of clothes from another Marks store for £49.95 in cash. Then I walked to the leather-coat rack and took my new purchase to the cashier. The sales girl had just begun comparing my signature on the check with my signature on the check-guarantee card when, suddenly, alarm bells started ringing everywhere in the store. Without saying a word, the cashier slammed down my check and card, stepped back and began striding quickly toward the exit.

I froze. Obviously this was it: time to raise my hands slowly and give myself up to the SWAT team hiding behind the brassiere department. Near me, young men in short-sleeved shirts and ties burst from unobtrusive service doors and joined the growing exodus of customers and staff. A siren wailed in the distance. My face felt hot, my hands were cold and sweaty.

I looked around. No one seemed to be interested in me! Since I had no idea what was going on, I simply picked up my checkbook and card, turned to go, and turned back to take the coat as well. Calmly, I walked to the exit and left the store among a group of stragglers.

A police cordon had been formed outside the doors, and a crowd of onlookers stared at the ambulances and patrol cars. Policemen rushed left and right with purposeful looks on their faces. It was only by chance that I heard one of them say something about an IRA bomb warning. Apparently, it was yet another hoax.

I could not help but smile to myself. Desperate criminals are supposed to feel particularly clever and superior in such situations, but what made me grin was the ironic parallel between myself and the policemen. All of us were caught in webs of our own misperceptions and misunderstandings. In the store, I had felt the overwhelming terror of the cornered animal, because of an alarm bell that had rung not for me but for a nonexistent bomb. Outside, the police were cursing their luck at having wasted their time on a false alert, while next to them stood one half of the most wanted couple in Virginia.

The greatest irony of that situation was completely beyond my apprehension, of course. Almost exactly a year before I had promised Liz to play the role of Macbeth, the criminal and murderer, to save her life; and now, only one year later, I had become that role, if not a murderer then at least a criminal with dozens of fake passports and a wad of stolen money in my pocket. During the funerals in Lynchburg I had nearly killed myself out of guilt and terror, but all I felt that day in Knightsbridge was relief at not being arrested, and satisfaction at having gotten a £50 coat without even having to pass a bogus check. My conscience, which had been the original motivator in my decision to save Elizabeth from the electric chair, had virtually died in the last twelve months of ever-growing deceit and desperation that had grown from that decision to help. Later, much later, I would understand that immoral acts, even if committed for the best moral reasons, change the character of the actor.

Standing in front of Marks & Spencer in 1986, however, I could not have cared less about what I had become, morally or in any other way. Liz was all that mattered, and her survival justified any action, including the criminal variety. My own existence only had meaning insofar as it sustained hers. That was the nature of the folie à deux in its final stages in London.

As soon as Elizabeth and I had spent our last check from the Holte account, we took a bus west to Bath, a small tourist town famous for its beautifully preserved Georgian architecture. We fled our first bed-and-breakfast when we discovered that the hotel owner's husband was an inspector on the police force of the nearby city of Bristol. Since we had plenty of cash, Liz and I decided to rent a small holiday apartment in the center of town.

During the second week of March, we opened accounts at a Midland Bank branch. This time we were Christopher Platt Noe and Tara Lucy Noe, Canadian exchange students at the University of Bath. Because we were able to deposit several thousand pounds immediately, the bank clerk arranged for us to receive check-guarantee cards within days. The cards soon arrived, but Elizabeth and I then had to wait a couple of weeks for Christopher and Lucy's special high-interest checking account checkbooks.

We did not mind waiting. Liz and I had plenty of money, spring was on its way, and the rolling green hills around Bath afforded us many wonderful hikes. For the first time since we had fled the U.S., we began to feel that we might survive over the long term. Our fraud scheme was working out so well that we did not have to fear starvation, and further research at the local library revealed that we could in fact become very wealthy while on the run.

During our travels around London, Elizabeth and I had seen scores of small jewelry stores, often several in each shopping district. These shops were in fierce competition with one another and offered huge discounts as well as "instant credit of £500 if you have a check-guarantee card." For a £50-check down payment we could thus buy £500 worth of gold coins, which were untraceable and easily converted to cash anywhere in the world. After only one week of shopping for coins, our 120 checks would be worth not £6,000 but £60,000 (about $90,000 then) in gold. Of course, the bank would report a fraud of that size to the police, but Liz and I would still be protected by our forged Canadian identities. We dreamed of making enough money to afford full plastic surgery and genuine passports from some South American country, so we could live legitimately again.

But before we expanded our fraud to gold coins, we had to acquire more working capital. That meant only one thing: Christopher P. and T. Lucy Noe would have to do some serious shopping at Marks & Spencer. To be on the safe side, Elizabeth and I decided to disguise ourselves, lest some cashier recognized Chris and Lucy as Tim and Julia. After an unsuccessful trip to Bristol, we finally found a London store that sold professional makeup supplies to film studios. I bought a terribly expensive reddish-blond mustache to match my newly dyed hair, while Liz's hair turned black and once was even hidden beneath a long wig.

During our second stay in London in the last week of April, we lived in a holiday apartment just off Baker Street, the home of Sherlock Holmes. Once again we spent our days taking the Underground between Marks & Spencer stores. At night, we indulged ourselves at rather expensive Cypriot, Swiss, and Chinese restaurants in the West End. Life was beautiful, and our future as successful international con artists seemed bright.

Then one day Elizabeth had a clever idea. Until now, she had only entered each Marks & Spencer store after she saw me leave upon completion of my refund-and-purchase operation. I had decided that this precaution was necessary because the alternatives either halved our profits or risked our detection. If we entered a store at the same time we would logically have to shop together as husband and wife, which meant the two of us could pass only one check at each visit to a store instead of one each. But if we entered a store at the same time and shopped separately we risked some bright cashier noticing by our matching checkbooks that Christopher Platt Noe and Tara Lucy Noe were not shopping together as they should be. So I thought it best only to enter each store one after the other.

Unfortunately, my cautious approach meant that one of us always had to stand on the street waiting for the other. Liz felt this was a waste of time. If we went into the stores at the same time and took care not to go to the same cashier, then we would finish our daily quota of checks much earlier in the day.

I hesitated, but Elizabeth quickly explained her idea of a system to avoid our going to the same cashier in the stores we visited. I would always go to the taller, lighter-haired, or male cashiers, while she would join the lines for the shorter, darker-haired, female cashiers. To me this system seemed prone to confusion and mistakes. But I told myself that I only resisted Liz's suggestion out of injured pride, because she was now making an improvement on my fraud scheme. Going home early to our apartment sounded good, too.

Somehow our arrest on April 30, 1986, was almost anticlimactic. We had just finished a long day's check-writing at our last Marks & Spencer in the wealthy London suburb of Richmond. At Kew Gardens Underground station the subway car's doors failed to close. Suddenly, a plainclothes policeman stood in front of us, waving his badge, asking us to accompany him.

Later, we learned that Elizabeth's system had indeed failed: we had entered the same cashier's line. Of course, the cashier had noticed immediately that Christopher P. Noe should have been shopping with his wife T. Lucy Noe, who had paid only a minute ago with the same kind of joint account checkbook. The cashier had informed the store detective. And of course the store detective had coincidentally run into an off-duty policeman on the street, who then made the arrest at Kew.

On the platform at Kew Gardens there was a moment when the off-duty policeman was in an office, and only the diminutive female store detective in her high heels stood between us and freedom. If only we had bolted! But somehow I could not bring myself to punch her. It would have been so . . . rude.

So we stayed. Our run was over.

9

Arrest and Interrogation

"Pleading guilty to something you didn't do"

April 1986–December 1986

THE AMERICAN PSYCHIATRIC Association's definition of folie à deux states that, "if the relationship with the [. . .] person who already has a disorder with persecutory delusions [. . .] is interrupted, the delusional beliefs will diminish or disappear" in the secondary partner. For me, the return to sanity began about two weeks after the police led Liz and me away to separate patrol cars after our arrest at Kew Gardens station. Like a heroin or cocaine addict in cold-turkey withdrawal, I was suddenly and permanently deprived of the only thing that made my life worthwhile or even possible: Elizabeth.

That shock was compounded by the trauma of being ingested by the criminal-justice machinery. Suddenly, I was no longer a person but a thing, a lump of meat thrown into the maws of the meat grinder called law enforcement. I was not Jens Soering, but a wrist handcuffed to another wrist. I was not the son of Klaus and Anne-Claire, but a finger, to be inked and rolled across a fingerprint card. I was not the lover of Liz, but a mouth, which was ordered to talk about the frauds by two interrogating police officers. I was not a highly intelligent and accomplished scholarship winner, but a stomach, into which the cell-block sergeant had to throw some cold food before the shift changed. The machine had consumed me and made me its own.

On May 2, 1986, two days after our arrest, I saw Elizabeth briefly at a court hearing where we were remanded into custody until our trial. We hardly had time to exchange a few words before being torn apart again. Because England's pretrial prisons, called remand centers, were grossly overcrowded at that time, I and many other unconvicted prisoners were housed in underground holding cells at various police stations across London. Two and sometimes three of us spent twenty-four hours a day in cells designed to keep one suspect safe for a few hours. Without TV or books or, for that matter, windows or toilets, we had nothing else to do but talk.

I learned a lot about stealing cars, dealing drugs, and breaking into houses during those days. When it was my turn to entertain my cellmates, I said nothing about the murders in Virginia, of course, but instead revealed to those youngsters the ineffable glory of loving and being loved by the most wonderful woman in the world. Never before had I told anyone so much about my feelings for Liz. During the previous year and a quarter, no opportunity for such self-revealing conversations had arisen because we had almost never been apart. And now, when I missed Elizabeth so much, talking about her was one way to relieve the yearning.

One of my cellmates listened more attentively and with more understanding than the others. As I recall, he did not express his opinions on my relationship with Liz but simply asked some pointed questions. If love was the attraction and bond between two people, did this not necessarily imply that there had to be two individuals, separate and more or less equal, in order for love to exist between them?

Yet did I myself not say that Elizabeth and I had merged our personalities into a common whole, because we wanted to be inseparable? Without our individuality, could we really call our feelings for each other *love*? What would be a better term for our relationship? Exactly why did I like disappearing as an individual by melding with Liz?

The more questions this cellmate asked, the longer I took to answer. His questions did not leave me when he was transferred a few days later for a court appearance. Without him to guide my examination of the relationship with Elizabeth, I fell back on the same tools I always used when I wanted to work on a problem: pen and paper. As a gesture of spiritual gratitude I even addressed my diary-letter to my cellmate, although I did not want him or anyone else to read it and had no way of sending it to him even if I did. *Obsessive* is how I described my bond with Liz; I had recognized that I needed to find some sense of a separate self again. But reestablishing my and Elizabeth's individuality was only a means to the same old end for me, since the whole crux of the letter was that I wanted our love to be even more glorious than it already was. Still, the insight that our relationship did not amount to perfection was revolutionary.

Before I could develop these thoughts much further, however, Liz and I were rearrested at an English magistrate's court hearing on June 5, 1986, for interrogation on the Virginian–homicide charges. Elizabeth and I had already believed ourselves safe from the Bedford County authorities since no one had questioned us about the murders during the month since our original arrests for the English frauds. Later, we learned that Sheriff Carl Wells and Commonwealth's Attorney James Updike had not issued international arrest warrants for us after our escape from the U.S. to Europe in October 1985. Thus, it took the police in London more than four weeks to trace Liz's and my movements back from England to Thailand to Yugoslavia and finally to Virginia. Had those English detectives not been alerted by the suspicious passages in our Christmas 1984 diary-letters, they would never have bothered to contact American law-enforcement authorities, and the Bedford County investigators would never have heard that Elizabeth and I were in custody overseas.

I have still not heard a convincing explanation for Sheriff Wells and Prosecutor Updike's failure to make any attempt to find us after our flight in the fall of 1985. In addition to the fingerprint and blood type and, possibly, footprint evidence against Liz, our sudden departure was itself an implicit admission of involvement in the killings of Derek and Nancy Haysom. The homicide investigation made no further progress during our seven months on the run, so the decision to send Commonwealth's Attorney James Updike and Bedford County Investigator Ricky Gardner to London at the beginning of June 1986 was based on the same evidence available in October 1985. Why then had the Virginia law enforcement authorities not contacted Interpol immediately after our escape from the U.S. to Europe? Perhaps Sheriff Wells and Prosecutor Updike's reverence for the Langhornes, Gibbes, Astors, Benedicts, and Haysoms was so great that they preferred leaving the crime unsolved to accusing the scion of those illustrious families of murdering her parents.

In any case, I had no intimation of trouble as I was brought to a magistrate's court on June 5, 1986, for a brief procedural appearance on the English fraud charges. Suddenly, the door burst open and my court-appointed lawyer entered. Without a word, he flung down on my bench a copy of London's seamiest tabloid, the *Sun*, with the banner VOODOO MURDERS: TWO HELD. Apparently, the journalists had combined the gruesome nature of the killings with the passage about "voodoo" in Elizabeth's Christmas 1984 diary-letter to arrive at that sales-boosting headline. Since Liz had not told me anything about voodoo when she described the crime scene to me fifteen months earlier, I did not even understand at first why my attorney had shown me the newspaper until I began to read the article.

No more than two hours later I found myself back in the holding cells beneath the same police station where Elizabeth and

I had been questioned about the frauds more than a month prior. This time, however, I knew that I had to face and fulfill the promise I had made to Liz in the Marriott on March 30, 1985: I would have to "confess" to her murders to save her life. How the feelings, the memories from that terrible night came flooding back! During the four days of interrogations, the investigators required me to think about the homicides, and during the long nights, I stared at the ceiling while I counted the blue tiles on the walls and remembered, remembered.

As Elizabeth had explained to me in the hotel fifteen months earlier, her parents deserved it, since they were child abusers. The drugs made her do it, so the murders were not really her fault. *And if I don't help Liz, she'll fry! If I don't help her, she'll fry! If I don't help Liz, she'll fry!*

Nothing had changed since the night of the killings. Either I could be the executioner's accomplice, by telling the police the truth and sending the woman I loved to the electric chair; or I could be the hero, by "confessing" to the homicides and spending a few years in a German youth prison under the partial immunity my father's diplomatic status would grant me. So it goes without saying that I played the role of Macbeth, the murderer. I kept my promise.

Even today, I am glad I did not become part of the judicial process that would have sent Elizabeth to her death. I still believe the lesson of the Nazi era with which all German children are inculcated: that the worst form of murder is the killing of a citizen by his own government. But my "confession" cannot be retrospectively redeemed by interpreting it as romantic idealism. Sydney Carton understood the consequences of his sacrifice when he took Charles Darnay's place on the guillotine, while I was just a mentally unbalanced and fatally misinformed nineteen-year-old.

"It is a far, far better thing that I do than I have ever done. . . . " So says Carton on the scaffold, and so I told myself as I prepared myself for my "confession." For three days, from June 5 to June 7, I told the detectives as little as possible; before I placed my head on that guillo-tine, I wanted to ask my lawyer whether I would in fact be protected by partial diplomatic immunity. But even on June 5, the first day of questioning, I tried to protect Liz from execution by insisting that she had been in Washington when the murders occurred.

On June 7, while I was still trying to persuade the policemen to allow me to see my attorney, I nearly panicked and told the truth. An English detective sergeant named Kenneth Beever asked me, "Would you consider, under those circumstances, taking into account your answer, pleading guilty to something you didn't do?"

"Would I consider doing that?"

"Yes."

"I can't say for sure right now, but I can see, I can see it happen-ing, yes. I think it is a possibility. I think it happens in real life."

"I disagree with you, but don't let's get into any legal argu-ments now. I'm sorry. I think you answered my question."

"I mean, you know. I couldn't answer that question right now. I certainly hope that, I hope very much that it's not going to come to something like that."

But it did come to something like that. I knew that the English magistrate had ordered the police to stop interrogating me about the homicides by midnight on June 8, 1986. If I were to keep my promise to save Elizabeth's life I could not wait forever for my lawyer, and the investigators never did allow me to speak to him. So on the evening of June 8, I decided to admit to Liz's crime without having checked my legal status with an attorney.

The interrogation was conducted by Bedford County Investigator Ricky Gardner, who dictated these notes onto a tape recorder as soon as the interview was completed:

> Told by Beever that Soering wanted to talk with me. Brought to detective's office at 4:45 P.M. Read Miranda warnings to Soering at that time. Said he

understood and signed form. Said he would make statement only to me. Said that he did not want me to tape record the statement. I agreed and asked Jens to tell me what really happened. He began to make his statement.

Elizabeth and Jens drove a rental car to Washington, D.C., on that Friday night. Discussed killing her parents. . . . They were opposed to her seeing Jens. Thought that she could do better. . . . Elizabeth and Jens did not want to kill them. . . . Subject of killing them came up. He decided to drive to Lynchburg and confront her parents. . . . Drove rental car there on Saturday night. . . . Had knife with him. . . . Had not decided to kill Haysoms, just wanted to talk to them and try to convince them to let Elizabeth continue to see him. Left Washington in afternoon. . . . Drove to Loose Chippings. Knocked on front door. Answered by Mr. Haysom. He invited Jens inside. . . . Elizabeth stayed in Washington to set alibi in case trouble happened.

Jens entered front door. Mr. Haysom served Jens one or two stiff drinks. . . . Mrs. Haysom came down from upstairs. . . . Argued with Mr. Haysom about her painting. . . . Both were drinking heavy. . . . My drink was gin and something. . . . Mrs. Haysom wearing jeans. . . . Big argument between Elizabeth's parents about painting. . . . They invited Jens to have something to eat. . . . Led to dining-room table. . . . Sat with back to window looking over the hill through back dining-room window. . . . Mr. Haysom was to Jens' left side. . . . Haysoms arguing very loud. . . . They started yelling and arguing with me about Elizabeth. . . . Said they could have me

kicked out of U.Va. . . . Said they did not want Elizabeth to see me any more. . . . Argument got more
violent. . . . Head was ringing. . . .

Tried to leave. . . . Got up from my chair and
tried to walk behind Mr. Haysom. . . . He pushed
me back and I was slammed against dining-room
wall. . . . Hit my head against the wall, . . . Do not
remember how many drinks I had before I tried to
leave. . . . I did not drink much. . . . Did not hold
my liquor well. . . . After hitting wall, I pulled out
my knife and cut Mr. Haysom across his throat. . . .
Across his jugular vein. . . . He grabbed his throat
and yelled, "God, you must be crazy, man!" Blood
rushed out of his throat. . . . I froze. . . .

Just wanted to get out of there. . . . Heard Mrs.
Haysom screaming. . . . She was coming at me with
a knife. . . . Waving it at me. . . . Got knife away from
her. . . . Grabbed her and held her as a shield. . . . Mr.
Haysom got up from his chair and came at me. . . .
Used Mrs. Haysom as a shield. . . . My glasses were
knocked off in this fight. . . . Slashed Mrs. Haysom
across throat. . . . She went towards kitchen. . . . Mr.
Haysom hit me in the head. . . . Don't remember
any more. . . .

Left house . . . took tableware and clothes to the
dumpster at the end of the street. . . . Threw pants,
jacket and sneakers into dumpster. . . . Hit small dog
on way to dumpster. . . . Drove speed limit all the
way back to Washington D.C. . . . Met Elizabeth at
the movie theater. . . . She was scared shitless. . . .
Told her what happened. . . . She said, "Oh my God!"

Jens threw two knives into dumpster. . . . Went
back to house to wipe up fingerprints and blood. . . .

Swirled footprints in blood on floor. . . . Threw away
glasses and silverware in dumpster. . . . Turned off
lights when he left house. . . . Drove all the way to
D.C. in rental car. . . . Wrapped sheet around him. . . .
Jens' hand was cut in fight. . . . Didn't notice cut until
he got to dumpster . . . washed hand and wrapped it
in a towel. . . . Met Elizabeth outside *Rocky Horror
Picture Show* . . . Theater in Georgetown near hotel.
. . . Movie ended around 2 A.M.

Derek Haysom was waving a spoon at Jens
during the fight. . . . Most blood was in the dining
room. . . . Mr. Haysom was standing like a bear and
waved arms after he was stabbed in the throat. . . .
Didn't see either victim fall and hit the ground. . . .
Last time he saw Mrs. Haysom, she was walking
towards the kitchen and was holding her throat.

The interrogation was interrupted at this point for a break,
which lasted from 6:45 to 7:19. When questioning resumed, the
English detectives Kenneth Beever and Terence Wright joined
Ricky Gardner, so I had to repeat my description of the murders.
Consistency and accuracy were crucial to making my "confession"
convincing, and I tried my best to repeat my story without changes.
Only two new details were added, which Detective Gardner noted
in his transcription of his tape-recorded notes:

Jens showed me scars on his fingers which he said
were from the fight with the Haysoms. [. . .] When
he returned to Loose Chippings the second time,
both Mr. and Mrs. Haysom were on the floor and
not moving. . . . Mr. Haysom was lying in the dining
room with his feet out of the living-room door,
facing the front of the house. . . .

During the last twenty minutes of the interrogation the policemen asked me a few questions about my motive. Here I tried particularly hard to keep my answers short and simple, since I believed this to be the most unconvincing aspect of my "confession." After all, Liz's mother and father lived in Lynchburg and thus could hardly prevent their daughter dating me while we both lived at U.Va. But in trying to explain the supposed cause of Elizabeth's and my purported hatred of her parents, I had to be careful not to say anything that might point too strongly in Liz's direction. Detective Gardner recorded in his notes:

> Elizabeth was raped in Switzerland when she was younger. . . . He did not think that Mrs. Haysom was a lesbian. . . . Elizabeth was neglected by her parents. . . . Mrs. Haysom had affairs and enjoyed creating havoc in public. . . . Mr. Haysom switched off to Mrs. Haysom and Elizabeth referred to him as cold. . . . Photos of Elizabeth in the nude were taken by her mother and shown to visitor. . . . Jens saw these pictures. . . . Elizabeth showed them to him. . . . Read excerpts of Jens' January, 1985, letters to Elizabeth. . . . Voodoo is possible if people believe in it. . . . Burglaries were a possible excuse for the murders. . . . Dinner scene a coincidence. . . . Jens concluded, "I fell in love with a girl. We talked about killing her parents. I didn't want to do it, but I drove to their house and killed them. I got caught." Interview ended at 9:42 P.M.

When my statement ended at 9:42, the three investigators' questions should then have begun in earnest. Detectives Gardner, Beever, and Wright were all familiar with the evidence found at Loose Chippings, so they knew that too many details of my story did not correspond to the crime scene. The location and type of murder weapon, the location of the bodies, the clothing of one of the victims, the logistics of the fight, the state of the crime scene, the forensic evidence, even the number of killers—none of these matched my "confession." Normal police procedure would have been to interrogate me further, since false confessions are common especially in high-publicity crimes, and I had already alluded to the "possibility [of] pleading guilty to something [I] didn't do." But, as in the spring of 1985 when police failed to confront Elizabeth with the fingerprint and blood-type evidence against her, Bedford County law enforcement officials decided to handle the Haysom murder investigation in their own unique, nonstandard manner.

Most police officers would have had doubts about a confession that did not match the type and location of the murder weapon as discovered at the scene of crime. In my statement I told police I "had [a] knife with [me]," which I "pulled out" to kill the Haysoms, and that I "threw two knives into [a] dumpster" near Loose Chippings afterward. Although Detective Gardner did not note this in the transcription of the interrogation, I also described the weapon to him as a butterfly knife with a two-edged blade, and Liz later provided the investigators with a sketch of the knife. On our return from Washington to Lynchburg on Sunday morning, March 31, 1985, we had stopped to look at a store window display of knives on Wisconsin Avenue, so that we could describe exactly the same weapon when the time came to lie to the police. Unfortunately, Elizabeth and I chose the wrong knife. The medical examiner who performed the autopsies on Derek and Nancy Haysom concluded that all wounds had been made with a single-edged blade. And it was a single-edged kitchen knife, which crime-scene specialists discovered in the drawer to the dining-room table at Loose Chippings. The knife was part of a set, but only this one had blood residue on its blade, as if the killer had cleaned it hastily and returned it to the drawer to hide it in plain sight.

Not only the type and location of the murder weapon but also the location and description of the victims' bodies in my "confession" failed to correspond to the scene of crime. Liz had told me in the Washington Marriott that her father's corpse was in the door from the dining room to the living room. So I told Detective Gardner that, "Mr. Haysom was lying in the dining room with his feet out of the living-room door, facing the front of the house." In fact, Derek Haysom lay entirely in the living room, stretched across the door to the dining room at a ninety-degree angle. According to my "confession," Nancy Haysom was "wearing jeans," when she had really worn a flowery robe.

From the evidence at the crime scene it was also clear that the fatal attack in the dining room could not have occurred as I claimed. I told Detective Gardner that I "sat with [my] back to [the] window looking over the hill through [the] back dining-room window [while] Mr. Haysom was to [my] left side" at the head of the table.

Fingerprint experts indeed confirmed that Derek Haysom had eaten his bowl of ice cream at the head of the table. But the only other place setting was to Mr. Haysom's left, facing the back dining-room window, and here the killer had removed the fork and glass from the setting to hide his or her fingerprints. From that side of the table it was unnecessary and indeed impossible for me to "walk behind Mr. Haysom" to try to leave the room, and he could not have "pushed me back and [. . .] slammed [me] against the dining-room wall." Even if I had sat on the other side of the table and Mr. Haysom had pushed me, there was no "dining-room wall" against which I could have "hit my head" but only the huge back window. My lengthy narration of how I had supposedly murdered Elizabeth's parents thus made no sense.

Other details of my description also did not match the crime scene. Investigators found clear evidence that the killer or killers had taken a shower in the master bathroom to wash off blood, but nowhere in my "confession" did I refer to showering. The lights on the outside of the house had been left turned on, though I told police that I "turned off [the] lights when [I] left [the] house." At my trial, Commonwealth's Attorney James Updike cited the blazing outside house lights as evidence of my guilt; the switch was inconveniently located in the master bedroom, where a non-family member like me was unlikely to find it. But I had visited Loose Chippings twice in the spring of 1985, so I was well aware of the electrical eccentricities of the house.

Finally, there was yet another contradiction between my "confession" and the scene of the crime: the fingerprint, blood type and, possibly, footprint evidence that placed Elizabeth in Loose Chippings at the time of the homicides. And only one or two hours after I finished my statement the three investigators received the strongest possible corroboration of the forensic evidence incriminating Liz. Detective Beever asked her, "You knew he was going to do it, didn't you? Did you?"

"I did it myself."

"Don't be silly."

"I got off on it."

"You did what? What does that mean?"

"I was being facetious."

"OK then. Now tell me the truth, please, without being facetious. You did hate your parents?"

"I did not hate my parents."

Elizabeth's claim that she did not hate her parents was no more true than her assertion that her admission to murder had been a facetious joke, but by then she was safe. The policemen had their confession, mine, and they wanted no further complications.

Why did Detectives Gardner, Beever, and Wright allow Liz to explain away her admission of guilt as a joke, even though her confession was corroborated by forensic evidence? Why did these same investigators accept my statement as true in spite of its obvious inaccuracies and the absence, at that time or later, of any fingerprint or blood evidence linking me to the crime scene? Perhaps because my claim of responsibility for the killings was so very convenient from Sheriff Wells and Prosecutor Updike's point of view. My "confession" reduced Elizabeth's role in the crime to that of an accomplice, so the venerable names of Virginia were saved from complete disgrace. Liz did not even believe that I would actually carry out the murders, according to Judge William Sweeney, a lifelong friend of Nancy Haysom's brother, Risque Benedict. The real culprit was that foreigner, that German: me.

Before I move on, I must mention one other important reason why my "confession" should be considered untrustworthy: I was never able to repeat the same story without changing various significant details, depending on what my audience at the time seemed to want to hear. Fifteen years after I "confessed" in that London police station, the study of the phenomenon of false confessions became a serious scientific and legal subdiscipline both in the U.S. and in Europe, and experts discovered that one of the hallmarks of a typical false confession is its constant mutability. On every retelling the story changes—and so it did with me.

Notice, for instance, that even on June 8, my "confession" changed. I actually "confessed" twice: once to Investigator Ricky Gardner alone and then to all three detectives together. On the second retelling of the story, I added the details about the supposed cuts on my fingers as well as the position of Derek Haysom's body. My aim in adding these details was to lend my "confession" the air of verisimilitude, but in fact I made two mistakes: DNA tests performed twenty-five years later showed that the blood at the crime scene did not match my DNA profile, and Mr. Haysom's body was actually found in the living room, not the dining room.

I "confessed" one more time, as I will explain below: this time, to a German prosecutor, as part of a legal ploy designed to gain my extradition to Germany. On this occasion, too, I told an entirely different story. Now I emphasized the role that alcohol had allegedly played in the commission of the crime. Why?

Because I had been advised that the influence of alcohol was considered a mitigating factor under German law. If German law had considered bubble gum to be a mitigating factor, I am sure I would have added that to my story, too.

As far as I was concerned, the whole story was a lie, since I had been in Washington when Elizabeth killed her parents. So what did it matter if I changed the lie around, adding and subtracting details as I went along? The really big lie was that I was the killer.

Today, I am naturally horrified by my moral idiocy at that time. Telling all those lies was an incredibly evil thing to do, because Derek and Nancy Haysom were dead—and they and their relatives deserved the truth to be known. Instead of honoring their memory and giving their family members and friends peace and closure, I told untruth after untruth after untruth, thereby forever tainting the victims' deaths and their loved ones' lives. Lies actually hurt people—and I, with my lies, am the one who caused that hurt, that harm.

Beyond that, the truth is a central value in and of itself. I learned this the very, very hard way, over the next thirty years, as I have tried to extricate myself from my lies. Regardless of who is hurt by the truth, the truth in and of itself matters. It is worth telling.

On one level, that is what all of my previous books and especially this one are about: recording the truth, even if no one believes it—just saying it, for itself.

As far as my various lies of 1986 are concerned, I can find some sort of limited excuse for myself for the first lie: I really *was* trying to protect Elizabeth from execution when I took the blame for her crime. But once one tells an enormous lie like that, one loses one's moral bearings completely, as one can see from my negative example. The first lie—that I was the killer—somehow made it acceptable to tell more lies. I despise who I was back then, in 1986.

As far as the alleged reliability of my "confession" of June 8, 1986, is concerned, I do believe that the continual mutations of my story are a significant factor to consider when determining the credibility of my statement to Investigator Gardner. If I had been telling the truth, why did my story keep changing?

When interrogations ended on Monday, June 9, I finally began to worry about the suffering I caused my family, and my greatest regret from that time until today is that I failed to think of them before I made my foolish decision to protect Elizabeth's life by taking the blame for the homicides she committed. After I was transferred from the police station to another cramped underground holding cell for unconvicted prisoners, I wrote my father and mother a letter in which I advised them to leave me alone and forget about me. Most parents would, I think, have done just that. Mine did not. As soon as they could, my father and mother flew to England to visit me in prison. I wish oh, how I wish! that I had shown them the same love and concern in 1985 and 1986.

One of my parents' first actions was to hire private lawyers for me, and they in turn asked two of the UK's senior forensic psychiatrists to examine both Liz and me as neutral, unbiased "friends of the court." Since the doctors reached the same medical conclusion, I will quote here only the December 15, 1986, report of Consultant Forensic Psychiatrist Henrietta Bullard, MB, BS, MRC PSYCH, DPM.

The introductory paragraph listed the material she had read in preparation for her examination of Elizabeth and me: the transcripts of all our police interrogations, as well as the "exhibits and affidavits relating to the United States Department of Justice's request for extradition." In the first formal section, Dr. Bullard reviewed my "Personal Background" and summarized the lies and fantasies Liz had told me, which I described in chapter 2 and subsequently. The report then continued with the "Examination of [my] Mental State":

During the first interview [conducted in July 1986], he was anxious and constantly expressed his concern for Miss Haysom. He felt she was the first person he had ever been able to relate to and that he could not exist without her. He believed that her parents would have been able to separate them and, above everything, he had wanted to protect and love her. During the second interview [conducted several weeks later], he spoke more about Miss Haysom and, while talking, it gradually dawned on him that he had been cheated and conned, and that her stories of gross neglect and physical and sexual abuse were unlikely to be true. He broke down into tears and began to describe their relationship and its unreal quality. I felt that, until this moment, he had no insight into how gullible and suggestible he had been. This emotional reaction was one of anger, bitterness and overwhelming sadness.

He gave a good account of his background, his family relationships and, in particular, his relationship with Miss Haysom. Miss Haysom was the first woman with whom he had had a close relationship and she flattered his vanity and boosted his self-esteem. At the time of their first meeting, he was only eighteen and both immature and inexperienced. There developed between them a symbiotic relationship in which he lost his personal identity and feeling of autonomy. His dependence on Miss Haysom and his need to be with her and share all his experiences strengthened. He described how he accepted her values and relied on her judgment. He was swept along by her enthusiasms and by the belief that he fulfilled her craving for excitement and sexual fulfillment.

During [additional interviews in] the last six months, he has gradually gained some insight into the shallowness of a relationship which was based on one partner's emotional hold over the other. He has recognized how, in order to sustain his beliefs in his own powers and attributes, he lost his critical faculties and subjugated himself to the will of another. There is no doubt that he was living in the fantasy world of Miss Haysom, and that his judgment was seriously at fault.

Opinion: Soering is a young man of just twenty who, at the time of the killings, was aged eighteen. He had the misfortune to meet a very powerful, persuasive and disturbed young woman whom he believed and trusted implicitly. He became tangled in her web of deceit and lies, and began to live with her a life of fantasy and unreality. He seemed devoid of judgment and was not only taken in by her fantastic stories but came to agree with her as to the ultimate solution. He was flattered by Miss Haysom's apparent emotional and sexual needs for him, and her suffering became his suffering. There existed between Miss Haysom and Soering a "folie à deux," in which the most disturbed partner was Miss Haysom. It is easy to see how an immature, sensitive and altruistic young man might become the prey of a woman such as Miss Haysom.

At the time of the offence, it is my opinion that Jens Soering was suffering from an abnormality of mind due to inherent causes as substantially impaired his mental responsibility for his acts.

Dr. Bullard's report concluded by explaining the legal significance of my "abnormality of mind" if the Haysom murder charges were tried in an English, as opposed to a Virginia, court. But as I struggled to free myself from the folie à deux during the summer and early autumn of 1986, my lawyers and psychiatrists' wrangling over my future was the least of my concerns. I remember spending one entire session with Dr. Bullard crying uncontrollably from the moment I walked into the examination room in the prison hospital to the moment I left to return to my cell. As the two doctors tore apart Elizabeth's lies, they ripped my universe and myself to shreds since I had ceased to exist other than as a subordinate part of the Liz-and-Jens union. By the time Dr. Bullard and her colleague were finished, I felt that I did not know Elizabeth Roxanne Haysom, and I believe I largely still do not.

For the rest of 1986 and much of 1987, however, I coped with the pain of the folie à deux's destruction by convincing myself that I pitied and even loved Liz, that I could perhaps even rescue her from her mental illness. Our fates were still joined, if only through the murderous horrors of our shared past. Life had meant us to be together.

But Elizabeth soon noticed the change in my attitude and, in one of the fits of paranoia to which her borderline personality disorder made her susceptible, she wrote me a bitter final letter in April 1987. Then she waived further appeals against her extradition, returned to Virginia, and made her bargain with Commonwealth's Attorney James Updike. Pleading guilty as an "accomplice before the fact," Liz was convicted on two counts of first-degree murder and sentenced to two consecutive terms of forty-five years imprisonment. She became eligible for parole in 1995.

It was the press reports of her sentencing hearing in October 1987 that finally killed my remaining illusions of love for her. Never had I lied about her, never had I tried to save myself by harming her. At that time, I had not even told anyone that she, not I, had killed her parents, though my motivation to be silent on this subject was not purely altruistic. As I sat on the prison recreation yard reading the newspaper clippings my parents had sent me, I was overwhelmed by the same emotions as during the psychiatrists' interviews more than a year earlier: I did not know this person called Elizabeth Roxanne Haysom. How could she tell such horrible lies about me, the man who had saved her life?

To answer that question and to explore all the other mysteries of our relationship, I wrote a document entitled "Legal Notes and Arguments" between 1987 and 1989. Over hundreds and hundreds of pages, I listed evidence and explanations and arguments in strict outline format, refining and rewriting countless times. It was a sad and futile undertaking, but it kept me sane: all those cold, hard facts left no room for feelings. As long as I kept writing, kept building and rebuilding that dike of scribbled paper, plugging holes in the seawall whenever they opened up, the dark oceans of pain could not flood into my cell and drown me. My pen kept me safe.

But I could not avoid my emotions altogether. What saved me from bitterness was, I think, the sad circumstance I discuss in chapter 3: I still cannot remember a happier time in my life than the months I spent with Liz, even though I now know all of it was false. Every prisoner needs the memory of joy to keep his soul alive, so I could not afford to deny the happiness, however twisted, that Elizabeth had brought me.

So she returned to my English prison cell almost daily as a ghost of the past, to bring me pleasure and pain in equal measure. I can still remember how, in the dawn hours just before waking, I used to dream of her, dream of the old man as he leaves the garden, closes the rusty gate behind him, and walks into the forest of black firs beyond. Only the white flags of his breath remain hanging in the air, blending with the frosty morning fog. The cold pricks my skin with goose bumps. I turn away from the window.

Liz lies naked on the bed with her back to me, graceful even at rest. Beneath the duvet I melt into her smooth white skin: my face in her hair, my chest along her back, my lap around her buttocks, my legs next to hers. She sighs contentedly. Eyes closed, I breathe her salty warm night scent and taste her neck with a kiss. Sleep comes slowly and gently until another sound awakens me again: metal striking metal in five-second intervals, far off. Between my arms there is an emptiness where Elizabeth had lain, but I can still smell her. I only have to reach out, and she will be there. I know this is true, I know it. My eyes remain tightly shut.

Every five seconds metal slams on metal. Every five seconds the sound comes closer and closer. Another five seconds and *crash!* The wicket-window on my cell door bangs open, and the screw glances inside to make sure I am awake. His eyes are empty of all emotion.

—10—

Fighting the Death Penalty

"With the rope for my suicide under my mattress."

January 1987–January 1990

THE EXTRADITION PROCEEDINGS for my transfer from London to Bedford County began on January 1, 1987, after Elizabeth and I had served an eight-month sentence for check fraud. At that point, no one could have guessed that this legal battle would last three years, nor that my case would end up in the highest court in Europe. In fact, I remember sitting in the blue-tiled holding cell under Bow Street Magistrates Court and feeling fairly confident when it all began.

A few weeks earlier, the German government had sent a prosecutor to England to obtain yet another confession from me. This was absolutely necessary in order to extradite me to Germany. The U.S. government had already submitted an extradition request to the British government, and now the German government wanted to file its own request so I could be transferred to my home country. Under German law I could be tried there for the murders committed in the United States. But in order to be indicted in Germany, I had to provide the German prosecutor some sort of evidence to justify a murder charge: my confession. With that in hand, the

German government only had to use the usual diplomatic means to persuade the British government that it should deny the U.S. extradition and grant the German one.

However, a few weeks later my attorneys visited me in Her Majesty's Prison Brixton to bring me the worst possible news: Commonwealth's Attorney James Updike had indicted me on two counts of capital murder, which meant that he would seek the death penalty. He had never lost a case of this type, so my execution was virtually guaranteed my lawyers told me.

They would immediately file an appeal. But their attempts to help me were condemned to failure since the British government had decided to give Updike's extradition request precedence over the German request. In order to accommodate the American government, Great Britain was even willing to circumvent its own extradition guidelines. Normally, the British required assurances that the death penalty would not be carried out if the defendant were sentenced to death. Otherwise, it could not extradite a prisoner to a country where he or she was subject to capital punishment. But in my case, Great Britain had agreed that the judge at my trial in Virginia only had to read the jury a letter, stating that the British government opposed the death penalty.

My attorneys leaned over the table in the prison visiting room and looked deep into my eyes, like doctors who had to tell a patient that he was suffering from a fatal illness. For a moment there was only silence. Then they told me: *Don't get your hopes up.*

I asked them about the German-extradition request. It had been denied. The British government valued its "special relationship" with the United States more highly than its ties to a fellow member of the European Community. (This was long before the European Union came into being.)

I asked the lawyers, *What about my partial diplomatic immunity?* Thanks to my father I had that diplomatic passport, and during my time in the U.S. it had contained a large American diplomatic visa. How could it be that all this suddenly meant nothing? Surely there had to be some sort of mistake.

Apparently, the mistake was mine, my attorneys explained. My father was a vice consul at the German Consulate General in Detroit and therefore was considered a consular official by the American government—not a diplomat. In order to obtain diplomatic status, he would have had to work at the German Embassy in Washington. This differentiation was completely arbitrary since officers in the diplomatic service constantly switched back and forth between consular and diplomatic duties. My father, too, had had both kinds of assignments during his career. But in contrast to all other countries, the United States extended diplomatic immunity only to the family members of embassy personnel, not to family members of consular personnel. Because of this bureaucratic subtlety, I would now be executed my lawyers told me.

So there I sat in the small, shabby visiting room and tried my very best to control my mounting panic and anger. This had not been part of my promise to Elizabeth! I had not promised to save her life by going to the electric chair myself. Five years in a German juvenile prison—that was supposed to have been the extent of my "sacrifice," as she had called it in one of her letters. Somehow I had been tricked, cheated, fooled. But now my main priority had to be caution, to avoid getting myself into even more trouble. With a nervous stutter I asked my attorneys what my legal status would be if I were innocent.

They gasped with shock. *For heaven's sake, anything but that! Not innocence, please!* In order to have any chance at all of obtaining a binding guarantee that the death penalty would not be carried out, it was absolutely essential that I did not withdraw my confession during the extradition proceedings. If we admitted that I had even the slightest defense against the murder charge, then the appellate judges would immediately conclude that I did not need any binding assurances. No innocent man could possibly be convicted in an American court at all. Legally, it was absolutely essential for us to maintain the so-called seriousness of the risk of execution, my lawyers explained.

If I wanted to live, no one could know that I had not killed the Haysoms. Even back then I had to smile at the poetic irony. If anyone found out I was innocent, I was a dead man. Liz had saved herself by playing the role of Lady Macbeth, the accomplice to murder—as we had discussed and planned after she had killed her parents. Now I only had one hope of saving my own life: I had to keep playing the role of Macbeth the murderer.

So I left the visiting room of Brixton prison and returned to my housing unit—to prisoners who were not just pretending to be murderers, but actually were. After my interrogation at the beginning of June 1986, I had been transferred, away from the petty criminals in the underground holding cells of various police stations, and to the heaviest boys in the "A-Secure" unit of the largest remand (i.e., pretrial) prison in London. The reason for this transfer was purely bureaucratic. All prisoners awaiting extradition for murder were automatically classified as high risk, presumably because they were assumed to be international contract killers. The fact that, in reality, I was a young, soft, and slightly crazy diplomat's son was irrelevant.

Because of this classification as a "Category A" prisoner, I spent the three-and-a-half years from June 1986 to my extradition in January 1990 with England's most dangerous inmates as they awaited their trials—almost all of them involved with organized crime, terrorists of various stripes, as well as the occasional mass murderer and serial killer. Most of the organized crime members were professional bank robbers from the East End, with their own subculture and language ("Cockney rhyming slang"), as well as a few genuine Italian Mafiosi, Israeli drug wholesalers, and Jamaican drug distributors. Among the terrorists there were members of the IRA, INLA (socialist Irish nationalists), and "Orange Order" (Northern Irish protestants), as well as Sikhs, Kashmiris, Tamil Tigers, and Iranians. Mixed in with all these was the German "voodoo murderer," as the English tabloids continued to call me.

If you think this was terribly dangerous for me personally, you would be mistaken. The petty criminals of my first few weeks behind bars had been a much greater danger, because they had all been drug-addicted teenagers without any self-control as they went through their withdrawal. By contrast, the organized crime members and terrorists were all grown-up, mostly not addicted to drugs, and comparatively intelligent.

Perhaps surprisingly, they were also in some sense moral creatures. The organized crime members from the East End had a code of honor that would have made Karl Marx proud. The uniformed guards on armored trucks were not to be injured, since they were members of the working class just like the robbers, whereas the bank managers in their tailored suits were fair game. Among the terrorists, the Irish were genuinely proud of the fact that they only killed police officers, soldiers, and politicians, but not innocent civilians. Murdering noncombatants was something only the British government did, the Irish claimed.

Of course, the moral values and ethical guidelines of organized criminals and freedom fighters were completely absurd. But at least the inmates of the "A-Secure" housing unit had some sort of value system that constrained their actions and made them somewhat predictable. They lived by rules, and as long as I respected those rules, I could get along with them easily enough.

Apart from the comparative civility of "Category A" gangsters and terrorists, however, Her Majesty's Prison Brixton had little to recommend itself to discerning convicts. In fact, various human rights panels and commissions regularly condemned Brixton as "the worst prison in Europe." Every other month or so, a gaggle of do-gooding bureaucrats would come to inspect the place, tut-tutting ostentatiously and raising their bushy eyebrows at the shameful conditions they encountered. The "governor" of Brixton always brought these visitors to "A-Secure" because our little unit was the least-awful corner of his facility. Nothing, however, could satisfy the sharp-eyed prison inspectors, and they hurried off to write their condemnatory reports.

As far as we inmates could tell, all that humanitarian paperwork produced no changes at all. But at least our suffering was officially documented, validated, and acknowledged. Also, at least a few of those human rights commissioners were fairly good-looking ladies, which made a nice change from our hairy, smelly fellow prisoners.

Brixton was built in 1847 and had not been modernized since. As with so much else from the Victorian Age, the prison looked very imposing from the outside, almost like a cathedral, but inside it was pure hell.

Instead of toilets there were only plastic buckets, into which both occupants of the narrow cells had to defecate and urinate. With a little luck you had two opportunities a day to empty your bucket. As a result, all of Brixton stank overwhelmingly—no, not of feces and urine, but of shit and piss.

And it had stunk like that for nearly one-and-a-half centuries, from the time it was built until I lived there. The walls, the plaster, and the paint had absorbed the stench of 140 years, so that a malodorous cloud hung over the prison and clung to its inmates. Sometimes, it actually stung your sinuses; you simply could not get used to it.

In addition, the prisoners of Brixton themselves smelled since you only got a shower and fresh clothes once a week. The stench of ancient and new shit and piss thus competed with the smell of your own and your cellmate's armpits. There was athlete's foot and unwashed underwear.

Added to that was the boiled cabbage, which was served at literally every meal and somehow intensified all the other smells.

For those who have never had to live in this kind of poisoned atmosphere, it is probably impossible to imagine how awful it is to be
subjected to such an assault on your nose at all times—even in your
sleep. Thirty years later, I still shudder when I think about it.

Almost all of the roughly one thousand inmates in Brixton
had to bear the stench in double cells, into which they were locked
for twenty-three hours a day. But in the "A-Secure" housing unit,
where I lived with the organized crime members and terrorists, we
had single cells and were locked in "only" twenty-one hours a day.
Most importantly, we could shower every day. So we could live
relatively well, apart from the general stench.

For me, those twenty-one hours of confinement to the cell
were undoubtedly more difficult than for the other "Category A"
inmates. I was the only one under indictment for capital murder,
under direct threat of the death penalty—and the only one whose
lawyers were telling him that he was beyond all help. *Don't get
your hopes up*, my lawyers had told me. And I took their advice
literally.

I had a little litany that I repeated to myself during the daily
twenty-one hours of solitude, almost as if I were praying a rosary:

- I would be extradited from England to Virginia.
- I would not receive a binding assurance that the death
  penalty would not be carried out.
- I would be sentenced to die.
- I would be strapped to the electric chair and executed
  through one or, if necessary, several shocks.
- I would die, just as everyone has to die (that was my
  consolation back then)—only, I would die a bit sooner
  and in a somewhat less pleasant way than most others.

Then the litany would start over: "I would be extradited from
England to Virginia" and so on—like dominoes, with one leading

to the next. The most important domino: I would not get my hopes up, not even a little, not at all.

Over the years, all the courts rejected my lawyers' appeals against my extradition, just as they had predicted: Bow Street in June 1987, the High Court of Appeals in December 1987, the House of Lords in July 1988, and the European Commission for Human Rights in December 1988. My attorneys were obviously very knowledgeable, judging by how successfully they had foretold these defeats in January 1987.

From a legal point of view, my situation really was hopeless. The death penalty was no longer in use in Europe, but several countries kept it in their legal codes at least on a formal basis—including England. As a result, the European Convention for Human Rights did not condemn the death penalty per se, and thus my lawyers could not argue in court that executing me would violate my human rights.

Instead, my attorneys had to argue that, firstly, Virginia's method of execution (the electric chair) was inhumane; and, secondly, that the long wait until I was executed (the so-called death row phenomenon) was inhumane. To support these arguments, they collected all sorts of reports and statements about executions that had not gone as planned, and about life on Virginia's death row, where inmates awaiting their deaths apparently whiled away their time by raping one another.

My lawyers sent me their appellate briefs, including all those reports and statements. In my single cell in the "A-Secure" housing unit, I had twenty-one hours a day by myself, without TV and with only a few books. So I had lots of time and hardly anything to do—apart from reading those appellate briefs, reports, and statements. A few of those also included photos.

Very interesting. Very, very interesting. So this—this was my future. Because, after all, I had been told not to get my hopes up. Not even a little bit.

That was decades ago—decades!—but I still remember it all so well. I remember:

- how the hairs on the arms of the men being executed all stand on end and sometimes catch fire;
- how the smell of an execution in the electric chair is reminiscent of grilled pork—and how this smell cannot be washed out of the witnesses' clothing afterward;
- how flames often shoot out of the electrode attached to the left calf;
- how the eyeballs sometimes pop out completely and hang down on the cheeks;
- how the mouth fills with blood, from biting the tongue— and how this blood sometimes sprays out with the final, dying breath;
- how sometimes a second or even a third shock is necessary, because the condemned man simply refuses to die.

Yes, I remember it well, so very well. Despite the decades. Despite the decades.

Because I did not get my hopes up, not even a little bit, I made plans to deny the damned Americans the pleasure of killing me. Throughout the years from 1987 to 1989, I kept a rope under my mattress, made from a torn-up bedsheet. I had made up my mind to kill myself before I could be extradited to America.

Once I was transferred to the United States, I would be kept under strict observation to prevent my suicide; I knew this from the reports I had read about living on death row. Therefore, I would have to kill myself in England, before I was extradited.

So every time another court ruling in the extradition proceedings approached, I would prepare myself: practically, with my homemade rope; and psychologically, through visualization. I planned and thought through every step: I timed exactly when the guards made their rounds; I knew how and where to hang myself. My own death was my only possible revenge. I refused to give them the pleasure of taking my life. My death was my victory.

That was how I lived from 1987 to 1989. With the rope for my suicide under my mattress. With death in my bed.

Trial and Error

"If it had not been for that [sock]print . . . "

January 1990–June 1990

O N JULY 7, 1989, the European Court of Human Rights announced its decision that extraditing me to Virginia to face the death penalty would constitute "torture or inhuman or degrading treatment," a violation of Article 3 of the European Convention on Human Rights. Since this ruling in effect outlawed capital punishment, the press and TV news programs across Europe celebrated the decision as the most important in the court's history. Across the Atlantic Ocean, the public reaction was somewhat different. A nationally known U.S. senator from New York, Alfonse D'Amato, bitterly condemned those interfering liberal Europeans for daring to lecture America on human rights, and for depriving law-abiding Virginians the pleasure of watching an animal like me fry.

As noted in the court's written opinion, the European Court judges expected me to be deported to Germany after their ruling, so I could be tried in my own country on the American murder charges. The British government began to make preparations for my transfer, but at the same time it was negotiating furiously with the United States. For more than half a decade, Britain had sought the extradition of an IRA terrorist named Joe Doherty, for the shooting of an English Army captain in Northern Ireland. Because Irish-American pressure groups claimed he was a political prisoner, however, this accused murderer remained in a federal facility while his supporters had a street in New York City renamed in his honor. The British government had hoped to trade my extradition for his until the European Court spoiled this plan.

Eventually, it was Commonwealth's Attorney James Updike who had to give in to accommodate the wishes of the British and U.S. governments. By dropping the capital-murder indictment, he cleared the way for me to be extradited to Bedford County without violating the European Court decision forbidding the death penalty. But he managed to express his frustration at being denied the opportunity to have me executed by choosing a special day on which to announce that I would after all be sent to Virginia, not Germany: August 1, both his and my birthday. After a fruitless petition to the High Court of Appeals in London, I was returned to America on January 12, 1990.

Television cameras met me at every airport through which I passed on my journey back: Gatwick in London, Charlotte in North Carolina, and finally Roanoke on the border of Bedford County. The media of central Virginia had covered every twist in the story since the discovery of Derek and Nancy Haysom's bodies in 1985, and now local journalists were driven to a frenzy as they awaited the main event. Because Elizabeth had pleaded guilty as an "accessory before the fact" in 1987, some pretrial news reports even described me as a murderer, without using the usual qualifying adjectives such as "alleged" or "accused." To most residents of the Roanoke–Bedford–Lynchburg area, there seemed to be no doubt about my guilt.

I spent the five-and-a-half months between my arrival in America and the first day of my trial in Bedford County Jail, an old-fashioned facility with only about fifty cells. Unlike the enormous Victorian remand prison in which I had spent most of the previous three years and eight months, with its vaulted, cathedral-like wings and foot-thick stone walls, the holding tanks and cells at this jail were essentially barred metal cages—and tiny cages at that. My fellow prisoners were different, too. They were not awaiting trial for crimes like terrorism, as in London, but for offenses like hunting deer out of season.

Most of my time before the trial was occupied with pretrial hearings at Bedford County Courthouse. Every few days, it seemed, Sheriff Carl Wells himself would drive me to this imposing building, located in the heart of the sleepy little town of Bedford. A typical Southern temple of justice, the courthouse had a red-brick exterior, enormous white columns, and wide marble steps leading up to the grand front entrance. All that was missing was a pair of Civil War–era cannons with pigeons roosting in the barrels.

If the exterior architecture was meant to impress, then so was the theatrical esthetic of the courtroom itself. It had clearly been built in the days before TV, when a good trial was the only entertainment to be had. Beneath the high ceiling, row upon row of dark wooden benches led up to the raised platform at the front of the room, which was dominated by the biggest judicial bench I have ever seen. No set designer could have provided a finer stage for the greatest show in town: the comeuppance of Jens "the Beast of Bedford" Soering.

If I seem to belabor the air of theater surrounding my trial, that is because the first of many pretrial hearings at Bedford County Courthouse dealt with the prejudicial influence of the media on potential jurors. The judge's ruling clearly demonstrated that the last lines of the play had been written before the actors ever walked onto the stage.

Because of the intense local publicity, my legal team—Richard Neaton of Detroit and William Cleaveland of Roanoke—filed a motion for change of venue, that is, a request to move the trial. Winning this motion would normally have been a foregone conclusion, since no other case in Virginia's entire history had been subjected to as much heated media attention as mine. If any trial qualified for a change of venue, surely it was this one.

But Bedford County Circuit Court judge William Sweeney disagreed. In fact, he refused to hear arguments from either prosecution or defense on this subject. Instead, he ruled that the four years' worth of newspaper and TV reports had indeed prejudiced potential Bedford County jurors—and that the solution was to import a jury from neighboring Nelson County.

As my attorneys pointed out immediately, however, Nelson County was subjected to precisely the same publicity as Bedford County: the same newspapers, the same radio stations, the same TV stations. If these media sources had prejudiced Bedford jurors, then they equally prejudiced jurors from Nelson. However, Judge Sweeney refused to budge. He had already made his decision, based on a car trip he had undertaken through Nelson County a few days earlier.

When the time came to empanel the jury, it turned out that the judge's plan had gone awry—or succeeded, depending on his actual intent. An astonishing fifteen potential jurors, out of a pool of thirty-eight, said that they believed me to be guilty before the trial started, and that it was my responsibility to prove my innocence. While those fifteen were dismissed, several others who believed me to be guilty were in fact placed on my jury. How was this possible? Because Judge Sweeney asked them if they could lay aside their previously formed opinion and look at the evidence with fresh eyes. If the potential jurors said *yes*—they thought they could set aside their belief in my guilt—then they were allowed to join my jury.

The judge also overruled the defense's objection to TV cameras in the courtroom. At that time, Bedford was one of only two localities in the state whose courts permitted live broadcasts as an experiment, and the novelty of this technology attracted viewers across Virginia. The entire trial was shown on cable TV, with highlights rebroadcast every evening. Public fascination with the case soon reached new heights, and local entrepreneurs profited handsomely from pirated videocassette recordings of the legal drama.

In another pretrial motion, the defense asked Judge Sweeney to excuse himself from presiding over the case due to his links to the Haysoms' relatives. The judge admitted that he and Nancy Haysom's brother, Risque, had remained in contact ever since attending the Virginia Military Institute (VMI) together for two years during the late 1940s. In fact, Judge Sweeney referred to the victim's brother by only his first name several times during the hearing and acknowledged thinking well of him. He also admitted attending a party in the Haysoms' honor in 1983. Nevertheless, the judge decided there was no actual bias or even the appearance of impropriety, so he denied my lawyers' motion.

From March 1–5, 1990, Judge Sweeney heard the defense's motion to suppress my "confession" of 1986. This was the most important of the many pretrial hearings. If the police were found to have denied me access to an attorney during questioning, my statements would not be admitted as evidence at trial. Credibility was the central issue, as in most such motions. Should Judge Sweeney believe my claim that an English policeman had threatened to hurt Liz if I did not agree to speak to the detectives without my lawyer present? Or should the judge believe one American and two English investigators, who all insisted that my right to an attorney had not been violated?

The prosecution argued that I had knowingly and willingly consented to questioning without counsel. Except for the first two sessions at 3:35 and 6 P.M. on June 5, 1986, I had signed Miranda waiver forms before each interrogation. Someone as intelligent and educated as I could hardly claim that I had not understood my rights, and there was no evidence of physical coercion. Those portions of the interrogations that had been tape-recorded contained fairly polite interviews without direct threats.

But I testified that I had only signed the waiver forms and talked to police because I had feared for Elizabeth's safety. The English Detective Sergeant Kenneth Beever had come to my holding cell alone and told me that Liz might fall down and hurt herself if I did not drop my demands for a lawyer.

In court, my American attorneys argued that the chronology of events on June 5 supported my claims. At the 3:35 and 6 P.M. sessions, I refused to sign the Miranda waiver forms, insisted on my innocence, and requested a lawyer. Police records confirmed that I was returned to my holding cell at 6:45 P.M. specifically because of my demand to see an attorney.

What I could not prove through documentation or witnesses was that Detective Beever issued his threat at some time between 7 and 7:40 P.M. But this allegation was hardly implausible, given the English police scandals of the late 1980s and early 1990s. First to be released by the London High Court of Appeals was the Guildford 4, a group of Irish youngsters who spent fourteen years in prison for an IRA terrorist bombing that they did not commit; Americans learned about this miscarriage of justice through the movie *In the Name of the Father*. In the following years the convictions of the Birmingham 6, the Maguire 7, and scores of nonpolitical prisoners were also overturned, because the English police had used violence or the threat of force to obtain false confessions in all these cases. Judge Sweeney, however, ruled that this pattern of abuse was irrelevant and cut off my lawyers before they could introduce a photocopy of an English police handbook on interrogation, which advised officers to take all steps necessary so suspects would not take advantage of their right to an attorney.

At 7:45, shortly after Detective Sergeant Kenneth Beever threatened to harm Elizabeth, I asked the station's desk sergeant for permission to telephone the German Embassy. Instead of reaching a consular officer who could contact my lawyer, I was only able to speak with the embassy night watchman. As soon as he learned of this attempted telephone call, Detective Beever fetched me from my cell, and at 8:05 I signed the first of many Miranda waiver forms.

Since I had been returned to my holding cell at 6:45 expecting to see my attorney soon, I had no reason to waive my right and speak to the police only seventy-five minutes later unless I had been forced to do so. I was certainly in no rush to unburden a guilty conscience. Although I admitted during the 8:05 interrogation that I had been at the scene of the crime, I retracted that partial confession the next day and did not admit to killing Derek and Nancy Haysom until the evening of June 8.

The defense was also able to produce some undisputed evidence that threw doubt on police credibility on the specific issue of granting me access to a lawyer. Bedford County Detective Ricky Gardner testified at the suppression hearing that I had made only an equivocal request for an attorney during the 6 P.M. interview on June 5, and his typed summary of this session, written on June 9, 1986, also implied that I had not directly asked for counsel. But the contemporaneous handwritten notes of the 6 P.M. interrogation, made by English Detective Constable Terence Wright, showed that my request for a lawyer had been very explicit indeed. Why would the Virginia investigator take the risk of lying in court about this issue, unless he realized that his actions had not conformed to Miranda requirements?

Unfortunately, my attorneys were unable to learn everything that happened at this interrogation session because Detective Wright's handwritten notes had been altered. One of the four pages had been removed and replaced by a page from an interview with Liz in a different color ink. In reversing the convictions of the Guildford 4 and all the other innocent prisoners, the High Court of Appeals in London had ruled that such tampering with interrogation transcripts was indirect but conclusive evidence of the police violation of suspects' rights.

Like Detective Gardner, Detective Beever also failed to tell the truth on at least two indisputable occasions. At 4 P.M. on June 5 he told my English lawyer over the telephone that I did not wish to see him, although at that time I was demanding counsel. The next day, Beever promised on tape to fetch my attorney; but when the lawyer arrived at the station two hours later, he was only permitted to speak with Elizabeth.

Finally, my attorneys were able to produce the British police station logbook entry for my interrogation: "To be held incommunicado," a clear order to deny me my right to a lawyer. Curiously, only my logbook entry contained this (arguably illegal) order; Elizabeth's did not.

In spite of my attorneys' arguments, Judge Sweeney found the convoluted explanations of the police more believable than my claim that I had been denied a lawyer. The "confession" was admitted into evidence and is reproduced here in chapter 9.

The trial itself began on June 1, 1990, with yet another hearing on Judge Sweeney's bias. That very morning—the first day of the trial—the local *Albemarle* magazine published an interview with the judge in which he openly declared me guilty. According to him, Elizabeth was surprised when I "took the dare" and killed her parents.

What made Judge Sweeney's statement to *Albemarle* especially outrageous was that he thereby proved himself to be a liar. In an earlier court ruling—his "letter opinion" of February 13, 1990— the judge claimed that he "was careful not to comment on the guilt or innocence of Jens Soering." Clearly, this was not true.

Even this did not suffice to persuade Judge Sweeney to remove himself from my trial. Amazingly enough, all subsequent state and federal appellate courts agreed with him. So, after opening statements, the prosecution presented its first evidence: Liz's and my diary-letters from the Christmas 1984 holidays, which I discussed in detail in chapter 2.

After the police witnesses had finished reading out those letters, Mrs. Massie testified how she had discovered the bodies of Derek and Nancy Haysom on April 3, 1985. During cross-examination, my lawyers asked this lady whether she thought Elizabeth had been present at Loose Chippings when the homicides occurred. She managed to say *yes* before Commonwealth's Attorney Updike jumped up to object. Judge Sweeney then ordered the jury to disregard Mrs. Massie's opinion and had it stricken from the record. This exchange was in fact a replay of Liz's sentencing hearing of October 1987.

Mrs. Massie and one of Elizabeth's half-brothers had testified then that they thought Liz had been in her parents' home during the attack. But even in 1987, Prosecutor Updike and Judge Sweeney had not allowed them to explain their reasons for this belief.

Before Mrs. Massie left the witness stand at my trial, my lawyers questioned her about one other subject: the cleanup of Loose Chippings at the end of May 1985. In chapter 6, I described how Mrs. Massie and one other member of the group had observed Elizabeth removing her shoes and comparing her feet to the bloody sockprints on the floor. Since the jury eventually based its verdict on the sockprint evidence, I cannot help but wonder now whether the jurors overlooked this testimony, given so early in the trial.

The connection between Liz and physical evidence at the scene of the crime grew stronger when forensic experts took the stand next. The prosecution's scientists could not of course deny the incriminatory findings I discussed in chapter 5: Elizabeth's fingerprints on the vodka bottle and her relatively rare blood type on the damp rag. But Commonwealth's Attorney Updike did his very best to prevent any suspicions falling on the star witness who would testify against me later in the trial. He questioned his own forensic experts as if he were a defense lawyer, forcing them to explain how a suspect's fingerprints could appear at a crime scene even if not present during the murders, and how the prosecution's own blood-typing tests could have malfunctioned and falsely implicated Liz. All in all, it was a very curious performance.

The prosecution's scientists also had to admit that no fingerprints of mine had been found anywhere at Loose Chippings. This too was rather curious because, according to my "confession," I had spent the better part of an hour in the Haysoms' cottage drinking alcohol, eating a snack, committing a particularly violent double murder, leaving and returning by the front door, cleaning myself up at both the kitchen and the bathroom sinks, and wiping the dining- and living-room floors on my hands and knees—all without wearing gloves. Since crime-scene specialists had used all available technology, including lasers and the luminescent chemical luminol, it was nearly miraculous that they had not found my fingerprints somewhere, if indeed I were the killer.

Even more curious was the discovery of a human hair in the bloodstained bathroom sink, where I had supposedly washed myself after killing Elizabeth's parents. This hair did not belong to Derek or Nancy Haysom or me. Yet it was highly unlikely, if not impossible, that the hair could have fallen into the sink much before the homicides because the water would have washed it down the drain when the murderer turned on the tap to rinse the blood off his or her hands. Perhaps most curious of all, the scientific experts claimed that they had somehow forgotten to compare Liz's hair to the hair in the bloodstained sink.

There was, however, at least one tenuous forensic link between myself and the scene of crime. A few spots of type-O blood, my type, were found on the way from the living room to the bathroom at Loose Chippings, as well as on the inside of the front door. But once again, the sample was too small to be subtyped, so those drops could have been left by any of the forty-five percent of the population with this, the most common of all blood types.

Although it could be argued that those droplets might have been mine, they were found in proximity to other physical evidence that was definitely not left by me. The attacker had lost his or her type O en route to the bathroom, yet the hair that the killer then dropped into the bloodstained sink was not mine. Also, unsmeared prints of a bloody socked heel on the bathroom floor were much narrower than the heel on sample footprints I provided police. And halfway between the location of the type-O blood and Mr. Haysom's body, detectives found a shot glass carrying, on one side, Mr. Haysom's fingerprints and, on the other, fingerprints whose owner was never identified. The shot glass was discovered on a small, round side table directly next to Derek—a highly significant location, since both Derek and Nancy Haysom's blood had high levels of alcohol. No other glasses were found at the crime scene.

At trial, my attorneys argued that the blood, the hair in the sink, and those fingerprints indicated the presence of a second murderer, apart from Liz. In later years, the presence of this second killer was further substantiated by shoeprint evidence, DNA tests, and even a new witness. But of course, no one knew this in 1990. What *was* known, even back then, was that the Bedford County Sheriff's Department had initially concluded, from the state of the crime scene, that this crime must have been committed by two perpetrators. In April 1985, the Department had issued an "all points bulletin" seeking two persons unknown, possibly in possession of a knife.

I myself have no doubt that Liz had an accomplice at the crime scene—but to this day I do not know his or her identity. Naturally, Elizabeth will never name this person; if arrested, he or she would confirm that Liz herself had killed her parents, and then she would never be paroled. Had Sheriff Wells and Prosecutor Updike's investigators done their jobs professionally, had they not let themselves be bullied by the Haysom brothers' lawyer into dropping Elizabeth as their prime suspect in April 1985, then perhaps their highly publicized manhunt, properly focused, could have caught her accomplice.

When the forensic experts finished their testimony, Commonwealth's Attorney Updike introduced the damning "confession" that I had made to detectives in London in 1986. Before the jury and the courtroom TV cameras, secretaries and sheriff's deputies reenacted how I allegedly stabbed and slashed Derek and Nancy Haysom on March 30, 1985. The "confession" was lengthy, and many details were accurate. Also, my story seemed to be corroborated, however weakly, by scientific evidence. In 1986 I claimed that I had been cut during the fight and showed investigators two tiny scars on the fingers of my left hand. These injuries seemed to account for the type-O blood found at the crime scene. In cross-examination, my lawyers pointed out the many discrepancies between my "confession" and the physical evidence at Loose Chippings, which I discussed in chapter 9.

Next, the prosecution called a witness named Harrington who testified that he had seen bandages on my fingers and a large bruise under my eye while I stood next to Liz's roommate, Christine Kim, at the Haysoms' funeral service in Mrs. Massie's house five years earlier. No one else could corroborate this man's testimony: not college students with whom I had attended classes after the murders; not the many other acquaintances of the Haysoms who had attended the funeral service; not even members of the Haysom family. Prosecutor Updike even stipulated that Christine Kim could not remember whether I had any injuries at the service. Strangely enough, Mr. Harrington only went to the police with his tale of seeing wounds on me after I mentioned the scars on my fingers during my London "confession," more than a year after the funerals. My attorneys were unable to discover whether this witness Harrington was related to Colonel Harrington of U.S. Army Intelligence, the friend of Derek and Nancy Haysom who captured Elizabeth in Berlin after she ran away from England.

Showing Detective Gardner those scars during questioning in 1986 was stupid even by my standards, but I was worried that he would not believe my "confession" if I did not offer at least some corroboration. It was only in the second half of the interrogation session, after Detectives Beever and Wright entered the room, that I decided out of desperation to add this detail. If the policemen had examined the shape of the scarred tissue on my fingers they would have become suspicious: the marks were thick triangular ridges like those commonly left by broken glass, not the thin white lines usually made by knife cuts. In fact, I had received those scars as a child in Cyprus, when I broke a marmalade jar while trying to capture a butterfly. Later in the trial, when it was my turn to testify, I showed the jurors my fingers so they could judge for themselves.

After Mr. Harrington left the stand, Commonwealth's Attorney Updike re-called police witnesses so they could read out the incriminating passage Liz had planted into the diary that we kept during our travels on the run. Supposedly, I had worried about leaving my fingerprints on a coffee mug I used during an informal interview with Bedford County detectives in October 1985. In chapter 6, I explained how Elizabeth had tried to provide seemingly objective evidence pointing at me, as insurance in case I did not live up to my promise to accept the blame for her killings when we were arrested. This plan was a bad one, however, since my fingerprints could not have been found at Loose Chippings. Moreover, the other fantastical passages about "white slave transfer points," laser brain surgery, and the IRA terrorist Rover cast even more doubt on Liz's story of fingerprints on mugs.

At last, Prosecutor Updike was ready to introduce his star witness: Elizabeth Haysom. My lawyers and I knew, of course, that she would claim I had killed her parents while she had remained in Washington. During cross-examination, my attorneys planned to question Liz closely on the many changes in her story of how she allegedly arranged an alibi for me. Neither she nor Prosecutor Updike knew that I had saved the actual movie-ticket stubs from the weekend of my killings; my father later found them in my college dorm room. Through this documentation, the defense hoped to prove that Elizabeth was not the one who had remained behind in Washington, and that she had in fact driven to Lynchburg to commit murder.

But then occurred yet another one of those bizarre turns of events that so frequently altered the course of this case. Not long after my arrest in 1986, my father had contacted John Lowe, a well-known Virginia criminal defense lawyer, to discuss his representation of me at a possible trial. Realizing the importance of the movie tickets, my father had faxed this attorney copies of these and other documents that he had found in my room. Mr. Lowe eventually did not join my defense team, but like any good lawyer he kept his records intact including the faxes my father had sent him.

On the eve of Liz's grand appearance on the witness stand, John Lowe decided to turn over the faxed copies of the tickets to Prosecutor Updike. So flustered did he become that he asked for a short recess in court, to allow him to digest the startling news. He realized immediately that a busy night lay ahead of Elizabeth and him, since they would have to correct large portions of her upcoming testimony. For my attorneys and me, Mr. Lowe's decision to help the Commonwealth's Attorney was a major disaster, of course, though we were lucky in one respect: those old faxes of the tickets were so unclear that the starting times of the films were illegible. At least the defense would still be able to prove Liz a liar on that subject.

The following day, after Prosecutor Updike completed the direct examination of his star witness, my lawyers took Elizabeth through the many mutations of her account of her supposed activities in Washington on March 30, 1985. During the London interrogation of June 8, 1986, she claimed she had purchased two tickets for *Witness* around 2 P.M. and two more tickets for *Stranger than Paradise* at 4. However, these ticket purchases were not made with the intent to provide an alibi for me.

Then, a little later in the same interrogation, Liz reversed herself on the latter point: the tickets were meant as an alibi, after all.

Upon her return to America in 1987, she was interrogated again on May 8. This time, Elizabeth changed her story completely. While she had agreed to provide an alibi, she had in fact purchased only one movie ticket all night long, for the midnight showing of *The Rocky Horror Picture Show*.

At her sentencing hearing on October 5, 1987, Liz came up with yet another version. She bought all the tickets but attended none of the movies, and the alibi was only hatched later—after the murders.

If Commonwealth's Attorney Updike had not obtained those faxed copies of the movie tickets, Elizabeth would presumably have repeated her sworn testimony from 1987 at my trial in 1990. But through lawyer Lowe's help she knew that she now had to revert to a variation of the tale she told Detective Gardner in London in 1986. Liz again claimed she had purchased sets of two tickets at 2 and 4 P.M., though she added a detail from her 1987 story about ordering a bottle of alcohol by room service.

Thank goodness the small print on those faxes was illegible! During cross-examination my attorneys produced the original ticket stubs for Elizabeth and the jury to study up close. The two *Witness* tickets could not have been bought for a 2 P.M. showing, as she alleged, since newspapers for that day listed 2:50 P.M. and 5:05 P.M. starting times, and the stubs for *Stranger than Paradise* read 10:15 P.M., not 4 P.M. Her story of purchasing a bottle of alcohol via room service was also untrue, since the hotel testified that the bill was too small to account for both alcohol and two meals. Finally, Liz had no explanation for the check I had cashed while she was in Lynchburg. The reverse of the original canceled check bore my signature, details from my driver's license, the imprint of my father's VISA card, the stamped date of March 30, 1985, and the hotel receptionist's initials. I had been forced to write this check because Elizabeth had taken most of our cash with her in the rush to depart earlier that Saturday afternoon.

However, movie tickets were not the only subject on which Liz changed her story dramatically between 1986 and 1990. There was also the murder weapon. At first, during her June 8, 1986, interrogation, she claimed that the two of us had bought a double-edged "butterfly" knife for my brother's birthday and even drew a sketch of this weapon. The only problem with that tale was that Derek and Nancy Haysom were murdered with a single-edged weapon.

After her extradition to Virginia, Elizabeth told the police on May 8, 1987, that we had bought the "butterfly" knife not for my brother's birthday but "to kill my parents."

Six days later, she came up with a new version. She had not been with me when the knife was purchased and did not know whether I had used it.

At her October 5, 1987, sentencing hearing Liz testified under oath that I had told her I had used a steak knife and only brought up the "butterfly" knife six months later. The story about a birthday gift for my brother had been a lie.

Now at my trial, Elizabeth again testified under oath—but this time, the birthday story was true. However, she stuck with the claim that I had used a steak knife, and the "bagged and tagged" steak knife with blood residue, which police had found in the dining-room table drawer, was passed around among the twelve jurors.

For the prosecution, this was wonderfully dramatic, of course. The members of the jury could actually touch the very knife used to commit this awful crime. Unfortunately, the bloodstained steak knife did not fit my "confession" at all. As can be seen in Investigator Ricky Gardner's transcription of my June 8, 1986, interrogation in chapter 9, I claimed that I "had [a] knife with [me]" which I "pulled out" to kill the Haysoms, and that I "threw two knives into [a] dumpster" near Loose Chippings afterward. Where did the bloodstained steak knife fit into this picture?

Until recently, my answer to that question would have been that the steak knife was the real murder weapon, but Elizabeth had been the one wielding it, and my "confession" had obviously been a lie. However, almost exactly twenty-six years after the murders, in March 2011, a new witness came forward and described seeing Liz with a young man other than me, and in possession of a bloodstained, single-edged, hunting-type knife. As always with Elizabeth, the truth is hidden behind so many layers of lies that this is probably forever beyond reach.

Yet I still believe there was a brief moment when she spoke the truth: June 8, 1986, when she told the police, "I did it myself. . . . I got off on it." If one studies the crime scene photos, one can see that, indeed, the perpetrator "got off on it."

Even Prosecutor Updike must have despaired of his star witness at my trial in 1990. So devastating were the discrepancies between Liz's testimony and the actual evidence that he did not even attempt a redirect examination, and according to post-trial newspaper articles, the jury did not believe her tales. What mystifies me even today, however, is that the Virginia State Bar took no steps to censure John Lowe for giving the prosecution material that he had received in confidence when my father discussed the possibility of hiring him. Perhaps John Lowe did not suffer the wrath of the Virginia State Bar because he moved in the same elevated social circles as Derek and Nancy Haysom once had; in fact, my lawyers later learned that he and the Haysoms had been acquaintances and possibly friends.

But the questionable manner in which Mr. Lowe helped Commonwealth's Attorney Updike and Elizabeth get her story a little straighter was not what was foremost in my mind while she was on the stand. This was the first time I had seen Liz in person since our brief joint appearances at the London extradition court in early 1987; a three-year interval had transformed both of us completely. Looking across the courtroom at the woman I had once loved beyond reason, I was shocked most of all by her appearance. I remembered her as attractive, with an athletic physique and, at the end, beautiful long hair. Now her body was emaciated like a heroin addict's, her face aged far beyond its years, and her hair chopped short in a butch style. Where had Elizabeth's physical magnetism gone, that strange allure that a reporter at her 1987 sentencing hearing had described as "unconventional beauty"?

More than anything, I wanted an opportunity to talk with Liz, so I could discover how I had fallen under her spell in 1984 through 1986. To what extent had she bewitched me, and in what measure had my own weakness made me susceptible to her magic? Such a conversation was impossible now, as I well knew. In any case, it was doubtful that she could give me the answers to my questions, since my attorneys had learned from Elizabeth's prison medical files that she had been prescribed psychotropic drugs. Having observed the terrible effects of these so-called medicines on other inmates in England, I was almost glad that one part of Liz's personality had remained undamaged. She still had that icy calm that allowed her to weather my lawyers' cross-examination when less practiced and accomplished liars would have broken down. In that respect, at least, she was still my girl, the same old Elizabeth who could not resist a little of the old POT.

The prosecution's last major witness was a certain Mr. Robert Hallett, a retired FBI lab technician (not a full Special Agent) who had specialized in tire, belt, and shoe impressions. Strangely enough, Commonwealth's Attorney James Updike chose this man to testify about a subject that lay outside his area of professional expertise: the analysis of the bloody sockprints found at Loose Chippings. Mr. Hallett's only qualifications in the field of forensic footprint morphology were that he had attended some of the sessions of a short FBI course on the subject, and that he had collected some sample footprints of FBI agents for comparison. No scientific publication bore his name; no university had awarded him a relevant degree: examining footprints was merely his hobby.

When Mr. Hallett took the stand, he showed the jury a so-called overlay: a translucent photograph of a sample ink footprint I had provided, laid over a life-sized photo of the bloody sockprint LR3 from the crime scene. The resemblance between the two was remarkable. The toes of my sample looked like the toes of the sockprint from Loose Chippings; the ball of the foot in my ink print was similar to the ball of the foot of LR3; only the heel of my sample footprint was half-an-inch longer than the heel of the bloody sockprint, a difference of at least two whole shoe sizes. Not just the length, but the width of my heels also differed from heel prints found at the crime scene. While the LR3 heel was too smeared for comparison, police also found clear, unsmeared heel prints in the blood on the floor of the master bathroom at Loose Chippings. The bloody heels measured 4½ inches in width, and my ink-sample heels were all at least 5 inches wide.

At my trial, however, Prosecutor Updike's belt-and-tire witness, Robert Hallett, argued that the difference between the heels of the bloody sockprint LR3 and my sample footprint could be explained away. My ink samples supposedly contained a "double impression" in the heel, which made my foot appear longer than it really was. Just why he was allowed to give the jury this opinion is something of a mystery, since Judge Sweeney had explicitly ruled at the beginning of the trial that Mr. Hallett would not be accorded the status of an expert witness qualified to interpret evidence, as opposed to merely stating facts. Without any professional training or background, Robert Hallett's opinion testimony could only be irrelevant and misleading, so the judge at one point stopped him from explaining how a socked foot could have made the LR3 impression—clearly a matter for expert interpretation. But when it came time for Mr. Hallett to testify how my foot allegedly left a "double impression" on the ink samples, Judge Sweeney made an exception to his own ruling on expert-opinion testimony and permitted this nonexpert to persuade the jurors that a difference of half-an-inch, or two shoe sizes, did not matter.

What really persuaded the jury panel was Robert Hallett's photographic overlay comparing one of Liz's sample footprints to the bloody sockprint at Loose Chippings. Hallett chose an ink sample of hers that bore little resemblance to LR3. Neither the toes nor the balls of the feet nor the heels appeared similar. Since the jurors only saw the one footprint of mine that looked like the sockprint and the one ink sample of Elizabeth's that differed, they concluded that I, not she, had made the LR3 impression at the crime scene. Thus, Mr. Hallett seemed to have proved true the prosecution's theory of the case: I had killed the Haysoms by myself just as I had "confessed" in 1986.

With that, Commonwealth's Attorney Updike closed the prosecution case. My attorneys and I had expected him to call Rick Johnson, the forensic scientist whose work I discussed in chapter 6. He had prepared the original reports on sockprint LR3 in 1985; his professional background was better than Robert Hallett's; and he was available to testify at my trial in 1990. Yet Prosecutor Updike chose the nonexpert Mr. Hallett to introduce his footprint evidence. As a result the jury never learned that, according to Mr. Johnson's report of June 7, 1985, LR3 was left by a man's size 5 to 6 foot; he clearly did not believe in "double impressions" that magically eliminated the half-inch difference between my size 8½ feet and the bloody print at the Haysoms' cottage. Nor were the jurors informed of Rick Johnson's August 29, 1985, report, which found that one of Liz's half-brothers could not be eliminated as a suspect on the basis of his footprints because his ink samples contained too many similarities to LR3. Commonwealth's Attorney Updike's choice of footprint witnesses thus was wise from a strategic point of view, given all the facts that only Rick Johnson, but not Robert Hallett, could give the jurors. However, I think it is fair to ask whether this clever prosecution strategy really served the ultimate purpose of the trial: finding the truth, the whole truth.

After Mr. Hallett left the stand, the defense opened its case, which was based almost entirely on my own testimony. As if that were not enough pressure, I also had to contend with a whole series of curious distractions while I told my story. First, the courtroom's air conditioner broke down, and the temperature inside soon rose even beyond the extremes of the Virginia June heat outside. Then the lights began failing intermittently, plunging the whole court into darkness on several occasions. Strangely enough, the air conditioning and lighting systems experienced such problems only when I was testifying. Nevertheless, I managed to maintain my composure and give the jurors my version of the events of March 30, 1985, as I have done here in chapters 4 and 9.

If I made any progress at all in persuading the jury of my innocence during direct testimony, however, I lost it all during cross-examination by Commonwealth's Attorney Updike. He did a masterful job of leading me into destroying myself.

Perhaps the key exchange revolved around a passage in a letter I had sent Elizabeth roughly four years earlier, while we had been in prison in England. She had apparently given Mr. Updike this letter as part of the deal she cut with the prosecution in 1987, after her return to Virginia. In the letter, written shortly after our interrogations of June 5–8, 1986, I referred to Bedford County law enforcement officials as "yokels." *Why had I done that?* Mr. Updike now wanted to know.

And I smiled.

I smiled out of a mixture of embarrassment, fear, and stress. I found most of the things I had said and done while with Elizabeth to be deeply humiliating now, years later, and the arrogance and stupidity of the "yokel" remark was especially painful in retrospect. Also, the entire rest of my life was at stake in this trial, so I was scared. Plus, after more than a day of testifying, I was reaching exhaustion. Under those circumstances, most people would smile; this is, in fact, an almost involuntary response, which primatologists have observed in chimpanzees who feel threatened.

But the jurors did not think about frightened chimps who smile to placate an aggressor. They only saw a smart-aleck foreigner grinning at his own murder trial. I looked almost psychopathically arrogant—and guilty.

However, I managed to answer the prosecutor's question: I had used the word "yokel" because I had been amazed that the police could have believed my pathetic, error-filled false confession.

So was this all a joke to me? Commonwealth's Attorney Updike asked. No, I answered.

Did I want to make a fool out of the people of Bedford County? No, but he was making a fool of me now.

Twenty years after this exchange between myself and the prosecutor, I had the opportunity to watch a video clip of this part of my cross-examination, for the first time in two decades. It made me wince. It helped me to see, once again, that throughout those years, my worst enemy was not Elizabeth Haysom or Investigator Ricky Gardner or Commonwealth's Attorney James Updike—but myself. If the false confession of 1986 had not been bad enough, my performance at my trial in 1990 was even worse. I talked my way into prison, twice.

During the closing arguments at my trial, my attorneys drew the jury's attention to one seemingly insignificant piece of evidence, which, under the defense's theory of the case, explained Elizabeth's motive for killing her parents. Crime-scene specialists had found a necklace lying on the floor in front of an open dresser drawer in Liz's upstairs bedroom at Loose Chippings, and they had carefully photographed and logged it because it was so obviously out of place. Now, my lawyers pointed out that Elizabeth herself could hardly have left her room in that condition when she visited her parents' cottage on the weekend of March 23–24 to celebrate her father's birthday. Her mother would certainly have straightened up before March 30, the night of the homicides. So that necklace most likely had been dropped on the floor at the time of the killings, as the investigators who took note of it had also surmised.

There was additional evidence that the necklace had been part of Liz's motive. In the letter she wrote me during her spring 1985 skiing vacation with her half-brothers (discussed in chapters 3 and 4), Elizabeth had threatened to steal her mother's jewelry, and at my trial she admitted taking an expensive watch and ring on the weekend of March 23–24. Her parents would undoubtedly have discovered this theft and then threatened to withdraw the gift of a small account at the Bank of Bermuda, which she had recently been promised for her upcoming birthday.

To Liz, this money represented freedom from the suffocating control of her mother and father—parents whom, because of her borderline personality disorder, she feared and hated with literally insane intensity. So she probably drove to Lynchburg on March 30 to plead for forgiveness or, if that failed, to win her liberty by any other means. My attorneys and I knew Elizabeth took along an ally, quite possibly the drug dealer to whom she owed the money that she hoped her parents would give her. But only she knew who left the O-type blood, the hair in the bloodstained bathroom sink, and the fingerprints on the shot glass.

When these four people met in Loose Chippings that night, violence was almost preordained. Derek and Nancy Haysom were highly inebriated, Liz admittedly used drugs, and the highly charged subject of the argument was money and missing jewelry. Perhaps she went upstairs to her room before the murders to fetch the necklace, which police later found on the floor, or perhaps her accomplice decided to arrange his or her own financial restitution after the killings. Unless Elizabeth decided to tell the truth, the actual sequence of events inside the Haysoms' cottage would remain a mystery, my lawyers told the jury.

After prosecution and defense had concluded their arguments to the jury, Commonwealth's Attorney Updike and my lawyers negotiated with the judge precisely what instructions on the law jurors should be given. This part of the trial might seem arcane and even unimportant to laymen, but in some ways how the jury is charged is the most important part of any judicial proceeding. Through the instructions, the judge tells the jury which possible verdicts are available to them, and what elements of proof (or evidence) jurors must believe beyond reasonable doubt to be true in order to reach each of the possible verdicts.

Still not persuaded that this is actually important? Then observe what Judge Sweeney did at my trial. Naturally, he granted the prosecution the jury instruction that Commonwealth's Attorney Updike requested on murder in the first degree. To find me guilty of this crime, the jury would have to believe that I killed Derek and Nancy Haysom intentionally and with "malice aforethought"—a legal phrase meaning, essentially, that I had base, cruel motives. This was the theory of the case that Mr. Updike had argued throughout the trial, so it was reasonable to grant him that jury instruction.

Then my lawyers asked Judge Sweeney to give the jury an instruction on the crime of accomplice after the fact. From the first day of the trial onward, it had been my attorneys' argument that this was what I was guilty of: when Elizabeth told me that she had killed her parents, I helped her cover up the murders. Therefore, it was reasonable for the defense to request and receive an instruction on its theory of the case, just as the prosecution had been granted an instruction on its theory. That would have given the jury a clear choice: to find me guilty of what Commonwealth's Attorney Updike claimed I had done, or to find me guilty of what I claimed I had done. (Incidentally, accomplice after the fact is a misdemeanor, not a felony, and carries only one year in prison as punishment.)

But Judge Sweeney refused to grant the defense an instruction on its theory of the case—unless my lawyers agreed to let the jury hear an instruction on the crime of accomplice before the fact, as well. On the face of it, this made no sense at all, because neither prosecution nor defense had argued during the trial that I was an accomplice before the fact. So why did the judge try to force the defense to accept a jury instruction of this type? Essentially, it was to lay a trap for my attorneys and me. Judge Sweeney knew that my lawyers could not possibly agree to allow the jury to consider a verdict of accomplice before the fact, for the simple reason that this amounted, in law, to first-degree murder. What the judge had tried to do was offer the jury two ways to convict me of first-degree murder: one, the prosecution's theory of the case, that I was the killer; two, his own theory, that I might have been an accomplice before the fact. In effect, Judge Sweeney hoped to double the prosecution's chances of reaching a guilty verdict.

My attorneys refused, so the jury never heard any instruction on the defense's theory of the case at all. Either the twelve jurors had to find me guilty of first-degree murder, or they had to acquit me completely and let me walk out of the courtroom a free man. However, as every observer of the legal system knows, juries are usually reluctant to grant complete acquittals, especially in a case like mine, where I clearly was guilty of a lesser crime. So Judge Sweeney's clever legal maneuver had the effect of helping the prosecution, by removing the option of convicting me of that lesser crime, accomplice after the fact.

If you think the above explanation is an example of an embittered prisoner griping about minor technicalities, you would be wrong. The legal system as a whole is well aware of the fact that judges have the power to influence verdicts by controlling which instructions, which verdict-options, the jury hears. In fact, the specific tactic that Judge Sweeney used in my trial—making a jury instruction on the defense's theory of the case conditional upon another jury instruction that favors the prosecution—is so well known that there is a long line of appellate-court rulings, all the way to the U.S. Supreme Court, which clearly forbids this precise maneuver. According to the Supreme Court, the resulting convictions must, without exception, be overturned and new trials ordered. Allowing judges to manipulate juries and verdicts though jury instructions can never be tolerated . . . except, of course, in one case, as I learned eleven years later, when the U.S. Supreme Court refused to hear my petition for a writ of habeas corpus.

Nevertheless in 1990, at the end of my trial, when Judge Sweeney forced my lawyers to decline a jury instruction on the defense's theory of the case, my attorneys were quietly pleased. They told me that this was a "slam dunk," guaranteed-winning argument in the appellate courts—if I were convicted in the next few hours. Little did they know how greatly the American court system would change over the next decade and how difficult it would become for convicted defendants to overturn their judgments on appeal.

While my lawyers and I sat in a small room on one side of the courtroom and discussed these issues, the jury argued over my future in its own chamber on the other side of the courtroom. According to newspaper reports:

> There was [a] six–six split over Soering's guilt when [jury] deliberations began. But juror Jake Bibb said the physical evidence in the Haysom home ultimately convinced him and his colleagues of Soering's guilt.
>
> "What he wrote didn't convict him [and] what people said didn't convict him," Bibb told the [Charlottesville, Virginia] *Daily Progress*. "It was what he left behind. If it had not been for that [sock] print, I would have found him innocent," Bibb said.[4]

---

4 *University Journal*, University of Virginia, Charlottesville, vol. 12, no. 91, June, 1990.

On June 21, 1990, the jury returned guilty verdicts on both counts of first-degree murder and recommended two life sentences as punishment.

—12—

After the Verdict

"I'm innocent."

June 1990–September 1990

As I sit in my prison cell in 2016, twenty-six years after the reading of the verdict, I can picture that moment precisely in my mind's eye. My attorneys and I had been asked to stand as Judge Sweeney read the words, "On the charge of murder in the first degree, we find the defendant guilty." Then he asked me if I had anything to say. I shrugged my shoulders very slightly, arched my right eyebrow a little, and said, "I'm innocent." And for the next twenty-six years, I have not stopped repeating those words at every opportunity: *I'm innocent.*

Why do I remember that moment in court so clearly? Because I have watched myself say "I'm innocent" over and over and over again on TV. Over the next two-and-a-half decades, dozens of TV news segments and true-crime TV shows have used this clip. The truth is that I do not really remember standing in court and saying those words from a first-person viewpoint, standing in my own shoes. Instead, I now remember that moment from the third-person point of view of the TV camera staring at me. Like you, the readers of this book, I too have become a kind of observer of my own life: the life of the most notorious defendant and prisoner in Virginia's modern history.

Here is a partial list of the true-crime, "info-tainment," and talk-show TV programs that have produced segments on my case: *Larry King Live, Geraldo Rivera, Inside Edition, Hard Copy, Justice Files, FBI Files, City Confidential, Court TV, On the Case with Paula Zahn, Wicked Attraction, Cold Case Files, Southern Fried Homicide* (really!), and the German TV shows *37 Grad, Auslands, Brisant, ZDFzoom, Markus Lanz, Johannes B. Kerner* (twice), and *Focus-TV* (twice). I have been told that National Geographic TV, an English TV station, and even an Australian TV program have also produced segments on my case, and there are undoubtedly more of which I am not aware. The list above does not include serious, news-style segments and interviews, which also frequently recycle the old TV footage of my trial; I can recall at least eleven of these just in the last six years. According to a 2007 retrospective feature article in the *Virginian–Pilot*, I "was 24-hour cable gabfest fodder before there were 24-hour gabfests."

In late 2007 and early 2008, I was able to speak at some length with a true-crime TV assistant producer who explained to me why her industry was producing segments on my case again and again, even two decades later: the availability of TV footage. As noted, my trial unfortunately was held at a turning point in legal and TV history, when television cameras were first being introduced into courtrooms. Virginia had just begun a (then-controversial) "cameras in the courtroom" experiment, limited to just two courts in the entire state. One of those was Bedford County. My trial was the first high-profile case ever to be conducted before TV cameras in that state.

No doubt this was the real reason why Judge Sweeney refused to move my trial to another county, one that had not been subjected to years of prejudicial pretrial publicity. He wanted his moment of fame and glory in TV Land. And what was the harm? I was guilty anyway, right?

Today, of course, everyone is used to watching trial footage on TV, and there is even talk of televising proceedings of the Supreme Court. But in 1990, cameras in the courtroom were a novelty for the judge, the lawyers, jurors, and the TV audience. Many members of the legal profession objected strenuously to the televising of trials, fearing that the presence of cameras would influence the way all participants in the trial acted—to the detriment of the defendant.

Five years later, in 1995, the infamous O. J. Simpson trial substantiated the fears of early critics of the "cameras in the courtroom" experiment. Judge Lance Ito played to the camera so shamelessly that he became fodder for late-night TV comedians, and defense counsel Johnnie Cochran took risks that he might not have taken but for the lure of televised showmanship. Even more troublingly, the jury seemed to have been influenced by the possibility that a conviction could spark off race riots similar to riots that followed the acquittal of the white police officers involved in the beating of Rodney King.

In the years following the Simpson trial, more and more prosecutors asked judges to ban cameras from courtrooms, especially in high-profile trials—no doubt because they feared the same sort of public humiliation that ended the career of Simpson's prosecutor Marcia Clark. More and more judges agreed to these requests to exclude TV from spectacular or salacious trials, perhaps because they feared becoming the next Judge Ito. So, over the last decade-and-a-half or so, many of the really entertaining, "juicy" trials have often been covered only by photographic (still) cameras, or no cameras at all.

According to the true-crime TV assistant producer who recounted these developments to me, the comparative difficulty of obtaining TV footage from relatively recent high-profile trials means that producers like her keep having to return to the brief "golden age" of the early 1990s, when judges such as Sweeney and Ito had not yet developed the necessary discretion and judgment to protect defendants from the negative influence of TV cameras. That is why my trial keeps being recycled endlessly by true-crime programs: it is a good source of comparatively scarce raw material.

Ironically enough, even Judge Sweeney seemed to have learned some sort of lesson from my 1990 trial. In November 1996, there was an evidentiary hearing in my case for petition for a writ of habeas corpus, which was held in Bedford County Courthouse. TV cameras could have been allowed; in fact, by then, cameras were permitted in all Virginia courtrooms. But this time the assistant attorney general (representing the prosecution) requested that TV cameras be excluded, and Judge Sweeney complied.

The fact that the evidence introduced at this evidentiary hearing was highly favorable to me surely had nothing to do with the judge's decision not to allow cameras—perish the thought. But that is a subject for a later chapter.

Meanwhile, back on June 21, 1990, I made that statement which later became so beloved by true-crime TV producers: "I'm innocent." With that, the sheriff's deputies put handcuffs on me and marched me out of the courtroom to a waiting car in front of the courthouse steps. Outside, there was an enormous crowd of people who wanted to see "the monster" after he'd been condemned, and the deputies actually had to form a wedge with me at the center to force a way through the throng. Later on, I was told that a man on a bicycle had been arrested near the courthouse that afternoon— carrying a gun.

I spent that evening alone and in a daze; the other inmates in my cell-block kept their distance. At some point, we were all locked into our tiny individual cells for the night, so I could proceed with my plan. Those bastards in the courthouse could convict me of something I did not do, but they could not force me to accept their punishment. I had the power to deny them that pleasure. So I put a plastic bag over my head and tied it tight around my neck with a shoelace.

Although I cannot remember saying "I'm innocent" at the end of my trial—I can only recall the image replayed endlessly on TV—I definitely remember the feeling of that bag over my head: the slick touch of the plastic on my face, the stale humidity of the air inside the bag as I kept breathing in and out, the rising panic as my lungs began to scream for oxygen. . . . In the end, the panic was too strong. I tore a hole in the plastic and started gulping down sweet breaths of fresh air. Then I untied the shoelace and removed the bag, and I laid back down on my bunk.

Another terrible defeat: first the jury's unjust verdict in court, now my failure to make my escape through suicide.

They had won. They had convicted me and sent me to prison, and there was no way out—not even by killing myself. Somehow, I would have to deal with this reality.

A day or two after I tried to commit suicide, a sheriff's deputy unlocked the door to the cell-block and told me to step outside. I was not scheduled to go anywhere at that time—no court date, no legal visit—so I did not like the sound of his order at all. Was I about to receive a second installment of Southern–style justice—a nice, thorough beating by a bunch of overweight deputies?

Reluctantly, I stepped outside the cell-block and let the heavy, metal door clank shut behind me. "Follow me," the deputy said, and he started down the hallway toward the laundry room. Now, as everyone with a minimal experience of jail or prison knows, laundry rooms are some of the most dangerous places in the whole joint: isolated, noisy, and full of dark corners. Laundry rooms are where you go if you want to get raped or killed.

When I turned the corner into the laundry room, I saw that no one was there—another bad sign. The only thing missing now was for the deputy to pull out his nightstick and start educating me about the importance of obeying the law in Bedford County. But then he surprised me. "I believe you," he told me. "You didn't kill those people. What happened in court was a god-awful shame.

You're innocent. I just wanted you to know that I'll be praying for you."

And that was it—no beating, nothing. Slightly stunned, I followed the deputy back to the cell-block. His actions were so absolutely extraordinary that I simply did not know how to respond. Taking me aside like that to express his compassion and his belief in my innocence was an act of great courage. Imagine what his boss, the sheriff, would have said if he had found out. What this meant to me at that time was that there was hope. If one deputy could already see the truth now, just a day or two after my conviction, then potentially others could come to see the truth, too. I could . . . I could . . . yes, I could fight!

That deputy turned out to be only the first of many, many people who reached out to me in Bedford County Jail to comfort me. Over the next few months, I received over 400 letters from residents of Bedford County and the neighboring cities of Lynchburg and Roanoke—of which only two were "hate mail." All kinds of different people wrote me: a teenaged girl from the social housing projects, a great-grandmother whose family tree was at least as distinguished as the Haysoms', a mathematician at a midwestern university, an African-American manual laborer, even a relative of a different sheriff's deputy. But not everyone in Bedford was as kindhearted as these letter-writers. One day, a sheriff's deputy came to the cell-block with a stack of yellow T-shirts. He told me that the prosecutor's wife had had them printed up, and she wanted me to sign them with an indelible marker so she could sell them for an even higher price. Then the deputy unfolded the T-shirt and showed me the logo: I SURVIVED THE SOERING TRIAL—LOCAL YOKEL.

Looking back, I can see the humor in this situation: the prosecutor's wife asking the victim of her husband's wrongful prosecution to help her profit a little from the circus atmosphere. In a way, that just about sums up my entire decades-long experience with the Virginia criminal-justice system.

Speaking of the court system, I cannot end this chapter without relating my attorneys' first attempts to overturn my conviction on appeal. The verdict of June 21, 1990, was an end of sorts, but in most ways it was merely the start of a legal struggle that continues to this day. During my stay at Bedford County Jail in the summer of 1990, my lawyers fought the first few skirmishes in that endless war—and were resoundingly defeated.

In fact, the first shots of the war were not fired by my attorneys at all, but by one of the local residents who wrote me after my trial and, in the case of this particular penpal, even visited me a few times. A smart young woman who ended up moving to California, she had the clever idea of visiting the library of E. C. Glass High School in Lynchburg.

Yearbooks from the mid-1940s showed that Judge William Sweeney and Nancy Haysom's brother, Risque Benedict, had grown up, attended high school, and participated in at least four extracurricular activities together. There was even a photo that appeared to show the two friends arm-in-arm. When the defense had asked Judge Sweeney at the pretrial hearing to reveal the extent of his relationship with the victim's brother, he had failed to disclose this information. The judge had mentioned only the two years that he and Mr. Benedict had spent together at college, thus creating the impression that their friendship was not as close or as long as it really had been.

During August 1990, my lawyers also discovered that either the Commonwealth's Attorney or his footprint witness had failed to disclose crucial evidence, as required by law. At trial, Mr. Hallett had shown the jury an overlay comparing one of my sample footprints to the bloody sock impression at Loose Chippings, as well as another overlay of one of Elizabeth's ink samples over LR3. Whereas my sample resembled the bloody print at the crime scene, Liz's differed from it, leading the jury to believe that I, not she, had made LR3. "'It was what he left behind. If it had not been for that

[sock]print, I would have found him innocent,' [juror Jake] Bibb said," in a post-trial interview with *University Journal*.

When my lawyers reviewed the original sample ink footprints in the prosecution's files, however, they discovered that the very first of Elizabeth's ink samples resembled the sock impression at the crime scene as strongly as my sample print did. Clearly, either one of us could have left LR3. But for his trial overlay, Robert Hallett had chosen another ink sample of Liz's that differed from the bloody sockprint, to mislead the jury into believing that she could not have made LR3 at all.

The implication of the sockprint evidence in its entirety thus was exactly opposite to the false impression created by Commonwealth's Attorney Updike's nonexpert witness. There was no unique identification of myself as the owner of the foot that left the bloody print at Loose Chippings. Not only I, but also Elizabeth, and even one of her half-brothers according to Rick Johnson's August 29, 1985, report could have made the LR3 sock impression. The jury had based its verdict on Mr. Hallett's misinformation.

Finally, my attorneys obtained the records of the theater that ran *Stranger than Paradise* on March 30, 1985; the original owners had meanwhile sold the theater. Box-office records show that ticket numbers 27014 to 27263 were sold for the 6, 8, and 10:15 P.M. shows. My stubs bore the numbers 27140 and 27141, and according to the cinema's owners, those tickets were almost certainly among the last sold for the 8 P.M. showing or among the first for the 10:15 P.M. showing. Printed on the tickets was the time of 10:15 P.M.—the time I said I had seen the film. Liz had sometimes claimed not to have seen the movie at all, and at other times to have watched it at 4 P.M.

The theater records thus proved that the purchaser of the tickets to *Stranger than Paradise* could not have been a murderer. Driving just below the 1985 speed limit of 55 MPH, it would have taken four hours to cover the two hundred miles from the movie theater to Loose Chippings. Even if the purchaser of the tickets had left Washington at 7:45, he or she would not have arrived at the Haysoms' cottage until 11:45 P.M.

Yet there was absolutely no indication at the crime scene that Derek and Nancy Haysom had been preparing to go to bed. It was highly unlikely that Mrs. Haysom would have warmed up a slice of leftover meat loaf at such a late hour, or that Mr. Haysom would have joined in with a bowl of ice cream. The Haysoms and their murderer had eaten that snack together much earlier in the evening, when the purchaser of the movie tickets could not have been anywhere near Lynchburg.

Prosecutor Updike did not dispute that whoever attended *Stranger than Paradise* had an ironclad alibi; he simply contended that it had been Elizabeth, not I, who had bought the tickets. The real significance of the box-office records was that they eliminated the theory espoused by Nancy Haysom's best friend, Mrs. Massie, and one of Liz's half-brothers at her sentencing hearing in 1987: that she and I were both at the scene of crime. One of us must have been in D.C. to buy the tickets.

That conclusion necessarily led to another one. If the forensic evidence proved that Elizabeth was at Loose Chippings during the murders, then only I remained as a possible purchaser of the tickets to *Stranger than Paradise*. As such, I could not have been a killer.

In September 1990, my lawyers submitted a motion for a new trial to Judge Sweeney and requested a hearing to present this new evidence. The judge denied the motion because my attorneys had used the terminology "set aside the verdict" instead of "vacate the judgment" in their written brief. He could have allowed my lawyers to amend their brief, using the correct terminology. But what would have been the point? As Judge Sweeney put it to *Albemarle* magazine, I "took the dare" and committed the crime.

Shortly afterward, I was placed in a brown sheriff's department van wearing handcuffs linked to a belt chain and leg irons. My property sat next to me in a brown paper bag. Then I began the long, long ride to my very first "real" American prison, Southampton Reception Center near Capron, Virginia.

—Part II—

The Evidence

Bill Sizemore

The Star Witness

"I have lied and I have deceived."

F ROM THE MOMENT I met Jens Soering in 2006, my brain rebelled at the notion that he was a monstrous killer.

This bookish, nerdy, mild-mannered man was the person who singlehandedly carried out two gruesome, Mansonesque knife murders? I couldn't wrap my head around it. Yet that was the story-line propounded by the police and prosecutor, and endorsed by the judge and jury in 1990: that his girlfriend Elizabeth Haysom planted the idea, then stayed behind in Washington, D.C., while Jens drove to Bedford County and killed her parents in a rage-filled orgy of slashing and stabbing.

My three-hour interview with Jens in a visiting room at Brunswick Correctional Center left me with nagging doubts about the validity of that story-line. And the weeks I spent investigating the case for my newspaper, the *Virginian–Pilot*, only fueled those doubts.

In the ten years that have passed since I first wrote about the case, a cascading series of new revelations and experts' conclusions have raised still more troubling questions about whether justice was served.

As any student of the American justice system knows, it is not a criminal defendant's responsibility to prove his innocence. It is

the responsibility of the state to prove his guilt "beyond a reasonable doubt." Was that standard met in this case? I will leave it to the
reader to decide.

In 1990, just in time for Jens' trial, a lurid true-crime book about
the Haysom murders called *Beyond Reason* was published. It was
premised on the prosecution's theory of the case—essentially,
Elizabeth's version of events: that she established an alibi in
Washington while Jens drove to Bedford County and carried out
the murders. The first scene in the book has Jens showing up alone
at the door of the Haysom home on the night of the slayings.

The author, Ken Englade, stuck to that scenario even while
acknowledging that Elizabeth was a pathological liar capable of
conjuring up fantastic stories with no basis in reality.

He dutifully reports her allegations to Sheriff's Investigator
Ricky Gardner that Jens not only killed her parents but also plotted
to kill his own parents, Elizabeth's half-brother Howard, and
Gardner himself. She said she talked him out of committing those
crimes, telling him: "You can't just go around killing people you
don't like, Jens."[5]

Oh, and there was one more victim Jens had in his sights,
Elizabeth told Gardner: his grandmother. "[H]e wanted to hook her
up to some kind of electric gizmo and torture her until she gave us
money," she said. "Then afterwards we obviously would kill her."[6]

When I investigated the case in 2006, I was struck by Elizabeth's
multiple and contradictory accounts about central elements of the

---

5   Ken Englade, *Beyond Reason: The True Story of a Shocking Double Murder, a Brilliant
    and Beautiful Virginia Socialite, and a Deadly Psychotic Obsession.* New York: St.
    Martin's Press, 1990, p. 132.

6   *Ibid.*, p. 238.

case—a red flag for anyone trying to assess the credibility of the prosecution's star witness. I counted five different stories she told about the murder weapon and five more about the alibi:

About the Murder Weapon

1. During their weekend in Washington, she and Jens bought a "butterfly" knife for Jens' brother's birthday.—*Police interview in London, June 8, 1986*

2. They bought the knife "to kill my parents."—*Police interview in Bedford, May 8, 1987*

3. She wasn't with Jens when the knife was bought and doesn't know if it were used.—*Police interview in Bedford, May 14, 1987*

4. Jens first told her he used a steak knife, then brought up the butterfly knife six months later. The story about a birthday gift was a lie.—*Testimony at her sentencing hearing, October 5, 1987*

5. The birthday story was true after all. Jens used a steak knife for the murders.—*Testimony at Jens' trial, June 13, 1990*

About the Alibi

1. She attended two movies Saturday afternoon, buying two tickets each time, but not for the purpose of creating an alibi.—*Police interview in London, June 8, 1986*

2. She arranged the alibi.—*Later in the same police interview, June 8, 1986*

3. They had agreed on the two-ticket alibi, but she bought only one ticket all day, for a midnight show.—*Police interview in Bedford, May 8, 1987*

4. She bought the tickets but didn't attend the movies. The alibi wasn't hatched until after the murders.—*Testimony at her sentencing hearing, October 5, 1987*

5. The alibi was hatched before the murders. She remembers the second movie showing around 4 P.M. The time on the ticket stubs is 10:15.—*Testimony at Jens' trial, June 13, 1990*

Elizabeth even contradicted herself on the fundamental question of murderous intent. At her 1987 sentencing hearing, she testified that whereas she had fantasized about getting her parents out
of her life, she never meant for Jens to kill them. "I was indulging
in some grotesque, childish fantasies. I was feeling hate and resentment and frustration but I wasn't thinking about murder," she said.
"And it seems that he was."

But at Jens' trial three years later, when Prosecutor James
Updike asked Elizabeth if she had wanted Jens to kill her parents,
she replied: "Yes, I did. I think it would be true to say that when
Jens left me on Saturday afternoon to go down to see my parents,
that I was much more concerned that he would not kill them than
that he would because . . . . "

"Why?" Updike asked.

Elizabeth chuckled and said: "Well, the whole idea of Jens
killing anybody is so utterly fantastic."

Speaking of things fantastic, Elizabeth Watson, a family friend,
testified at the sentencing hearing that Elizabeth once told her "a
Middle Eastern sheik had offered her father a number of camels
for her hand."

"Were there occasions when you doubted her veracity?"
Updike asked.

"I think there certainly were, but I attribute that to drugs,"
Watson replied.

At one point in her own testimony, Elizabeth claimed the
German Embassy had been phoning her at Bedford, sending her
money and advising her how to conduct her case.

Sounding a bit incredulous, Judge William Sweeney interject-
ed: "You've been getting phone calls from the German Embassy at
the jail here?"

"Yes," Elizabeth replied.

"What has been the nature of the calls?" the judge asked.

"They say things like Jens loves me, Jens needs me, I'm

responsible for his life, his life's in my hands," Elizabeth said. "They say things like they fear for my life, that time is running out for me, that I should be quiet in thought and word and deed."

It was an extraordinary claim: a foreign embassy meddling in a criminal case and sending money to a jailed defendant. But there was no further exploration of the subject.

Elizabeth did not respond to an interview request for this book. But testimony confirming her fabulist tendencies came from no less a source than Elizabeth herself. At one point in her sentencing hearing, Updike asked: "You're capable of lying and deceiving should it meet your needs then?"

Elizabeth replied: "I have lied and I have deceived."

Later she elaborated: "I lived in—I'm sure you can tell from my letters that I lived in a world of fantasy to a large extent. I deceived people. I lied to them."

Finally, Updike asked in exasperation: "Ms. Haysom, how are we supposed to know what's true? You have told so many things, haven't you?"

Elizabeth replied: "Yes, I have, sir."

—14—

The Judge

"It was like 'Double-dare You.' I think she was shocked he took the dare."

ONE OF THE earliest issues to arise in the years-long trail of legal appeals that followed Jens' conviction for double murder in 1990 centered on the judge who presided over the case.

Circuit judge William Sweeney had been on the bench twenty-five years at the time of the Haysom murder trial. He ultimately served for more than thirty-five years, making him Virginia's longest-serving sitting circuit judge when he retired.

Jens' lawyers asked for a change of venue, arguing that due to the intense media coverage the sensational case had generated, any jury composed of Bedford County residents would be hopelessly biased. Judge Sweeney denied that request, offering the defense only one concession: the trial would be held in Bedford but the jurors would be brought in from neighboring Nelson County. Jens' lawyers protested that Nelson County residents would be just as biased, since they got their news from the same newspapers and TV and radio stations that served Bedford. But the judge stuck to his guns.

The defense also took aim at Judge Sweeney himself, arguing that he was potentially biased because of his acquaintance with the Haysom family and should therefore recuse himself from the case. The lawyers presented evidence that the judge had been a classmate of Nancy Haysom's brother, Risque Benedict, at Virginia Military Institute and that he had attended a dinner party welcoming Nancy Haysom back to the Lynchburg area when she and her husband retired there.

Judge Sweeney countered that his relationship with the Haysoms was not close enough to warrant recusal. He would stay on the case.

Just how close was the relationship? I put that question to Judge Sweeney when I visited him at his Lynchburg home in 2016. He was eighty-eight then, but still had vivid memories of the Haysom case, undoubtedly one of the highest-profile trials of his career.

He had carefully considered recusal, the judge told me, but ultimately decided that he had no reason to withdraw from the case.

"I think I was forthright in stating that I did know the brother of the lady victim, but he was not a close friend of mine," he said. "He did go to Virginia Military Institute, but I never roomed with him. . . . When he graduated, as I recall, he went to California and the only time I would see him would be at a reunion of VMI. I never discussed the case in any way with him either before or after the trial, and he never tried to discuss it with me."

"What about high school?" I asked the judge. I showed him a copy of the 1945 yearbook from E. C. Glass High School in Lynchburg. It shows that Judge Sweeney and Risque Benedict were both in the senior class and participated in several extracurricular activities together, including the Chemistry Club, the Civics Club, the Athletic Association, the Honor League, and the National Honor Society.

In the back of the yearbook there is a collage of candid photos under the heading "Famous Personages." One picture depicts two lanky young men standing arm in arm, dressed identically in white

shirts and dark pants. There is no caption, but the pair bear a striking resemblance to Judge Sweeney and Risque Benedict.

The judge didn't dispute that he is the young man on the left.
As for the youth on the right, he first said, "I don't think that's
Risque." A moment later, he conceded that "it could have been."
But he still insisted that "we were not close."

Jens' legal appeals also drew attention to a cover story in
Albemarle magazine, published just as Jens' trial got underway in
1990, which featured interviews with several key figures in the case,
including Elizabeth Haysom and Judge Sweeney. In a key passage,
the judge offered a scenario of what happened on the weekend of
the murders.

"Sweeney says he imagines the couple discussed the idea of
murder," according to the article. Then it quotes the judge directly: "As far as the acts themselves, I don't think she planned all that
out. It was like 'Double-dare You.' I think she was shocked he took
the dare."

That quote amounts to an endorsement—on the eve of Jens'
trial—of Elizabeth's story, or at least one variation of it: that she
inspired the bloody crime, perhaps unwittingly, and Jens carried
it out.

When I asked Judge Sweeney about that, he turned vociferous.
"I absolutely deny that I made any statement in any way indicating
that I had made up my mind about guilt or innocence," he said. "I
just categorically deny it. I didn't say anything like that."

Later, I tracked down Amy Lemley, the author of the magazine
piece, and she was equally adamant that she got the quote right. She
said she was shocked that the judge would say such a thing.

"There's absolutely no question that he said that to me," Lemley
told me. "To my mind, he certainly should have recused himself."

The Virginia Court of Appeals, however, didn't see it that way.
In its 1991 ruling denying Jens' appeal, the court opined: "The
fact that the trial judge . . . made extrajudicial statements that were

reported in the media, which . . . may have acknowledged that evidence existed of the petitioner's involvement in the crimes does not establish bias or prejudice requiring recusal."

The Virginia Supreme Court concurred shortly afterward, delivering one in what became a long series of post-trial legal defeats for Jens.

The state's two highest courts also were not bothered by Judge Sweeney's refusal to instruct the jury that they could convict Jens as an accessory after the fact. That may sound like an esoteric legal technicality, but as Jens explains in chapter 11, it was a crucial point. The judge's decision left the jury only two options: convict Jens of murder or declare him innocent. It's easy to see why the jurors, faced with such a brutal crime, would have been loath to let Jens off the hook altogether—and, in fact, Jens has never claimed total innocence. He has always acknowledged that he is guilty of helping to impede the investigation and cover up the crime—the very essence of accessory after the fact, a misdemeanor punishable by no more than a year in jail.

But had the jury been inclined to believe Jens, Judge Sweeney's ruling left them no way to deliver a verdict consistent with his story. According to Gail Starling Marshall, one of Jens' later appeals' lawyers, that alone should have been enough to get the jury's verdict overturned.

"There is a very clear law that if there is any evidence to support the defense's theory of the case, that instruction must be presented to the jury," Marshall told me.

Here's how the appellate courts justified upholding Judge Sweeney's ruling: Jens' attorneys failed to request their preferred-jury instruction in the proper manner.

After the defense asked for an instruction on accessory *after* the fact, Prosecutor James Updike responded by advocating an instruction on accessory *before* the fact, noting that Jens admitted participating in the movie-ticket alibi on the day of the murders.

Jens contended that—in his mind, at least—it was an alibi for a drug deal, not for murder. Nevertheless, Judge Sweeney ruled that the jury would be given both accessory instructions or none at all. Since a conviction of accessory before the fact would have carried the same penalty as an outright murder conviction, Jens' attorneys decided not to press for any accessory instruction.

In the end there was no formal request from the defense for its preferred-jury instruction. Therefore, the Court of Appeals ruled, there was no error by the judge.

What Jens' attorneys should have done, Marshall told me, was to insist on their desired instruction and then, when Updike requested an instruction of accessory before the fact, the defense should have lodged a formal objection.

That was only one of several instances, according to Marshall, when Jens' out-of-state lead attorney, Richard Neaton, went astray because he was unfamiliar with the intricacies of Virginia–trial procedure. The list of particulars against Neaton will be fleshed out in succeeding chapters.

Judge Sweeney told me he knew from the get-go that the Haysom murder case "was going to be a very, very difficult case." Yet he doesn't rank it as his toughest case ever. He reserves that distinction for the 1976 civil case in which the city of Lynchburg annexed additional territory from neighboring Campbell and Bedford counties. He received death threats during that one, he told me.

As for the Haysom case, he professed no regrets about how he handled it.

"This was a fair trial," he said. "But having said that, most judges will tell you that there's no such thing as a perfect trial."

15

The Lawyer

"We have incarcerated an innocent person for this heinous crime."

IN 1993, JENS received disturbing news about Richard Neaton, the Detroit lawyer who had led his defense team during his trial and direct appeals. Neaton had been hired by Jens' father, a mid–level German diplomat who by the time of the murders had been posted to the German consulate in Detroit.

Neaton, Jens learned, had become the subject of a complaint by the Michigan Attorney Discipline Board. The charges included neglecting a client's lawsuit to the extent that he missed crucial deadlines, misleading a client about the progress of her case, preparing a fake deposition, misappropriating $11,000 of a client's funds, and failing to cooperate with the Discipline Board's investigation. Shortly after the filing of the complaint, Neaton moved to Florida and closed his law practice.

In his answer to the complaint, Neaton said he had suffered from a "mental or emotional disability [which] materially impaired his ability to practice law" since January 1989—eighteen months before Jens' trial. So, throughout Jens' pretrial hearings, his trial, and appeals, his lead attorney had been so mentally disturbed that, by his own admission, he could not properly do his job.

In December 1993, Neaton's law license was suspended.

In 1995, Jens filed charges of his own against Neaton. Researching the matter with no legal help, Jens persuaded the Discipline Board to find Neaton guilty on four counts: mishandling his appeal, misappropriating $5,000, creating phony affidavits with fictitious notary signatures, and refusing to return Jens' trial transcript.

Neaton's license was suspended a second time in June 1995 and finally revoked in 2001.

In his place, Jens' father hired Gail Starling Marshall, a former deputy state attorney general who had recently gone into private practice.

While working in the attorney general's office, Marshall had been largely responsible for the exoneration and release of Earl Washington Jr., the first Virginia inmate freed through the then still-new science of DNA testing. Interestingly, Washington had given a false confession—just as Jens claimed to have done. Over the following years, as more and more prisoners proved their innocence through DNA, it became clear that twenty-five percent of these wrongful convictions involved false confessions.[7]

As Marshall read her way through the voluminous transcript of Jens' three-and-a-half-week trial, she began to see more and more parallels between his case and Washington's. Eventually, she reached a conclusion that, nine years later, she repeated in a letter to the Virginia Parole Board:

> [T]here have been only two occasions in my 35 years of practice when, after a thorough investigation and review of the trial transcript of an individual convicted of a heinous crime, I have concluded, to a moral certainty, that the person was innocent of the crime for which he was convicted and serving time. The first such incident occurred in 1993–1994

---

7   Zak Stambor, "Can Psychology Prevent False Confessions?" *Monitor on Psychology* (American Psychological Association), September 2006.

[with] . . . Earl Washington. . . . The second occasion involved Jens Soering. . . .

[C]onfessions are sometimes false and . . . juries sometimes make mistakes. . . . Our system is not, and cannot be expected to be, infallible. . . . [W]e have incarcerated an innocent person for this heinous crime.

For the next seven years, Marshall took Jens' appeals through five courts, all the way to the U.S. Supreme Court. And for more than a decade after that, acting purely as his friend, she has continued to fight for Jens in other venues, including before the parole board and in innumerable media interviews.

"She has been the best and most loyal friend imaginable," Jens has written, "and if there is one single person responsible for my even being alive today, it is Gail Starling Marshall."

Marshall told me she reached her conclusion about Jens' innocence purely on the strength of the case record, and that conclusion was only reinforced once she met him in person.

Look at the kind of person Jens was as a baby-faced, mop-haired eighteen-year-old college freshman, she said. "He didn't drink. He didn't do drugs. He was a nerd. He had had a completely law-abiding, boringly nonviolent existence. Is this the kind of person who's capable or likely to do this kind of crime? The answer is, absolutely not.

"The evidence was so biased and so inflammatory and, in my view, unconstitutional. I don't find any of the evidence enough to overcome what I know about his character.

"I think his story—that he really thought he was going to be Elizabeth's romantic savior because he was so damn smart—is very believable. It's certainly something that I can picture him doing.

"He was very, very smart—too smart for his britches, as my mother used to say."

Even Elizabeth Haysom, at one point, agreed that Jens seemed

incapable of murder. "Jens is a wimp," she testified at her sentencing hearing in 1987. "You can't imagine him doing something like
that. It's extraordinary."

Other than Jens' confession, Marshall said the state's case was
paper-thin. There was no reliable physical evidence linking him to
the crime scene: no murder weapon, no DNA, no fingerprints.

The brutality of the crime suggested that the perpetrator had
gone berserk, Marshall said. Generally, that happens for one of
two reasons, or both: the person was on drugs and/or was driven
to fury by some life-altering personal experience with the victims.
Arguably, both of those factors applied in Elizabeth's case: she
admitted to using hard drugs and had made allegations of sexual
abuse by her mother.

As for Jens, there was zero evidence of drug use, and his only
contact with the Haysoms had been an uneventful lunch wherein
routine pleasantries were exchanged.

But he faced headwinds that had nothing to do with the
evidence, Marshall said, not the least of which was the mental and
emotional hurdle the jury would have had to overcome to decide
that Elizabeth—this seemingly demure, refined, soft-spoken young
woman with the lilting British accent—was the killer.

"It's very, very hard for a juror, or any individual, to come to the
conclusion that someone could kill their own parents," Marshall said.

Jens, on the other hand, was a convenient foil on whom to pin
the blame: a cocky, smart-alecky, know-it-all foreigner who had the
misfortune to be tried in Bedford, the community that suffered the
nation's highest per capita casualties at the hands of the German
army on D-Day. The outsized sacrifice of the "Bedford Boys," as
they came to be called, inspired the choice of Bedford as the location of the National D-Day Memorial.

Finally, Marshall said, Jens' fate was sealed by the multiple
failings of his own attorney, Neaton.

Marshall filed a series of habeas corpus petitions on Jens'

behalf—post-appeal legal pleadings alleging constitutional error—in the state and federal courts, all of which were denied. One of the principal pillars of those petitions was the claim of ineffective defense counsel.

Most of the complaints against Neaton were sins of omission—things he should have done but failed to do.

For instance, he never interviewed or called as a witness Keith Barker, the British attorney who was appointed to represent Jens during the crucial police interrogations in London in 1986. Before finally confessing to the murders, Jens asked repeatedly to be given access to his lawyer, but it was never allowed. When Marshall contacted Barker years later, she learned he would have been prepared to testify that he requested—by telephone and in writing—that he be present when Jens was interviewed. At no time, Barker said, was he told that Jens had requested counsel. Testimony to that effect would have bolstered the defense argument that Jens' confessions should not have been admitted into evidence.

In addition, Neaton failed to object when the prosecution harped on Jens' refusal to provide forensic evidence—fingerprints, footprints, hair, and blood samples—when he was first interviewed by Bedford detectives in the fall of 1985, before he and Elizabeth fled the country. In the absence of a search warrant based on probable cause, Jens' refusal to provide such evidence was a proper assertion of his constitutional rights under the Fourth Amendment.

Nevertheless, in his closing argument Prosecutor Updike repeatedly reminded the jury of it. Putting on his best folksy air, he declared: "Now we have moseyed around to the idea of getting Elizabeth's footprints . . . and her blood. . . . Asked her for them, she gives them. But . . . you put the same question to Jens Soering here, he comes down to the sheriff's department with the intent of charming us country boys. . . . So we mosey around to talking to Jens Soering and what does Jens Soering want to do? He doesn't want to give any blood, he doesn't want to give any footprints. . . . The star witness in this case was Jens Soering by virtue of his conduct, by virtue of his refusal to give the samples."

Those comments by the prosecutor were extremely prejudicial and improper, Marshall believes. But Neaton let them pass.

Updike is now a circuit judge. Neither he nor Neaton responded to interview requests for this book.

Ironically, once forensic samples were obtained from Jens after his arrest, none of them could be reliably linked to the crime scene. His fingerprints were not found there, nor was his hair. None of the blood in the house was proved to be his.

As for footprint evidence, that turned out to be central to the state's case and Jens' conviction. But years after the trial, Gail Marshall was able to make a strong argument that it was completely bogus. Neaton's failure to do so in 1990 was perhaps his biggest mistake of all.

Unfortunately for Jens, that discovery came far too late to help him.

16

The Sockprint

". . . no evidence whatsoever that Mr. Soering was at
the scene of the crime."

THERE WAS PRECIOUS little physical evidence with which to make the case against Jens, but Prosecutor Updike made the most of what he had. And Judge Sweeney gave him plenty of latitude to do it.

The centerpiece was the smeared, bloody, sock-covered footprint recovered from the wooden floor at the Haysom home. It was placed into evidence in tandem with the extensive testimony of Robert Hallett, the retired FBI lab technician who was allowed to testify about it even though it lay outside his area of professional expertise.

Because he was not qualified as an expert, Hallett was not permitted to testify as to any "causal relation" between Jens and the sockprint. But he did the next best thing. He made a transparent overlay of Jens' footprint, placed it on top of the bloody sockprint, and the two seemed to match perfectly.

Media interviews with jurors after the trial revealed that the sockprint was the decisive piece of evidence in their deliberations. One said the jury was split six–six at the outset, but the bloody sockprint and Hallett's overlay, with its red dots and arrows, were enough to persuade him of Jens' guilt.

Upon reading that, Russell Johnson, a fully qualified foot-print expert, was so outraged that he wrote a letter to the editor of the Roanoke newspaper declaring that the sockprint evidence was worthless, junk science.

Five years later, Jens' habeas attorney Gail Marshall secured an affidavit from Johnson in which he expanded on his opinion after examining the evidence firsthand. He pointed out that because it was covered by a sock, the bloody footprint displayed no dermal ridges—the swirling patterns in the skin that differ from one indi-vidual to the next.

Moreover, Johnson noted the length of the print couldn't be precisely determined since there was evidence of movement as the foot made contact with the floor. Hallett conceded this point in his testimony, stating, "There appeared to have been a slide in the heel before it came to rest."

In the end, Johnson concluded that Hallett's exhibit suggested a similarity between the sockprint and Jens' foot that did not exist. Hallett's overlay "is misleading and implies a degree of precision to the jury that in fact was not present," Johnson said.

There were multiple footprint samples from both Jens and Elizabeth in police files. A full comparison of Jens' prints with the bloody sockprint "provides no evidence whatsoever that Mr. Soering was at the scene of the crime," Johnson said. In fact, he added, "I can state that the crime scene print matches in size only with Ms. Haysom's print."

A second qualified footprint expert consulted by Marshall reached a similar conclusion.

Even the state attorney general's office, responding to one of Marshall's pleadings in 1997, conceded that the footprints in the house "could not be sized with precision."

Experts such as those Marshall found were available in 1990, but Neaton didn't put any of them on the stand to rebut the pros-ecution's witness. His failure to do so was a fatal flaw in the view of

Dennis Dohnal, a veteran Virginia trial attorney who later became a federal magistrate judge.

In an affidavit secured by Marshall, Dohnal said Neaton's performance was "deficient . . . to the point of falling below the acceptable level of reasonable competence."

Even the state's own forensic lab report about the bloody sockprint, had it been made available to the jury, would have completely undermined Hallett's exhibit and implicated Elizabeth, not Jens. That report concluded that the sockprint corresponded to a woman's size 6½ to 7½ shoe or a man's size 5–6 shoe. Elizabeth wore a 7½ shoe, Jens an 8½.

Bolstering that was a separate report from a Bedford sheriff's deputy about a tennis shoe print that was also recovered from the crime scene. The deputy concluded that the print was left by "a woman or a small man or boy."

But neither of those reports was placed in evidence.

Jens' trial was the first Virginia case in which anything like the bloody sockprint evidence had been admitted. In the years since, the validity of such evidence has been sharply questioned in the legal literature.

A study in the *Virginia Law Review* in 2009 looked at 137 cases in which defendants convicted of serious crimes were later exonerated by DNA evidence. In sixty percent of those cases, the authors found, forensic analysts called by the prosecution provided testimony with conclusions misstating or unsupported by the empirical data.

One of those cases involved Robert Hallett, the witness who provided the crucial sockprint testimony in Jens' case. Hallett's testimony about a shoeprint helped put an Idaho man, Charles Fain, on death row for murder, kidnapping, and lewd conduct with a minor, only to be later invalidated by DNA evidence.[8]

---

8   Brandon L. Garrett and Peter J. Neufeld, "Invalid Forensic Science Testimony and Wrongful Convictions," *Virginia Law Review*, March 2009, p. 71.

Major Ricky Gardner, who investigated the Haysom murders as a rookie sheriff's detective in 1985–86, still keeps a copy of the bloody sockprint and Hallett's overlay readily accessible in his files. For years, he has used it in presentations about the case to college classes and community gatherings.

When I first interviewed Gardner in 2006, he told me he remained absolutely convinced of Jens' guilt. "I don't have any trouble sleeping at night; I never have," he said.

When I reinterviewed him ten years later, his mind-set was exactly the same. "As I've said before, he's right where he should be," he told me. "We had a three-week trial, and the twelve jurors that were brought in from Nelson County said that he was guilty, and nothing that I've seen or heard since then has changed my opinion on that verdict." The prosecution's theory of the case, he said, is "exactly what happened."

What about the sockprint? I asked. Hasn't that evidence been pretty clearly debunked?

Gardner parsed his answer carefully. The prosecution never made any overt claim that the print was Jens', he said. "That was never identified as his footprint. It was *compared* to his. . . . All Hallett did was make a one-to-one comparison with the two, and the jury looked at it."

That answer was reminiscent of an interview Gardner gave the German broadcaster ZDF in 2011. The German journalist showed him a video clip of an interview with Jens' attorney Gail Marshall in which she labeled the sockprint evidence "hogwash" and said it proves nothing about Jens' guilt or innocence.

"She is absolutely right. She is," Gardner responded. "But nobody ever said that was Jens Soering's footprint. Did you hear me say that? I didn't say that. I kept saying that was similar. Another piece in the puzzle."

The German interviewer was flabbergasted. "Is this not—don't get my English wrong—I don't want to say 'tricky,' but is this not a problem? Put it like this: To say: 'I'm not saying that this is Jens Soering's footprint,' but I try to *convince* everybody, the jury, that this is his footprint. It's a smart move, but is it fair?"

"Sure it's fair," Gardner replied. "Because it's a work product. . . . What wouldn't be fair [is] if somebody tampered with that or somebody distorted it, or if they could prove something like that. That wouldn't be fair. . . . I don't know where the trickery comes in."

Did the prosecution ever make a flat-out, explicit claim to the jury that the bloody sockprint was Jens'? It's arguable. Jim Updike may not have crossed that line in so many words, but in his closing argument he certainly walked right up to it and leaned over.

"And Jens Soering—here's this particular one with the markings," the prosecutor said, holding up the sockprint and Hallett's overlay. "That's designated Jens Soering, you can see that, and you can see what Bob Hallett did concerning designating this as his. . . . It matches and it fits like a glove."

David Watson, a private investigator and retired police master detective, was hired by Jens' defense team in 2011 and conducted a yearlong investigation of the case. He concluded that the evidence was insufficient to convict Jens beyond a reasonable doubt and that Elizabeth was the more likely perpetrator.

The sockprint evidence was "completely unscientific and prejudicial," Watson said in his report, adding that such evidence would never be admitted in a trial today.

Watson also concluded that the style of the Haysom murders—clearly a rage-fueled crime of passion—was completely out of character with Jens' logical, methodical personality. If Jens had wanted to murder the couple for any reason, Watson wrote, he would have used a gun.

Watson pointed to another piece of forensic evidence that, in his view, was far more illuminating than the sockprint display. It's an example of how such evidence can be more important for what it *doesn't* show as for what it does.

The investigator recounted what he called Elizabeth's "fantastical" account of how, after the murders, Jens picked her up in the rental car on a busy street in Georgetown dressed in nothing but "some kind of white sheet, and he was covered in blood from head to toe." Blood was "all over everything," she said—Jens, the sheet, and the car.

That cannot be true, Watson concluded, because of the luminol test that was performed on the rental car.

Luminol is a chemical that gives off a blue glow when it comes in contact with an oxidizing agent. Because of the iron in hemoglobin, it can be used to detect blood, even in minute amounts, at crime scenes. A thorough spraying of luminol inside the rental car by Bedford sheriff's detective Chuck Reid revealed no trace of blood.

When I asked Ricky Gardner to explain that, he was stumped. He shrugged and offered this bit of speculation: "The luminol wasn't any good? Luminol was a new technology at the time."

Elizabeth testified that at Jens' directive, she cleaned up the mess in the car—with Coca-Cola, no less. A representative of the rental car agency testified that the car was returned in immaculate condition—a remarkable testament to the cleaning power of Coca-Cola.

In the end, none of the subsequently discovered evidence debunking Robert Hallett's sockprint display made any difference. That's due in large part to Virginia's twenty-one-day rule, which says any post-trial evidence of innocence must be brought forward within twenty-one days of sentencing. After that, as the Virginia attorney general famously declared in the early 1990s, "evidence of innocence is irrelevant."

It's the strictest such rule in the nation. In the early 2000s, the state legislature tweaked the law to allow convicts to seek release based on post-trial evidence through a procedure called a writ of actual innocence.

But the legal bar for winning such a writ is exceedingly high. Only five have been granted in fifteen years. Jens' attorneys have told him it would be futile to try.

17

The Drifters

"... individuals of apparent criminal bent..."

IN 1996, SIX years after Jens' trial, his habeas attorney Gail Marshall got a call from George Anderson, a former Bedford County sheriff's deputy. He had some information that seemed relevant to Jens' case, the ex-deputy said.

Late one night a few days after the Haysom murders in 1985, Anderson said, he stopped two men who were walking along the Route 460 bypass outside Lynchburg and put them in the back of his patrol car for questioning. The pair, William Shifflett and Robert Albright, told the deputy that they had been to Lynchburg "to see a girl." After a few more questions, they were released.

A few days later, those same two men knifed another man to death in Roanoke in a manner eerily similar to the Haysom murders, stabbing him twenty-six times. Around the same time, Anderson found a knife—a Buck 110 folding knife typically used by hunters—stuffed in the upholstery of his squad car's back seat.

It was a striking coincidence. Death by stabbing is a relatively uncommon method of homicide. Fewer than one in five homicides in Virginia in 1985 were carried out with a knife.

But none of the information about Shifflett, Albright, the knife, or the subsequent murder was provided to Jens' defense attorneys, so this never came out in his trial.

Under a well-established legal precedent known as the Brady Rule, prosecutors are obliged to disclose exculpatory evidence— that is, evidence favorable to the defendant—to defense counsel.

In a petition that made its way to the state supreme court, Marshall argued that the information about the two drifters and the knife was highly relevant to Jens' case and, had it been made known to the jury, could have changed the outcome of the trial. The high court sent the matter back to Judge Sweeney's court for a fact-finding hearing.

At that hearing, a state medical examiner testified that the Buck 110 knife was consistent with the type of weapon used to kill the Haysoms.

At Jens' trial, the state had introduced into evidence a steak knife found in the Haysom home as corroboration of Elizabeth's story that Jens told her he used a steak knife for the murders. But that knife, which had been passed around among the jurors, was *not* consistent with the victims' wounds, the medical examiner testified.

Marshall also called to the stand Dennis Dohnal, the legal expert she had consulted on the effectiveness of Jens' defense counsel. He testified that the withheld evidence about the drifters and the knife "absolutely" would have had a reasonable probability of changing the outcome of the trial.

That evidence would have bolstered the defense theory that Elizabeth committed the murders, most likely with the help of one or more accomplices, Dohnal said. It was important to substantiate that theory, he said, because the jury would have been reluctant to conclude that any child could murder her parents in such a brutal fashion, or that Elizabeth alone was physically capable of over-powering two adults. Neaton hammered that theory home in his opening and closing statements to the jury: Elizabeth did it with an accomplice.

But in the absence of any supporting evidence, Dohnal testi-fied, "The comments of trial counsel . . . in both his opening and his

closing arguments, was little more than pure conjecture and speculation which the jury was free to discount in its entirety for lack of
any foundation whatsoever. He was left, so to speak, hanging out
there on a limb without anything with which to suggest the entire
theory of the defense."

Had he known about the two drifters, Dohnal said, Jens'
attorney could have reasonably suggested that Elizabeth "would
have been more likely to use an individual or individuals of apparent criminal bent, if not experience, and that she would not likely
depend on the ability (or inability) of one like Mr. Soering with no
history of violence or criminal tendency."

Judge Sweeney ruled—and the higher courts agreed—that
the information about the drifters and the knife was indeed exculpatory and should have been divulged to the defense, but was insufficient to overturn the verdict.

In short, the prosecution failed to fulfill its legal obligation to
Jens, but it didn't matter.

I asked Major Gardner, the sheriff's investigator, why the
information wasn't turned over to Jens' attorneys.

"Because we didn't know about it until years later," he said.
"We couldn't turn over what we didn't know."

That assertion is, at best, debatable.

George Anderson, the former deputy who came forward with
the information, testified under oath that the day after questioning
and releasing the two drifters, he reported the incident to a sergeant
who was involved in the investigation of the Haysom murders.

He would not be the last to suggest the possibility of alternative suspects in the slayings.

18

The Car in the Woods

". . . yet another significant element of doubt . . . ."

In 2011, another witness stepped forward to buttress Jens' contention that Elizabeth murdered her parents with the help of an accomplice.

Tony Buchanan, retired owner of a Lynchburg–area auto transmission shop, said that some three-to-five months after the murders in 1985, a car was towed into his shop for repairs, its undercarriage matted with grass and mud as if it had been sitting in the woods for a while. The tow-truck driver told Buchanan the two-door Chevrolet belonged to "some college kids."

Buchanan said in a sworn statement that when he looked inside, he saw that the floorboard on the driver's side "was full of dried blood." Beside the console between the front seats, also covered in dried blood, was a single-edged, hunting-type knife—the same type that was used to kill the Haysoms.

At the time, Buchanan attached no significance to the discovery, figuring that perhaps the car belonged to some deer hunters.

When the repairs were done, a young couple—a man and a woman—came to pick up the car and pay the bill. That stood out in his memory, Buchanan said, because it took longer than usual. The woman offered a credit card, and when Buchanan tried to process it, payment was declined. Buchanan called the Florida phone number on the back and was told the bank had stopped payment on the card. The young woman then called someone in Florida—probably a relative, Buchanan figured—and thirty minutes later the card was cleared for payment.

Although the woman paid the bill, Buchanan got the impression that the young man with her—tall, slender, with highlighted hair—was the owner of the car.

Buchanan hadn't been closely following the Haysom murder case, but a month or so later he saw a picture of Elizabeth Haysom in the local newspaper and did a double take. "That's the girl who was in here with that car," he told his employees.

Shortly after that, as the detectives began to close in on them, Elizabeth and Jens skipped the country and Buchanan put the matter out of his mind. When the pair were caught and Elizabeth were brought back to Virginia to face trial two years later, he said, "I just figured, well, they had the people that were guilty."

Another three years passed while Jens was fighting extradition. When he finally went on trial and Buchanan saw his picture in the newspaper, he was shocked. "That ain't the guy that was here picking that car up," he said.

Eventually, Buchanan said, he got in contact with Major Gardner, the sheriff's deputy who investigated the case, and told him he believed there may have been someone else involved in the murders. Gardner, he said, "more or less blew it off."

Gardner vehemently denies that he and Buchanan ever spoke.

"He's lying! It didn't happen," Gardner declared in the German documentary *The Promise.* "I don't know what Buchanan's motivation is. I don't know if he's trying to get his five minutes of fame or whatever. But I certainly don't appreciate him trying to interject himself in a homicide. Tony Buchanan has no credibility to me."

Buchanan is equally insistent that the conversation occurred, and that somewhere out there, another murder suspect is running around free. It has nagged at him for a long time, he said: "I probably thought about it a hundred times over the years."

When shown a photograph by Jens' parole lawyer, Buchanan picked out a fellow U.Va. honors student, a friend of Elizabeth's alleged drug dealer Jim Farmer, and said he looked like the young man who came to pick up the car from the woods. That man's name never came up in Jens' trial. When the film team tried to interview him for *The Promise*, he refused to talk.

If Buchanan's memory can be relied upon, it raises the possibility that Elizabeth drove the rental car from her weekend getaway with Jens in Washington to a rendezvous with her accomplice, then joined him in his car to travel to the Haysom home.

Jens' parole lawyer, Gail Ball, submitted Buchanan's statement to then–Gov. Bob McDonnell in 2011, seeking to get Jens paroled or pardoned. She pointed out that Elizabeth was in the area during the time when Buchanan said the car with the bloody knife was brought to his shop—first helping prepare the Haysom home for sale and later attending summer school at the University of Virginia.

Buchanan's story "adds yet another significant element of doubt to an already highly dubious prosecution theory of the case," Ball wrote the governor.

Imagine that the jury had heard from a witness who described "Elizabeth Haysom in possession of a bloodstained knife and accompanied by a young man *other than Jens Soering*," Ball wrote. "As a former Commonwealth's Attorney, you know that no jury would have convicted Mr. Soering under these circumstances."

And Buchanan would have been a credible witness, Ball said. He had nothing to gain by coming forward and, in fact, was opening himself up to potentially unwelcome scrutiny.

While Jens' petition was pending, Elizabeth sent a letter to the Associated Press, breaking a long silence, in which she reiterated her insistence that Jens was the killer. "If he were innocent, if he were in any way not guilty, I would shout it from the rooftops," she wrote.

Two months later, McDonnell's response to Jens' petition was almost anticlimactic. He was unmoved by Buchanan's story. "Nothing in the information provided by Soering or his attorney provides any basis for me to doubt the judgment of the jury in the case or the veracity of Soering's own confessions," the governor said in a May 2011 statement. "I decline to intervene."

Whatever the significance of the bloodstained car from the woods, linking it or its owner to the Haysom murders required some speculation. There seemed to be no hard evidence of an accomplice at the crime scene—until recently.

—19—

The DNA

"The real killer, a man with type-O blood, is still out there."

IN THE YEARS since Jens' trial, revolutionary advances in genetic science have yielded powerful new crime-solving techniques based on DNA, the unique biological roadmap that distinguishes each individual from the rest of the human race.

The past three decades have seen an increasing number of convicted criminal defendants exonerated on the basis of DNA evidence.

But DNA was not a factor when Bedford detectives collected physical evidence from the bloody scene at the Haysom home in 1985. The dozens of blood samples recovered from the house could only be analyzed using the much more rudimentary system that classifies human blood according to four general types: A, AB, B, and O.

Not surprisingly, most of those samples turned out to be the blood types of the victims: type A for Derek Haysom and type AB for his wife Nancy. But significantly for Jens, five of the samples—four from the front entrance to the house and one from the master bedroom—were type O, Jens' type.

In one of his confessions during the London interrogations, Jens had told the detectives that he cut himself in the struggle with the Haysoms, showing them two small white scars on his fingers as corroboration. Jens now says those scars were from a long-ago childhood accident, but he added that detail to his confession to make it seem more believable.

Type-O blood is the most common type, shared by forty-five percent of the population. But prosecutor James Updike made the most of what he had. If Jens cut himself at the scene, Updike told the jury during his closing argument, he most likely left some of his blood behind and—voila!—his blood type was found there.

"You have got type-O blood there, his blood type," Updike said. "It's not Nancy's, it's not Derek's; Nancy's got type AB, Derek's got type A. It's not Elizabeth Haysom; Elizabeth's got type B. Now where did that type-O blood come from? . . . That blood was put there at the time of the killing, and the person that put it there was injured during the course of the killings, which would make sense in a knife fight like this. He would have at least some kind of injury. He showed you all the cuts on his hand. . . . He was injured."

That might have been the end of the story, had it not been for the enterprising and meticulous work of a serologist at the Virginia Department of Forensic Science named Mary Jane Burton.

Alone among her peers, Burton developed a habit of preserving biological samples from crime scenes and attaching them to hundreds of case files where they could be accessed years later.

By the time those files were discovered in 2001, DNA science had advanced to the point that the samples Burton had filed away were capable of yielding much more precise information. After three prisoners were cleared of rapes that they did not commit through DNA testing of samples in Burton's files, then–Gov. Mark Warner decided a thorough search of those files was in order.

Under the Post-conviction DNA Testing Program launched by Warner in 2005, more than 500,000 old case files from the 1970s and 1980s were reviewed. By the end of 2015, eleven convicted defendants had been exonerated as a result.

One of the cases in which Burton had preserved forensic samples was the Haysom murder case.

In 2009, the forensic department reported that forty-two samples from the Haysom crime scene had been DNA–tested, and none of them could be shown to match either Jens or Elizabeth. In fact, in the case of eleven of those forty-two samples, both Jens and Elizabeth were definitively excluded.

Those findings were not sufficient to exonerate Jens, but they clearly raised significant doubts about his guilt, Attorney Gail Ball argued in a petition to then–Gov. Bob McDonnell in 2011 asking that Jens be paroled and deported to Germany.

"The prosecution and police have claimed for 20 years that Jens Soering cut himself while killing the Haysoms and bled at the crime scene," Ball wrote. "They had 42 opportunities to prove that theory and failed 42 times."

The DNA testing "raises the specter that an innocent man has spent nearly a quarter of a century in prison for a crime he did not commit," Ball told the governor. "That would be an affront to justice—and also a huge potential embarrassment to Virginia."

McDonnell, however, was unconvinced and declined to intervene in the case.

The problem with the 2009 forensic report, standing alone, was that the forty-two DNA–tested samples were not designated by blood type. Were any of the five specimens of type-O blood—Jens' type—collected in 1985 among the forty-two samples? There was no way to know.

Without that key piece of information, the most logical conclusion to draw from the 2009 report was that all forty-two samples were the victims' blood.

It wasn't until 2016 that Jens retrieved the original 1985 forensic report from a friend in Germany who had been storing the voluminous records generated by the case in her apartment. That allowed Jens and his current attorney Steve Rosenfield to compare the two reports side by side. When they did, a crucial fact emerged—an "amazing epiphany," Rosenfield called it later.

Thanks to a common numbering system, each DNA–tested sample could be traced back to the 1985 report and identified by blood type. The result: two of the five type-O samples—both collected from the front entrance to the Haysom home—were among those from which Jens has been definitively eliminated as the contributor.

What does this mean? Several things.

Neither of the victims had type-O blood, so those two samples didn't come from them.

Neither did they come from Elizabeth, who has type-B blood.

And there was one more thing. The type-O samples contained a Y chromosome, which means that they were left by a male contributor. So a man with type-O blood injured himself at the crime scene and left his blood. But that man was not Jens—he had a different genetic profile.

This discovery is compelling new evidence, Jens and his attorney say.

"It's no longer about believing me or not," Jens told me. "It's about science."

In light of the latest revelation about the type-O blood samples, the only way to argue that Jens was present at the crime scene is to postulate that he was there with a male accomplice who shared his blood type—a scenario that was never suggested by the prosecution.

"Following the Commonwealth's theory that the type-O blood left at the crime scene was somebody participating in the murders, Jens is eliminated," Rosenfield told me. "And the real killer, a man with type-O blood, is still out there."

Or as Rosenfield put it at a press conference announcing the discovery: "There is a killer still at large that the sheriff's department doesn't think is worthy of further investigation."

But that still wasn't the end of the story.

Weeks after the discovery about the type-O blood, Jens noticed something else while comparing the two lab reports: two more blood samples, taken from the front entrance and the kitchen, were type AB—Nancy Haysom's type—but the 2009 DNA analysis determined that they came from a *male* source.

That can mean only one thing: there were *two* unidentified men at the murder scene that night, not just one.

Who are those men? It's unclear. It's not even clear whether they are still alive.

Jens has long suspected that Jim Farmer—judge's son, fellow U.Va. honors student, and Elizabeth's alleged drug dealer—could have been her accomplice in the murders. If so, he took the secret to the grave with him. Farmer died in 2014 at forty-eight.

Attempts so far to link forensic evidence from the crime scene to potential suspects other than Jens and Elizabeth have come up dry.

There were several fingerprints recovered from the house that have never been identified, including some in a significant location: on a used shot glass found near Derek Haysom's body. Both victims had extremely high blood alcohol levels: 0.22, more than twice the drunk-driving limit. The prints from the shot glass have been compared against state and federal criminal databases, and no match was found.

Now, Rosenfield says, the DNA evidence should be subjected to a similar comparison.

But Major Gardner of the Bedford County Sheriff's Department, who was one of the original investigators in the case, dismissed the DNA findings as old news. "Based upon the totality of evidence that was presented in Jens' trial in June 1990, I remain confident that he perpetrated these heinous crimes," Gardner said.

❖

And what of Elizabeth? There is some evidence that she was at the crime scene. Two witnesses, including her half-brother Howard, testified that they believed she was present. "I personally am not satisfied with the explanation that her guilty plea provided," Howard Haysom said. "I think Elizabeth was in the house at the time of the crime and I have reasons for that, too." He was not given an opportunity to explain those reasons.

After Elizabeth's sentencing, Howard Haysom told a TV interviewer: "If my sister had been convicted of capital murder, I could have loved her, hugged her, and kissed her, and walked her to the electric chair if that was what the law called for."

The bloody sockprint that was used to convict Jens turned out to be closer to Elizabeth's foot size, according to experts consulted after the trial. Elizabeth was seen by witnesses comparing her foot to the sockprint during the cleanup of the house.

Fingerprint evidence links Elizabeth, not Jens, to the crime scene. Her prints were found on a half-empty vodka bottle on the liquor cabinet near her father's body.

Three Merit cigarette butts—Elizabeth's favored brand—were found at the scene.

The recent side-by-side comparison of the 1985 and 2009 forensic reports failed to implicate Elizabeth but doesn't completely eliminate her as a suspect either. The one sample of type-B blood—Elizabeth's type—collected from a dishtowel found draped over the front of the washing machine in the kitchen, near Nancy Haysom's body, was insufficient to yield a DNA profile for comparison.

Finally, it took three decades and the detective work of a filmmaking crew from Germany to turn up one more indicator pointing to Elizabeth as a likely suspect. And it is hotly disputed.

—20—

The Profile

"I settled on her daughter."

IN RECENT YEARS, the wall of solidarity maintained by those who put Jens in prison has begun to crack.

Major Ricky Gardner, the Bedford sheriff's deputy who has lived with the case since he was assigned to it as a rookie detective in 1985, remains steadfast in his insistence that Jens is guilty. But Chuck Reid disagrees.

Reid was an older, more experienced investigator who worked the case with Gardner for a year after the murders. He left the department for a higher-paying private-sector job in April 1986, shortly before Jens and Elizabeth were captured in London.

In a 2012 episode of the true-crime TV show *On the Case with Paula Zahn*, Reid recalled something that had eluded the multitude of journalists—me included—who have covered the case over the years.

Early in the investigation, Reid said, two specialists from the FBI were brought into the case and worked up a psychological profile of the killer. Their two-part conclusion: it was someone close to the victims. And it was a woman.

Not long after the Paula Zahn interview, two German documentary filmmakers, Marcus Vetter and Karin Steinberger, began a years-long investigation of the case that resulted in the *The Promise*, which premiered in Germany in June 2016. One of the first people they sought out was Chuck Reid.

Reid, in turn, led them to Ed Sulzbach, a retired FBI profiler. Oh yes, Sulzbach says on camera in the film. He remembered the case well.

"I got a phone call from the sheriff in Bedford County," he says. "And I drove out to Bedford County. My mission was to study the crime and come up with possible suspects. Mrs. Haysom was wearing her nightgown with a robe, and it occurred to me that Mrs. Haysom would never entertain strangers in such attire. Who might be close enough to her that she would feel comfortable entertaining in a nightgown and robe? We're dealing with somebody who's close to these people. And I suggested to the investigators, I settled on her daughter, because Mrs. Haysom was a very proper woman."

"Ed, did you all do any paperwork on that?" Reid asks Sulzbach in the film.

Yes, Sulzbach replies. Call the Richmond FBI office. It's in their files. "The FBI never throws anything away," he says. "It's still there, somewhere."

The filmmakers got to Sulzbach just in time. He died in May 2016. His obituary in the *Richmond Times–Dispatch* called him a "police legend" who became the model for a character in the books of best-selling crime novelist Patricia Cornwell.

When I interviewed Chuck Reid, he showed me a typewritten copy of field notes from 1985 that he had kept in a file at home for thirty years. It includes this sentence: "Special Agent Edward F. Sulzbach of the Federal Bureau of Investigation, who is trained in the field of compiling profiles of criminal suspects, viewed the scene and the evidence gathered during this investigation and stated that the suspect was female and knew the victims."

But no one in the sheriff's department or the prosecutor's office ever divulged the existence of such a profile to Jens' attorneys. And when his attorney Gail Ball requested a copy of the document in 2013 under the Freedom of Information Act, both the sheriff's department and the FBI said they couldn't find it.

That's because it never existed, Ricky Gardner told me.

"It's nobody that knows this case better than me, and that includes Chuck Reid. And he's lost his mind!" Gardner said.

The suspect profile "didn't happen," he said. "They can't find it because it was never done. And I'll tell you why I know it was never done. We talked about doing it, and it was volumes of paperwork. . . . It would have taken three college professors to fill out the questionnaires that you had to do, and we just didn't take the time to do that. . . . If there had been a written report on that, we would have been bound to turn that over to the defense as exculpatory evidence. I'm not ignorant."

When I showed Gardner the typed field notes I got from Reid, he said he'd never seen the document and couldn't say whether or not it was turned over to Jens' attorneys.

Jens was infuriated by the belated revelation of a profile pointing to Elizabeth as the killer. After decades of blaming himself for sealing his fate with his confession, he now believes he was framed by Gardner.

"He built his entire life on a lie," Jens told me. "They knew even before I was arrested about the suspect profile. For years, I thought it was all my fault. Now it turns out I never had a chance."

I also interviewed Carl Wells, who was the Bedford sheriff at the time of the Haysom murders. Like Gardner, he professed no knowledge of a suspect profile.

"I knew Ed Sulzbach, but I don't remember him being involved in this case," Wells said. "As sheriff, I knew nothing about it. I think, had it occurred, I would have known."

And like Gardner, Sheriff Wells said he remains confident that justice was done in the case. "It's never haunted me," he said. "I have a clear conscience." He added: "I have often thought it's an ultimate sin for two brilliant minds such as those two had to have been wasted. . . . What they could have accomplished! . . . But hindsight is 20–20 and foresight is total blindness, as my daddy used to say."

Apparently, Wells' memory has faded over the decades. A story published April 6, 1985, in the *Lynchburg News & Advance* contained this nugget: "Wells revealed Friday that FBI agents have also been summoned to piece together a personality profile of the killers."

When I went back to Chuck Reid, he was insistent that the suspect profile exists.

"Believe me, the FBI isn't going to come in there and send two special agents all the way in on a homicide like that just to sit down and discuss it and not write anything down," he said. "I didn't make that stuff up, and I know Ed Sulzbach didn't. . . . If they're saying they couldn't find it, it's because they didn't look for it. . . . If Ricky or anybody else thinks they're going to persuade me it didn't happen, they're barking up the wrong tree."

Despite the profile indicating a female perpetrator, the investigation didn't focus on Elizabeth in the early stages, Reid told me. In fact, he said, Elizabeth steered the detectives to another female suspect: the daughter of a local judge who had been engaged to marry one of Elizabeth's half-brothers.

When they interviewed the judge's daughter, Reid said, she relayed a chilling story.

"She told me and Ricky that the day of the wake, they were in the kitchen and Elizabeth looked at her and said 'I'm the devil and you're the sacrificial lamb,' kind of insinuating that 'I did it and you're going to pay for it.'"

The judge's daughter was eventually ruled out as a suspect.

When the investigation finally turned in Jens' direction, Reid reacted much the way I did when I met Jens twenty years later.

"When he came in our office that Sunday evening for an interview, I looked at him and I'm thinking, no way, no way," Reid said. "This little kid, this rosy-cheeked little boy? . . . It can't be this little guy that did that kind of damage."

In contrast to Gardner and Wells, Reid said he didn't sleep so well as he pondered the case. "I'd wake up out of a dead sleep at two or three o'clock in the morning thinking, 'Did it happen this way or that way?'" he said. "That's how consumed I was with it."

After he left for the private sector, Reid soon came to miss police work and returned to the sheriff's department in 1989. When Wells retired in 1995, Reid ran for sheriff and lost. After that, he became a jail administrator. He retired in 2011.

Considering the weakness of the evidence in the case, Reid has come to believe Jens was wrongly convicted.

"I just think Jens is innocent of this thing," he told me. "I don't think he was there. That sockprint—to me, without an expert, an expert did not testify to that—to me, that's not beyond a reasonable doubt."

"I've always felt that Elizabeth was there," Reid said, and that she had an accomplice. "There was more than one person that did this."

That theory is buttressed by the new DNA evidence and is also consistent with testimony at Jens' trial. A neighbor testified that she saw five or six cars parked in the Haysoms' driveway—suggesting that the couple may have had multiple visitors that night.

Gardner and Wells have a vested interest in continuing to uphold the prosecution's theory of the case, Reid told me. "I understand why Ricky and them are sticking to it, because you can get egg on your face real quick.

"As an investigator you've got to look at all angles and all alternatives. If these other alternatives are there, to me they're worth looking at. That's the first thing they teach you in law enforcement: Don't get tunnel vision."

Gardner and others who continue to insist on Jens' guilt are "cherry-picking the evidence," Reid said. "That's what tunnel vision does to you."

Of course, the prosecution had Jens' confession to help make the case. But now there are grave doubts about that, too.

21

The Confession

"There are significant doubts about the reliability of the confession."

WHATEVER THE WEAKNESSES in the case against Jens—notably the shaky physical evidence and a star witness, Elizabeth, with severe credibility problems—the police and prosecutor could always fall back on one undeniable, damning piece of evidence: Jens confessed to the murders.

Not just once, but three times.

Now an internationally renowned expert on police interrogations says those confessions should be viewed with extreme skepticism.

After a thirty-year career as a British police officer, Andrew Griffiths has taught police science on four continents and works as a consultant, lecturer, and author. At the invitation of Jens' attorney Steve Rosenfield, Griffiths conducted a months-long investigation of the Haysom murder case focusing on the four days of interrogations in London in 1986 during which Jens confessed.

Griffiths' twenty-one-page report, issued in July 2016, concludes that "in the case of Jens Soering there are significant doubts about the reliability of the confession he made, so as to render it unreliable when considered against other case information and the circumstances of his interrogation."

On the way to that conclusion, Griffiths enumerates a series

of what he calls "serious breaches" of British law governing treatment of suspects in police custody. Among them:

- The detectives who questioned Jens circumvented legally
  required time limits on interrogations.
- There were no legal grounds for the police to hold Jens
  incommunicado without access to a lawyer.

Griffiths also found it troubling that none of Jens' confessions
was captured on tape. Less than twelve percent of the total interrogations was recorded.

Moreover, Griffiths faults Ricky Gardner, the Bedford sheriff's
deputy who questioned Jens in tandem with two British detectives,
for making a premature assumption of Jens' guilt.

Griffiths cites a 2001 report from the Council of Europe's
Committee for the Prevention of Torture and Inhuman or
Degrading Treatment or Punishment reminding member states that
the purpose of an interrogation is "to obtain accurate and reliable
information in order to discover the truth about matters under
investigation, not to obtain a confession from someone already
presumed in the eyes of the interviewing officers to be guilty."

In Jens' case, Griffiths found, "it is obvious from the first interrogation that Gardner believes Soering to be guilty of the crimes.
This is significant and contrary to modern day best practise in relation to interrogating suspects."

"In effect, nothing of what Soering said was probed or challenged in a manner that demonstrated an investigative mind-set
or healthy disdain for his apparent willingness to take all of the
blame," Griffiths writes. "Rather, his brief confession was accepted
as complete evidence of guilt and an opportunity to close the case."

Chuck Reid, the original lead investigator in the case who quit
the sheriff's department before the London interrogations, says it
is quite plausible that Jens' confession was false.

"It's very well known that people have confessed to crimes that they didn't commit," Reid says in *The Promise*. Elizabeth "was such a manipulator to that young boy that, yes, he would take the rap for her."

Griffiths cites research showing that more than half of convicted defendants who make false confessions are in the sixteen–twenty age group and that within that group, the most common motive for a false confession is to protect someone else. Jens was nineteen when he confessed—as a high-minded sacrifice, he says, to save his girlfriend from the electric chair.

"I felt like such a hero," Jens has said. "I felt like a knight in shining armor who would rescue this fair damsel in distress. I thought I was doing something good and noble."

An exchange of letters between the two lovers after their arrest in London, featured in *The Promise*, sheds light on their frame of mind as they faced their police interrogators. One of the letters reflects Jens' belief—which turned out to be spectacularly wrong—that he could be tried for the crime in Germany and given a light sentence because of his father's diplomatic status:

ELIZABETH: "Promise me, Jens. Whatever it takes now, promise me you will not let me ruin your life. I've seriously fucked up mine. Don't let me destroy yours. I would kill myself if I discovered you were compromising yourself for me."

JENS: "You are in a horrible position, more horrible than mine. Let me clear a couple of things up— erase all written evidence of Bedford, cross it out. That's all I have time for, Sweetie. Always trust me. Always love me."

ELIZABETH: "I have been upset, scared, lonely, worried. You won't leave me to take the rap alone."

JENS: "If I go to Germany and get convicted, I will go

away for only a few years. Your parole board will give you early parole, especially when they take my early release into consideration, so in a few years we will hopefully both be out and together. Trust me and go with the flow."

To analyze the veracity of Jens' confession, Griffiths says, it is necessary to examine the details of what he said.

Perhaps the biggest red flag, in Griffiths' opinion, is the sharp discrepancy between Jens' description of Nancy Haysom's clothing (jeans) and what she was actually wearing (a flowery housecoat).

In addition, Griffiths says, Jens' account of where he was sitting at the dining-room table is inconsistent with crime-scene photos that show three place settings at the table, but none where Jens said he was seated. Jens also incorrectly described the position of Derek Haysom's body.

A competent interrogator would have probed and challenged the suspect about such inconsistencies, Griffiths says. Instead, "Gardner is too easily persuaded that Soering committed the murders in the way he described—despite the glaring contradictions in the detail of his account."

"Soering was a naive, love-struck teenager who was volunteering information," Griffiths writes. "The situation required an objective and enquiring mind to sift the generality of his story in order to find and test the crucial detail, seeking to establish exactly what took place and who was culpable, not to accept a superficial and inaccurate account."

In all his years in law enforcement, the Haysom murder case is one of the most unusual he has ever encountered, Griffiths told me in an interview. What made it stand out were the gruesome nature of the crime, the fact that the suspects were arrested and interrogated in a foreign country and, not least, the personal dynamics between Jens and Elizabeth.

"What makes Jens' case so intriguing is his willingness to put his hand in the flame—the voluntary nature of his confession," Griffiths said.

In Griffiths' opinion, the London interrogations were a classic case of confirmation bias—the tendency to interpret new evidence as confirmation of one's existing beliefs or theories—but with a twist.

"I think it's one of the major problems with most miscarriages of justice, and it's prevalent in this one," he said. "In most situations, confirmation bias is present when a suspect is denying the crime and the police officer has come to a premature conclusion that they're guilty and therefore spends the interview persuading them that they need to admit this and ignoring evidence to the contrary. . . . Now in this situation, Jens is trying to persuade Ricky Gardner that he has done it on his own."

Nevertheless, the principles of good police interviewing still apply, Griffiths said. Every crime has a before, a during, and an after. Often, it's the before and the after that produce the best evidence. For instance, he said, there was never any hard questioning about why Jens and Elizabeth went to Washington before the crime. Nor was there any probing of Elizabeth's account of Jens showing up after the murders draped in nothing but a bloody sheet—a story that, to Griffiths, "sounds very implausible."

And then there is the role of Christine Kim, Elizabeth's U.Va. roommate, who, according to Elizabeth's testimony, helped her construct a time-line of the weekend after the fact. That indicates she might have had some knowledge of the murders, yet there seems to have been no further probing of her role. When the film crew sought to interview her for *The Promise*, she refused to cooperate.

Also left unchallenged was Jens' claim to Gardner that he slashed Derek Haysom's throat as he sat at the dining-room table. If that is true, Griffiths wonders, how is it possible that there were only a few droplets of blood on the placemat at that table setting? According to the medical examiner's report, Derek Haysom suffered a massive wound that severed the trachea and all the major blood vessels in the throat. Why was there not a lake of blood on the table?

Finally, Griffiths believes it was a major failing of proper police procedure—not to mention a violation of British law—that Jens' confession was not recorded.

"Transparency in investigations is extremely important," Griffiths said. "This was a capital offense at the time that he was interviewed. It is in my opinion frankly crazy not to have a firsthand account of what that suspect said. You've got this inconsistency: some interviews over that three-day period were recorded and some not, and then it comes to the point where the most crucial one was not recorded.

"Ricky Gardner had crime-scene information. He was essentially a contaminated witness of that crime scene. . . . The bits of what Jens said that Ricky Gardner picked out for his notes are contaminated by his own knowledge and the fact that it's not recorded. It's a straightforward issue of accuracy upon which at that point a man's life depended.

"It's not sufficient in those situations to deal with gist, particularly where I think that even at that stage, any right-thinking person should have considered the fact that more than one person was involved."

Mistakes happen in police investigations. All over the world, that is becoming increasingly apparent, Griffiths said, and the Haysom case belongs high on that list. "Investigations of this nature are a huge responsibility. It's not the first or last mistake that's been made in such an important investigation. What's unfortunate for Ricky Gardner is that he's so heavily invested in that result. And he's not alone in that."

❖

When I interviewed Ricky Gardner, he made much of the fact that Jens confessed not once, not twice, but three times. Particularly significant in his mind is the third confession, one in which Gardner had no part. That's the one Jens gave to a German prosecutor and a German defense attorney several months after the London interrogations.

"Elizabeth wrote him a Dear John letter over the summer of 1986," Gardner told me. "She said, 'Look, I'm going to go back to Virginia and face the music. You do what you've got to do, but . . . I don't love you anymore. You're on your own.'

"Then in the fall of 1986, the German prosecutor and the German defense attorney came to England and interviewed Jens. What did he tell them? He told them the same story that he told me . . . the same confession, the same facts.

"She severed the relationship in July. She doesn't love him anymore. That would have been the time, in October or November, for him to say, 'Wait a minute. I lied in June. I didn't do this. Elizabeth did it.'"

But Jens says recanting his confession at that point would have been counterproductive, if not fatal. The interview with the German lawyers was part of a legal maneuver to avoid the electric chair by winning extradition to Germany. If that effort had succeeded, Jens would have been tried in his home country, where the maximum sentence under German juvenile law would have been ten years and Jens would have had to serve only about six-and-a-half years. Capital punishment would have been off the table.

But in order to get an indictment for murder, the German prosecutor needed evidence, so Jens was advised to give another confession.

"The whole point of that meeting was to give the German government something that they could staple to their extradition request," Jens told me. Recanting his confession then, he said, "would have cost me my life."

Jens' explanation has been confirmed in writing by his German defense attorney.

In the end, it was a moot point. The German extradition request was denied. Jens ultimately avoided execution by winning a precedent-setting decision from the European Court of Human Rights that forced the Bedford prosecutor to drop the capital charges.

Before I left Ricky Gardner's office, he had one more point to make about why he found Jens' confessions believable. It was something Jens said to Gardner during one of the London interrogations.

"Jens and I were sitting there talking. And he said, 'Did y'all find a dead dog on the side of the road? On the way back to the house that night, a dog ran across in front of me and I thought I hit it.'

"And I said, 'You murdered two people, almost decapitated both of them. And you were going back to the house to turn the light off and you thought you hit a dog and that bothered you?'

"And he said, 'That dog never did anything to me.'

"Now why would anybody that was making up a story, why would you think to interject something like that if it didn't happen? . . . Because he was telling the truth. You don't just pull something like that out of the air."

When I asked Jens about the dog story, he let out a small rueful laugh. In his usual thorough, methodical way, he said, he had embellished his confession with that anecdote precisely to persuade Gardner that he was telling the truth.

"When you tell a lie, you've got to add telling details," he said. "You try to make things believable. Looking back on it, it's awful. I did this incredibly stupid thing to the best of my ability."

22

The Motive

"The major question . . . is why did your parents die?"

DURING HIS EXCRUCIATINGLY long cross-examination of Elizabeth Haysom at her sentencing hearing in 1987, prosecutor James Updike kept asking one question over and over again in a multitude of ways: *Why are your parents dead?*

He never got what he considered a good answer.

The question of motive, a central element of any murder case, was always murky in the Haysom case. The prosecution's story-line at Jens' trial, parroted in innumerable media accounts, went like this: Derek and Nancy Haysom disapproved of their daughter's relationship with Jens, so the young lovers decided that they had to be gotten rid of. But there was no convincing evidence of that scenario presented at trial. According to Jens, it was just something he and Elizabeth cooked up after the fact, borrowing from the plot of *Romeo and Juliet*.

There was no testimony supporting that story-line from family members, friends, or classmates. When Elizabeth herself was asked about her parents' attitude toward Jens, she said this: "They felt he was too young for me, they thought that he was very brilliant, they thought that he tried very hard to be courteous and gentlemanlike. They didn't want me to spend too much time with him." But in the next breath, she acknowledged that was no different from how her parents felt about anyone she dated. "They didn't like any of the young men that I saw," she said.

As a practical matter, even if the Haysoms had strongly disapproved of the relationship, there was little that they could have done about it. Elizabeth was no longer living under their roof. She and Jens were both adults and were in Charlottesville, seventy-five miles from Lynchburg.

The one thing that was crystal clear was that Elizabeth harbored deep-seated anger and resentment toward her parents. But why? Updike wanted to know.

"Please tell us, why were you so bitter and frustrated and angered at these people who spent all this money on your education, and had done everything that they could for you?" the prosecutor asked. "Why were you so resentful, please?"

Elizabeth had a two-part answer. "At the time I believe I thought that when I needed them when I was younger, they weren't there for me," she said. "When I was at U.Va., they were overwhelmingly smothering me with attention."

"So you didn't like it when they didn't give you attention and you didn't like it when they did, did you?" Updike asked.

"Well, sir, it went from one extreme to the other," Elizabeth replied.

"What did they do so wrong?" Updike asked a little later.

"Probably not very much, sir," Elizabeth said.

By halfway through his cross-examination, the prosecutor was pleading with his witness for an answer. "I still don't understand why, Ms. Haysom, I don't understand why . . . why willing your parents to death, why concentrating on their death?"

"I'm afraid, sir, that it was a fantasy of mine for many years that my parents would die," Elizabeth said.

But why? Updike insisted. "I'm concerned about why your mom and dad got butchered as they did."

Finally, the prosecutor gave up in exasperation. "Let's just move on, Ms. Haysom," he said. "I think I've plowed that ground and I'm not getting anything but rocks."

But what about Jens? Updike wanted to know. If it were true, as the prosecution insisted, that Jens carried out the murders at Elizabeth's instigation, there had to be a reason.

"Would you tell us, please, Jens Soering's motive for killing your parents?" he asked.

"I don't know, sir," Elizabeth replied.

A little later, Updike tried again: "My question to you that I'm still asking, Why did he kill them at all?"

"I've asked him that many times," Elizabeth said.

Near the end of the grueling session, the prosecutor made one last desperate effort to get to the bottom of the issue. "Ms. Haysom, I just have a very few more questions for you," he said. "The major question that I'd like to ask you is why did your parents die?"

This time, Elizabeth offered an explanation that not only failed to support the official story-line but seemed to contradict it. Yes, it was true that she and her parents had been at loggerheads in the past, she said, but on a visit home a week before the murders, they had begun sorting out their differences and a reconciliation seemed to be underway.

"My parents died," she said, "because Jens and I were obsessed with each other and he was jealous of anything else other in my life. He was jealous of my parents."

"So he killed them out of jealousy?" Updike repeated.

"Yes," Elizabeth replied. "He killed them because he knew how important they were to me and that there was a reconciliation going on."

Finally, the prosecutor gave up. "Thank you, ma'am, I don't have any further questions," he said wearily, and slumped into his seat.

❖

There is another, more plausible motive for the murders that was not part of the prosecution's story-line. In fact, Updike went to great pains to discredit it.

Elizabeth had told several people—including Jens and the detectives, psychiatrists, and a probation officer who interviewed her—that she had been sexually abused by her mother. But child sexual abuse was still something of a taboo subject in 1985, and such allegations concerning a prominent, upper-crust family in genteel Virginia were apparently a bridge too far for the prosecution.

During his cross-examination, Updike confronted Elizabeth about her allegation, detailed in the probation officer's pre-sentencing report, that she had had a "full-blown sexual relationship" with her mother. Was that true?

There was a long pause. "I didn't put it that way, no, sir," Elizabeth finally replied.

"How did you put it?" Updike asked.

The question had come up in reference to the nude photographs her mother had taken of her when she was eighteen or nineteen, Elizabeth said. "I said that she was aggressively affectionate, and I believe when I have discussed this with other people that I said that she was a very lonely and affectionate woman and that is what she was seeking, it was nothing more than that."

She did tell the probation officer and other interviewers that her mother slept with her, Elizabeth added.

But there were logical reasons for that, weren't there? Updike pressed. "At times you would come home, there would be no beds available other than sleeping with your mother. . . . Perfectly innocent, wasn't it?"

"Mr. Updike, this isn't an issue I wanted to bring up," Elizabeth protested.

"My question is simply this: Your mother's been butchered," Updike said.

"Yes, she has, sir."

"During previous testimony yesterday you called her a liar and an alcoholic."

"I did not call her an alcoholic."

"Was she a sexual abuser, did she sexually abuse you? If she didn't for God's sake clear her name now!"

"She did not sexually abuse me."

"Thank you," Updike said. "And maybe the press and others will be just as eager to print the recantation as what's been printed previously."

If there was any lesbian relationship, Updike pressed further, wasn't it with the young woman with whom Elizabeth had run off to Europe in 1983?

"That's your terminology," Elizabeth responded.

"Did you sleep with her?" Updike asked.

"Yes, like I slept with my mother," Elizabeth replied.

And as far as the prosecution was concerned, that ended the matter.

What went unsaid was that a history of parental sexual abuse would have been a logical explanation for the kind of rage-fueled attack that took the Haysoms' lives.

The psychiatrists diagnosed Elizabeth as suffering from borderline personality disorder, a condition characterized by problems regulating emotions and thoughts, impulsive and reckless behavior, and unstable relationships with other people. It is often accompanied by substance abuse.

The causes of the disorder are not yet fully understood, but one of the leading candidates is childhood trauma, including sexual abuse.

It took three decades, but Elizabeth herself finally has said publicly that that was in fact the real motive for the murders. "My mother sexually abused me for eight years," she said in an interview with the *Richmond Times–Dispatch* in September 2016. "I felt trapped. . . . It was a horrid, horrid, ugly secret."

When she denied the abuse at Updike's prodding in 1990, she said that she was lying. She didn't want to discuss such a private matter in a public forum.

In London in 1986, during an interrogation by British detective Kenneth Beever, Elizabeth briefly contradicted the official story-line that Jens carried out the murders. But she quickly recovered:

> BEEVER: "You knew he was going to do it, didn't you?
>   Did you?"
> ELIZABETH: "I did it myself."
> BEEVER: "Don't be silly."
> ELIZABETH: "I got off on it."
> BEEVER: "You did what? What does that mean?"
> ELIZABETH: "I was being facetious."

From that time until this, Elizabeth has insisted that Jens was the killer, acting as her agent.

"My mother had this power over me," she said in the 2016 interview. "I could never have laid a hand on her. That's why I needed Jens to do it. . . .

"Am I to blame for the crime? Absolutely."

Elizabeth was never prosecuted for perjury based on her false testimony at Jens' trial denying sexual abuse—a powerful motive for murder that the jury never heard about.

23

The Long Slog

"How can a God who claims to be good allow his creatures to suffer?"

For nearly three decades now, ever since recanting his confession, Jens has been proclaiming his innocence to anyone who will listen. But when I first met him in 2006, his primary focus was on simply surviving the horrors of prison life.

One of his most successful coping mechanisms has been writing books. Against all odds—as a prisoner, for instance, he has no access to the Internet—he has published nine books, five in English and four in his native German. His books offer an incisive and compassionate inside look at America's massive prison-industrial complex.

It is a grim world, he writes: a Darwinian struggle for survival in which the strong prey on the weak. A recurring theme is sexual assault, which he says is common and widely ignored by guards. One of the first sights he saw after his arrival at Southampton Correctional Center in 1990 was the rape of a young man by his cellmate as a dozen other inmates stood by, cheering and applauding.

When he was moved to Mecklenburg Correctional Center in the summer of 1991, Jens was just turning twenty-five. "I was nothing more than another 'fresh fish,'" he wrote, "a pudgy guppy among highly experienced and hungry sharks." There, he himself was nearly raped by a muscular inmate who threw him against a wall as he exited the shower, releasing his grip only after Jens let out a bloodcurdling scream.

The U.S. Justice Department estimates that more than 200,000 inmates in American jails and prisons are sexually assaulted every year. That means far more men are raped each year in the United States than women—most of them in prison.[9]

Jens writes of mentally ill inmates who earn cigarette money by performing sex acts in portable toilets in the exercise yard, dubbed the "love shack" by prisoners. One such inmate once tried to castrate himself with an old razor blade.

Jens later did time in two prisons in Virginia's mountainous far southwest: Keen Mountain and Wallens Ridge. The latter is one of the state's two so-called supermaxes—super-security facilities. There, Jens was hit in the arm by a ricocheting rubber bullet in a barrage fired by a guard at another inmate.

In 2000, to his great relief, Jens was moved to Brunswick Correctional Center in Southside Virginia, which he found to be relatively humane after the trauma of the supermax. To be sure, he wrote, prison life was still "hell on earth," but at least "there were pretty flowers to look at while you burned."

One day in April 2004, Jens returned to his cell after breakfast to discover that his cellmate, "Keith" (not his real name), had hanged himself with a rope made of shoestrings tied to Jens' top bunk railing.

"What many of the rest of us have been asking ourselves," he wrote, "is why we are not following Keith's way of making parole."

Jens says he had suicidal thoughts constantly for fourteen years and used to keep 200 to 300 aspirin tablets in a Metamucil jar that traveled with him to three different prisons, ready to be used for an overdose.

---

9 Marie Gottschalk, *Caught: The Prison State and the Lockdown of American Politics*, Princeton: Princeton University Press, 2015, p. 137.

One of Jens' books, *An Expensive Way to Make Bad People Worse*, is a call for sweeping prison reform, written to appeal to fiscal conservatives. He argues that hundreds of thousands of inmates—including the elderly, the mentally ill, and nonviolent drug offenders—should not be behind bars because it is unnecessary, expensive, and often counterproductive.

Another of Jens' books, *The Church of the Second Chance*, contains an account of his six weeks in segregation—"the hole," inmates call it—in the fall of 2004. Inmates in segregation are kept in their cells except for three showers and three one-hour exercise periods per week. Although it is normally used as punishment for disciplinary infractions, Jens was never charged with any misconduct. In fact, he has never incurred a single infraction in his entire thirty years behind bars—an amazingly clean, if not unique, record.

He was never told why he was placed in segregation.

While in "the hole," Jens saw a depressing range of aberrant behavior among segregated inmates: drumming on their sinks all night, exposing themselves to nurses making their morning rounds, gouging chunks of flesh out of their forearms with sharpened pieces of plastic, smearing the walls of their cells with feces.

Interlaced with his accounts of prison life, Jens' books trace his spiritual odyssey from agnosticism to Buddhism to Christianity and back again. At times, they become dense theological treatises, drawing on the works of Christian thinkers like Martin Luther, St. Augustine, John Calvin, and St. Thomas Aquinas, reflecting what Jens has called his years-long "intellectual romance with Christianity."

By the time I first met him, he had become a devoted practitioner of centering prayer, a meditative technique that he traces back to ancient Christian mystics. "I spent six or seven years reading theology books," he told me. "Finally, that stopped working for me. Then I discovered centering prayer. It helped me deal with the reality of my situation."

For nine years, three times a day, he sat quietly in his cell for forty minutes at a stretch, wearing earphones to muffle the cacophony of prison life. Breathing deeply and deliberately, he silently chanted a single word—*Jesus*—over and over and over again. The aim was to reach a stiller level of consciousness and, ultimately, to dissolve his conscious self and experience the presence of God.

There were times, he has written, when he did in fact feel or see God as "a warm, golden-green, glowing light."

For a long time, he says, following that monastic regimen saved him from near-certain suicide.

In addition, he told me, his years of meditation helped him come to see that he bears a degree of moral guilt for the murders. He possibly could have prevented the crime, he says, by encouraging his girlfriend to seek professional counseling.

He also admits he is not totally innocent, even in the legal sense, because he helped cover up the murders. For years, he says, he prayed—individually, by name—for the Haysoms' siblings and children.

"I hurt all those people terribly," he said. "I should have told the truth from the very beginning."

Jens persuaded the authorities at Brunswick to let him set up a biweekly prayer-and-meditation group so he could share the technique with fellow prisoners. He also established a class in tai chi, a form of Chinese martial arts, and a fitness walkabout program for elderly prisoners.

But as the possible avenues for winning his freedom—court appeals, parole, pardon, repatriation to Germany—were closed off or appeared increasingly distant, Jens felt the walls closing in. His despair was multiplied by the loss of contact with his family. His mother died of alcoholism in 1997, a tragic end for which he assumes a large measure of guilt. His brother cut off contact with him long ago. In 2001, he and his father, who for years had been a source of emotional and financial support, came to an apparently unbreachable split.

One morning in July 2008, Jens' faith journey came to an abrupt halt. "When I woke up . . . my faith in God was gone," he wrote later. "Even in my current state of bewilderment and anguish, I could recognize that I had suffered some sort of psychological trauma or nervous breakdown."

In March 2009, he stopped his thrice-daily centering prayer sessions. "Why? Because there is no God," he wrote. "At least no God who matters to us humans." It came down to the "problem of evil," the conundrum that has bedeviled religious thinkers for centuries: "How can a God who claims to be good allow his creatures to suffer?"

Nevertheless, even though his faith has dissipated, Jens says he still believes in following Christ's directive that we are to love our enemies. Why? Because that is "the only way to respond to the absurd cruelty of life on this horrible planet."

Brunswick Correctional Center was closed in 2009 during a state budget crunch. Since then, Jens has been housed at Buckingham Correctional Center, a concrete fortress in central Virginia about fifty miles east of where the Haysoms were murdered. Jens' German friends refer to it sardonically as "Buckingham Palace." A plaque on the wall just off the lobby proudly cites the Buckingham chow hall for feeding the inmates at a lower per-person cost than any other prison in Virginia.

Just forty miles up Route 15 to the north, Elizabeth is serving her time at Fluvanna Correctional Center for Women. She has kept a far lower profile than Jens. She shuns most media interviews and has seldom pled her case in public.

She did find one outlet for her literary skills. For five years in the mid-2000s, she wrote a monthly column about prison life for the local weekly newspaper, the *Fluvanna Review*. She stuck to

mundane topics, often drawing on her activities behind bars: facil-
itating a computer-aided drafting class, working as a dog handler,
playing in a handbell choir. Even so, there are flashes of eloquence.
In one column, she describes watching a drenching rain after a long
dry spell from her tiny cell window: "Only the fruit grower, the
vineyard manager, the orchard foreman, the gardener, the farmer
follow the rain with loving attention. And prisoners. We watch the
rain. We watch the rain and vow never again to take any small pleasure for granted."

The columns are never self-revealing on any deep level, and
there are only occasional oblique references to the crimes for which
she was incarcerated. In one ironic twist, she writes about being
cast as Macbeth in an all-female version of the Shakespeare play—a
contrast to her role in the prosecution's theory of the case as Lady
Macbeth, the instigator of murder, not the actual killer.

In another column describing a typical day in prison, she
writes: "During the day I never forget I am an inmate, a prisoner, a
convict, a murderer. During the day I struggle to remember I am a
woman, an adult, a person. I could make my days easier by forget-
ting. But I also know I deserve the days I live. I therefore struggle
to remember who I am and face each day with awareness—this is a
punishment; it's meant to be tough."

The headline on the newspaper story I wrote about Jens in
2007 was NO HOPE. Yet, a decade later, he somehow manages to
cling to some shred of hope—even though he knows none of the
favorable evidence that has emerged since his trial guarantees him
a ticket out of prison.

"The essence of incarceration is despair," he wrote in his latest
book. "When you wake up in the morning, you know with absolute
certainty that today will be precisely like yesterday. And tomorrow
will be exactly like today."

Most prisoners start going crazy after twenty years behind
bars, he says—if, that is, they weren't already crazy when they came

in—and Jens has now passed the thirty-year mark. But "my life has been completely different from the lives of all my fellow inmates," he wrote. "Unlike them, I have always had hope, I have always believed that tomorrow or next year really could be *different* from today and yesterday. And that has kept me sane."

24

Political Winds

"It is not much of an exaggeration . . . to call me a political prisoner."

J ENS NEVER SET out to be a political football. But over the years of waging his high-stakes fight for freedom, that's what he has become.

Ambassadors, parliamentarians, and state lawmakers have weighed in on his case. Presidents have discussed it in head-to-head talks. A succession of governors has dealt with the thorny issues it presents. And in this take-no-prisoners era of American politics, it has become an issue in campaigns for the Senate and the White House.

Jens has also made friends in high spiritual places. One of his most stalwart supporters was the late Bishop Walter Sullivan, who led the Richmond Catholic Diocese for almost thirty years. While researching Jens' case in 2006, I interviewed Bishop Sullivan and asked if he were convinced of Jens' innocence. "Yes," he replied, "because I find him believable on all other things."

It was at Bishop Sullivan's urging that Tom Elliott began visiting Jens in 2005. A retired senior executive with the U.S. Department of Defense and a Catholic deacon, Elliott had been named coordinator of prison ministry for the Richmond Diocese and became a volunteer chaplain in the Virginia prison system. At Jens' request, he located a priest to conduct services at Brunswick

Correctional Center, where Jens was then housed. Over the next ten years, Elliott had monthly pastoral visits with Jens—occasionally in the company of Bishop Sullivan—and became a valued source of support and comfort.

On the drive home from one of those visits with Jens in 2009, Elliott recalls, Bishop Sullivan turned to him and said: "We've got to get the governor to do something for him." With the help of mutual friends, a private meeting was arranged between the bishop and then–Gov. Tim Kaine, a Democrat and devout Catholic, in October 2009, near the end of Kaine's term in office.

At the time, Jens had a petition pending with the governor seeking repatriation to Germany under an international treaty allowing transfer of foreign prisoners to their home countries. Kaine listened politely to the bishop, but Jens' petition posed a political problem for him. Because criminal sentences are much shorter in Germany than in the United States, Jens would have been freed long before 2009 if he had been tried and convicted for the Haysom murders in Germany. Under normal procedures, a transfer in accord with the repatriation treaty would have resulted in his immediate release, which undoubtedly would have stirred a storm of protest in Virginia.

Before he could consider granting Jens' petition, Kaine told the bishop, he needed assurances from Germany that he would have to serve some minimum amount of prison time there. Elliott then contacted Jens' German lawyers to see what could be done, and after weeks of negotiations Germany made a highly unusual if not unique concession: Jens would be found guilty in a German court and would have to serve a minimum of two more years.

The deal required Jens' consent, and he was reluctant at first to sign onto it, Elliott said, because it seemed tantamount to another false confession. But Elliott put it to him this way: "Look, two years in Germany or life in Virginia. What's your choice?" Jens relented, and soon after that, so did Kaine. Days before he left office in

January 2010, he granted the petition and Jens began making plans for the move to Germany.

Those plans proved premature, however. On his first working day in office, newly elected Gov. Bob McDonnell, a Republican, revoked Kaine's decision. Weeks later, the Virginia General Assembly weighed in with a unanimous resolution supporting McDonnell's move, declaring, "It is in the interests of justice and in fairness to Derek and Nancy Haysom that Jens Soering serve out his punishment in the Commonwealth."

Jens' lawyer Steve Rosenfield filed suit to enforce the repatriation, arguing that McDonnell didn't have the authority to reverse his predecessor's decision. But that legal effort ended in failure in 2012.

Jens was devastated by this turn of events, as was Bishop Sullivan. When Tom Elliott paid him a visit two weeks before he died in December 2012, the bishop extracted a promise from him: "Don't give up on Jens. Get something done."

Meanwhile, ex–Gov. Kaine had mounted a campaign for an open U.S. Senate seat. Among the first issues raised against him by Republicans was his attempt to repatriate Jens. The furor was relatively brief and never gained traction. Kaine won the election with fifty-three percent of the vote.

But that didn't stop Republicans from raising the issue again after Democratic presidential nominee Hillary Clinton chose Kaine as her vice-presidential running mate in 2016. In a conference call with reporters, state delegate Rob Bell of Albemarle County, a candidate for attorney general in 2017, called the repatriation attempt an "extraordinary step" that raised questions about Kaine's judgment.

Gov. Terry McAuliffe, a Democrat elected in 2013, denied a second repatriation petition from Jens in 2015, perhaps proving that fear of political repercussions from Jens' case is a bipartisan concern.

"It is not much of an exaggeration, and perhaps no exaggeration at all," Jens has written, "to call me a political prisoner."

As for Bob McDonnell, the governor who first moved to keep Jens locked up in Virginia, he ended up scrambling to stay out of prison himself. He was convicted on federal corruption charges in 2014 and sentenced to two years after doing favors for a businessman who showered him with more than $175,000 in luxury gifts and loans. The Supreme Court threw out the conviction in 2016 and he never served any time.

The decades of Jens' incarceration have spanned a sea change in American criminal-justice policy. At the time of his conviction and sentencing in 1990, the prison population was relatively stable and there was still some degree of political support for the concept of rehabilitation. For inmates who maintained a clean disciplinary record, it was still a realistic possibility to earn early release through parole.

That all changed in the 1990s as a new lock-'em-up ethos took hold. Along with many other states, Virginia took advantage of federal financial incentives to embark on a dramatic prison-building boom that added thousands of new cells. Criminal laws were overhauled to require much longer stays in prison. The incarcerated population increased exponentially. The prison budget of Virginia ballooned to $1 billion a year. In many isolated rural communities today, the local prison is the biggest employer in town. Parole was abolished for all crimes committed after January 1, 1995.

Since the crime for which Jens was convicted occurred before that, he became technically eligible for parole in 2003. But Virginia's five-member Parole Board sensed which way the political winds were blowing. Over a decade, the state parole rate dropped from forty percent to the low single digits. By the end of

2015, despite his unblemished disciplinary record, his volunteer work helping fellow inmates, and his success as a published author, Jens had been turned down for parole eleven times. That's despite an outpouring of support from his native Germany, where—like most of Europe—rehabilitation and mercy still enjoy popular currency.

Bernadette Faber, a middle-school teacher in southwestern Germany, first learned of Jens' plight from a German TV report in 2007. She recorded the newscast and replayed it for her students. "I was shocked," she told me. "I couldn't forget it for weeks. My students were shocked, too."

Along with dozens of other Germans, Faber wrote Jens and asked how she could help. From that outpouring emerged a devoted band of grassroots supporters. Faber has boxes of documents from Jens' case stored in her apartment. She helps maintain his website, which has a comprehensive trove of information about the case. For six years, she and her friend Anna, an actress who works as a clown in a children's hospital in Munich, have made annual trans–Atlantic trips to visit Jens in person.

"His family is gone," Faber told me. "We are his family now."

In June 2013, Jens' German supporters held a rally outside the chancellor's office in Berlin demanding that Jens' case be made a priority of the German government. Thanks in large part to their efforts, dozens of German parliamentarians and two successive presidents of the European Parliament have written the Virginia governor supporting Jens' parole or repatriation. One letter to Gov. McAuliffe in January 2014 was signed by 121 members of the Bundestag, the German parliament—about one-fifth of its membership. Chancellor Angela Merkel brought the case up with President Barack Obama on three occasions.

None of this has moved the Virginia authorities, however. At Jens' second parole hearing in 2006, the parole board member assigned to the case slept through much of the testimony. When

Jens' supporters protested, the board apologized, held a second hearing, and denied parole.

Ten days before Jens' eighth parole hearing in 2012, parole board chairman William Muse signaled what the outcome would be in a letter to a German parliamentarian who had written in support of parole. "You are correct in your understanding that Mr. Soering has been a compliant inmate and taken advantage of a number of programs. We expect that of all inmates," Muse wrote. "In reviewing any offender for parole, the Board considers not only the offender's conduct and treatment while in prison, but also the nature and circumstances of the crime. While the risk to public safety is of paramount importance, a low risk to re-offend and the offender's efforts at rehabilitation are off times [sic] offset by the serious nature of the crime and the sentence imposed. Simply stated, that balance has not yet tipped in Mr. Soering's favor."

Ironically, Jens' continued profession of innocence may have worked against him in the parole-board deliberations. At least one board member has suggested to his supporters that his lack of remorse is one of the factors impeding his release. Remorse implies an admission of guilt—a line that Jens resolutely refuses to cross.

Jens addressed that quandary in a seven-page letter to then–parole-board chairwoman Helen Fahey in 2006. Even though he is innocent of murder, he wrote, he is nonetheless remorseful because he did nothing to help his girlfriend Elizabeth when she told him that she had been sexually abused by her mother. If he had encouraged Elizabeth to seek professional counseling, he wrote, the murders might have been prevented.

"I failed to be my sister's keeper," he wrote. "I acted like a cold-hearted swine, and thereby caused the deaths of two people, and the godawful suffering of at least seven others. *I* am to blame *first*."

Problematic though it may be, Jens has doubled down on his innocence claim.

In August 2016, Attorney Rosenfield filed a "Petition for Absolute Pardon and Parole" with Gov. McAuliffe based on "incontrovertible scientific proof of absolute innocence."

First and foremost, the petition relies on the new analysis of DNA evidence that eliminates Jens as the source of the type-O blood collected at the crime scene. "The only way the Commonwealth can now argue for Jens' guilt is to assert that he committed the crime with an unknown accomplice, who was injured and left type-O blood at the scene," the petition says. "This accomplice cannot be Ms. Haysom, who has type-B blood. Until now, there has been no suggestion by the Commonwealth that there was a third murderer involved."

The petition also invokes the conclusion by Andrew Griffiths, the British expert on police interrogations, that Jens' confession is unreliable, as well as the newly expressed doubts about Jens' guilt from Chuck Reid, the original lead sheriff's investigator in the case.

"Thanks to DNA, we now know as an absolute, scientific fact that Jens is innocent and that at least one killer with type-O blood has gone unpunished for these crimes," the petition says. "Investigatory bias and false pride have resulted in Jens' life having passed in prison while someone guilty remains at large. That is a tragedy for Jens, but it is also a tragedy for the victims, their family and the citizens of Virginia."

On August 1, 2016, Jens turned fifty. More than three-fifths of his life has been spent in prison.

Elizabeth, who turned fifty-two in April 2016, will qualify

for mandatory release in 2032, when she is sixty-eight. But for Jens, because he was convicted of double murder, not even geriatric release is a possibility. Barring pardon or parole, he will die in prison. He is not optimistic about his chances for freedom.

At times, his despair has reached such depths that he shut himself off to visits—even from such faithful allies as Tom Elliott, his long-time confidant and spiritual adviser, and the friends who come from Germany every year to see him.

In an October 2014 letter, Jens asked Elliott to cancel a planned visit. "I've had enough," he wrote. "I give up. After 28 years (and 'change'), I finally get it: I won't be leaving prison alive. And I really don't want to talk about it. I don't want to pretend AGAIN that I'm really o.k. with all this, that there's still hope, that I'll never give up—and all that other cr*p. This is the same song-and-dance routine that I've put on for all my visitors since the very first one, my father . . . in 1986. I felt so sorry for him, and so bad for causing him so much trouble and heartache, that I told him what he needed to hear: that I was o.k., that there was hope, etc. It was the least I could do. And I've been doing the same shtick now for 28+ years. . . . But in reality I am NOT o.k., and in reality there is NO hope. And I don't want to pretend anymore."

Elliott insisted on visiting him anyway, and Jens eventually rallied from his depression. He has written more than once that "life is mostly about how you bounce back."

But he suffered a crushing blow in 2015 when Elliott was cut off from any contact with him by the Virginia Department of Corrections. Someone in the department had been monitoring the pair's mail and decided that their relationship had crossed the line from spiritual to personal. So all communication between the two—visits, phone calls, and letters—was prohibited. In order to reestablish contact, Elliott gave up his volunteer-chaplain status. He couldn't disagree that the relationship had become personal, Elliott told me. "I've known Jens since 2005. I've seen the problems that he's had because of being a German in the U.S., separated from his family. He's had relationship problems with his father. I have three sons around the same age as he is. . . . In some ways he's like a son to me."

As of mid-2016, Elliott had been allowed to resume phone calls and letters to Jens but was still awaiting permission for in-person visits.

The exculpatory DNA evidence discovered in 2016 buoyed Jens' hopes, but he maintains a hard-bitten realism born of repeated frustrations over the years.

"If this were any other case in Virginia or even in the United States, I would now be released, probably by the end of this week," he said when his pardon petition was filed. "This kind of DNA evidence has been the basis for immediate release in many, many other cases. . . . So I really should be treated the same as all those other DNA exonerations. But of course I will not be treated the same. My case has been a political football for many, many years. So I expect that everyone will make a great effort to keep me in prison, because that is the safest option for everyone involved."

The politicization of his case has filled him with anger, Jens wrote in an email to reporters. "But anger is a wonderful antidote against hopelessness. After now 30 years in prison (let me say it again: for a crime I didn't commit!), I am an immensely, titanically angry man. My anger is so great that hopelessness really doesn't stand a chance against it. When I came into prison in 1986 at the age of 19, I was a soft, naive, innocent child. Now, in 2016, I am 50 and still innocent, at least of any felony. But I am not even a little bit soft or naive—quite the opposite. I suppose on some level I regret that. But if I had not become the hard, angry son-of-a-bitch that I now am, I would not have survived."

25

Hope and Despair

"There was nothing there at all. . . . She is just a black hole."

WHEN I VISITED Jens in July 2016, he was still wiry and sinewy from his regular workouts in the prison gym, but there was something new. He was sporting a beard—his "beard of despair," he called it.

He had recently come into possession of a diary and a batch of letters kept for three decades by a fellow U.Va. student that propelled him back to those days in a particularly painful way.

The correspondence makes clear that—unbeknownst to Jens—the other man had an intimate relationship with Elizabeth Haysom at the very same time she and Jens were carrying on their steamy romance.

Within a week of declaring her undying love for Jens, Elizabeth joined the other student—along with two more men at one point—on a sexually adventurous skiing vacation in Yugoslavia over Christmas break in December 1984, three months before the Haysom murders.

"I do wish we could travel together again," Elizabeth writes the man. "I'll never forget that evening we ate squid in that Yugoslav restaurant and got taken home as souvenirs."

She revisits their fling repeatedly in subsequent flirtatious letters: "I remember that incredible evening we were in Sarajevo eating squid, drinking that horrible Slivovitz, going home with those slav businessmen. The drinking, the sex, the weird things that went on. Very strange!"

"Yugoslavia was great," the man wrote in his diary. "Elizabeth was grand. I'm afraid I've now been outclassed, but brilliance always cheers me regardless of its nature, fleeting or no."

The two stayed in contact by mail for years, through Elizabeth's incarceration in London and Virginia, her sentencing in 1987, and beyond. Occasionally, the man visited Elizabeth in prison. Their letters repeatedly express disdain and contempt for Jens. "He struck me as an uneven child/man, heavier on the former, unsure and over-bearing in an attempt to compensate," the man writes Elizabeth.

In one of her letters, Elizabeth includes a long account of her six months on the lam with Jens through Europe and Asia—but she never once mentions Jens. The passage is written in the first-person singular, as if she had been traveling alone. Jens is a nonentity. "Came home to England, was arrested, and spent quite a lot of time with Special Branch discussing my rather peculiar traveling habits," she writes breezily. "And then went to prison. So there we have it. My next 3 projects are to (1) bicycle China, (2) collect wild life in South America, (3) cross-country ski to Antarctica."

In another letter, Elizabeth refers to Jens not by name but as "the kid." "Officially, he is dangerous," she writes. "My own biased viewpoint is that he is a little boy who is desperate and thus is dangerous and unstable."

Reading the pair's correspondence brought Jens crashing up against a stark truth: his perception of his relationship with Elizabeth was nothing like her perception of it.

"That really hurt," he told me. "Even until then, I had a fantasy that there was something there. But there was nothing there at all. There was no relationship. She is just a black hole." It struck me then that for all his logical, methodical approach to life, Jens remains at some level a hopeless romantic.

He has written about how, after seventeen years in prison, a young woman who had read one of his books came to visit him and declared—much to his surprise—that she was in love with him. Having had only one serious girlfriend before that, Elizabeth, one that didn't work out so well, Jens was hesitant at first. But he invited the woman back for a second visit, and this time they kissed.

"My first kiss in over 17 years," Jens wrote later. "Frightening and wonderful at the same time—and oh so soft. . . . For the first time in over 17 years, another human being—this woman in my arms—was treating me as a human being, on the most basic and intimate level possible. I was not a prisoner during that kiss, neither for her nor for myself. All day long, for 17 years, I had been nothing but a convict, a number if you will: 179212, my inmate ID number. But for a few seconds in this woman's arms, I was Jens again: a man, a human, someone who loved and was loved in return."

After his visitor left, Jens returned to his cell-block, stepped into a broom closet, and wept.

❖

A student of the absurdist philosophers, Jens likens his plight to Albert Camus' take on the ancient myth of Sisyphus, the mortal condemned by the gods to spend eternity rolling a huge rock up a hill only to have it roll repeatedly back to the bottom. Sisyphus is the perfect absurd hero, Camus tells us, because his punishment is representative of the human condition. His struggle is perpetual and holds no hope of success. So long as he accepts that there is nothing more to life than this absurd struggle, Camus says, then he can find happiness in it.

"I want to keep my rock, but I'd like to roll it up some other hill," Jens told me. "Why shouldn't I have a little bit of happiness, after thirty years of hell? A little bit of romance even? Why shouldn't that be possible?"

Resources

Books by Jens Soering

One Day in the Life of 179212. New York: Lantern Books, 2012.

The Church of the Second Chance: A Faith-based Approach to Prison Reform. New York: Lantern Books, 2008.

The Convict Christ: What the Gospel Says about Criminal Justice. Maryknoll, N.Y.: Orbis, 2006.

An Expensive Way to Make Bad People Worse: An Essay on Prison Reform from an Insider's Perspective. New York: Lantern Books, 2004.

The Way of the Prisoner: Breaking the Chains of Self through Centering Prayer and Centering Practice. New York: Lantern Books, 2003.

Additional Resources

To learn more about the case, visit Jens' website: www.jenssoering.com.

To see a trailer for *The Promise*, visit the website: http://promise-movie.com/the-movie.

About the Authors

Jens Soering is the author of six books and three translations, including *The Way of the Prisoner*, a hands-on, practical approach to medieval mystical texts; *The Convict Christ*, a twenty-first century, North American take on liberation theology; and *One Day in the Life of 179212*, an homage to Aleksandr Solzhenitsyn.

Bill Sizemore retired in 2014 after a thirty-five-year career as a reporter with the *Virginian-Pilot*, the state's largest-circulation newspaper. He was a finalist for the 2007 Pulitzer Prize in explanatory reporting for a series of stories on Blackwater, the private military company, and he received more than twenty-five awards from the Virginia Press Association.

About the Publisher

LANTERN BOOKS was founded in 1999 on the principle of living with a greater depth and commitment to the preservation of the natural world. In addition to publishing books on animal advocacy, vegetarianism, religion, and environmentalism, Lantern is dedicated to printing books in the U.S. on recycled paper and saving resources in day-to-day operations. Lantern is honored to be a recipient of the highest standard in environmentally responsible publishing from the Green Press Initiative.

lanternbooks.com

green press
INITIATIVE

MIX
Paper from
responsible sources
FSC® C013483

FSC
www.fsc.org